"Teaming is a fresh new concept to organize the best knowledge available for creating and maintaining effective action."

—**Chris Argyris**, professor emeritus, Harvard University

"This is the ultimate book on teams and learning. Edmondson combines academic rigor and relevance in a unique way. A must-read for scholars and practitioners."

—**Bertrand Moingeon**, professor, directeur général adjoint, and deputy dean, executive education and academic development, HEC Paris

"Amy Edmondson is the best leader teacher I know. Her experience in the classroom and her deep understanding of how leaders lead in the real world rings loud and clear in this book."

—**Charlie Eitel**, founding partner, Eitel & Armstrong; and former chairman and CEO, Simmons Bedding

"Edmondson's insights that teams are verbs rather than nouns, and that leaders who focus on 'teaming' animate a more adaptive work environment, are a major advance in our grasp of leading, organizing, and learning. This is the work of a gifted, hands-on scholar at her best!"

—**Karl E. Weick**, Rensis Likert Distinguished University Professor, organizational behavior and psychology, Stephen M. Ross School of Business, University of Michigan

"*Teaming* is *the* book on how to lead and learn from innovative teams and dispersed networks. Amy Edmondson has gathered a wealth of evidence, experience, and illustrations to write the definitive playbook for learning and bringing out the best in collaborative endeavors anywhere."

—**Michael Useem**, professor of management, and director of the Leadership Center, Wharton School, University of Pennsylvania

"The always-insightful Amy Edmondson has produced a terrific book. She provides the best insights I have seen on failure and learning in teams. By distinguishing between types of failures across her Knowledge Process Spectrum, she shows how some types of failures should be discouraged and minimized while others are essential for learning and advancement. Easy to read, *Teaming* provides useful insights from start to finish."

—**Roger Martin**, dean, Rotman School of Business, University of Toronto

"*Teaming* shows how organizations can inspire every employee to voice new ideas, compensate every manager to reward the risk of experimentation, and recognize every leader who empowers the collective quest for learning and innovation. Edmondson has provided an articulate, indispensable guide for organizations to succeed in an age of unprecedented change and competition."

—**Sean Woodroffe**, vice president, human resources, Sun Life Financial U.S.

"Many of us have experienced or observed the drama of a hospital emergency room where life-and-death split second decisions are made, and where priorities and staff assignments shift unpredictably, even in the midst of caring for a patient. *Teaming* describes a new way of working that achieves superior outcomes in this chaotic environment, a setting for which past organizational theory has fallen short."

—**Ray Gilmartin**, professor of management practice, Harvard Business School; and former CEO, Merck & Co.

"Edmondson goes to the very heart of the single biggest challenge we face in the 21st century: while our problems are growing ever more complex, the expertise we bring to those problems is growing ever more narrow. Only through teams—or teaming, as Edmondson rightly argues—can we hope to learn across boundaries and tackle the problems we face today. Using captivating stories based on decades of research, this remarkably readable book explains why such learning is hard, shows how it's possible, and illustrates what it takes. Beautifully written and cogently argued, it's bound to be a classic.

—**Diana McLain Smith**, chief executive partner, New Profit Inc.; and author, *The Elephant in the Room: How Relationships Make or Break the Success of Leaders and Organizations*

"A must-read for managers at all levels who want to learn about cross-boundary teams and how to lead them. Based on her extensive research and consulting experience, Edmondson has written an authoritative, comprehensive, and engaging book that I will recommend to my students and corporate clients."

—**Michael Beer**, chairman, TruePoint Partners; and Center for Higher Ambition Leadership Cahners-Rabb Professor Emeritus, Harvard Business School

"No one has done more insightful research than Amy Edmondson on why effective teams are effective. Every team leader needs to know what she knows."

—**Chip Heath**, author, *Switch: How to Change Things When Change is Hard*

"Amy Edmondson has built a wide following for her studies on how organizations learn and grow through cooperative work and enlightened leadership. Her experience provides the rich soil from which this book has grown. It is packed with insight, drawn from cutting-edge research, and is squarely aimed at 21st century leaders seeking to build collaborative, self-reflective teams."

—**David Gergen**, senior political analyst, CNN; adviser to four U.S. presidents; professor, public service, and director, Center for Public Leadership, Harvard Kennedy School

"This book is both practical and profound. It takes us from the static organizational models and procedures of the past to the skills and practices of a knowledge economy, in which learning is the mainstay of success. *Teaming* is an extraordinary concept, filled with inspiration and possibility. My admiration for Amy Edmondson continues to grow with this contribution. This is a must-read for those in pursuit of habitual excellence, joy, and meaning in work, and success in the 21st century."

—**Julianne Morath**, chief quality and patient safety officer, Vanderbilt University Medical Center; and associate professor, clinical nursing, Vanderbilt University

teaming

How Organizations
Learn, Innovate, and Compete
in the Knowledge Economy

Amy C. Edmondson

Foreword by Edgar H. Schein

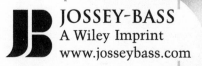

JOSSEY-BASS
A Wiley Imprint
www.josseybass.com

Published by Jossey-Bass
A Wiley Imprint
One Montgomery Street, Suite 1200, San Francisco, CA 94104-4594—www.josseybass.com

Jossey-Bass books and products are available through most bookstores. To contact Jossey-Bass directly call our Customer Care Department within the U.S. at 800-956-7739, outside the U.S. at 317-572-3986, or fax 317-572-4002.

Wiley publishes in a variety of print and electronic formats and by print-on-demand. Some material included with standard print versions of this book may not be included in e-books or in print-on-demand. If this book refers to media such as a CD or DVD that is not included in the version you purchased, you may download this material at http://booksupport.wiley.com. For more information about Wiley products, visit www.wiley.com.

Library of Congress Cataloging-in-Publication Data
Edmondson, Amy C.
Teaming: how organizations learn, innovate, and compete in the knowledge economy / Amy C. Edmondson ; foreword by Edgar H. Schein.
    p. cm.
Includes bibliographical references and index.
ISBN 978-0-7879-7093-2 (cloth); ISBN 9781118216743 (ebk);
ISBN 9781118216767 (ebk); ISBN 9781118216774 (ebk)
1. Teams in the workplace. 2. Organizational learning. I. Title.
HD66.E327 2012
658.4'022—dc23
                                    2011053064

Printed in the United States of America
FIRST EDITION
HB Printing 10 9 8 7

contents

part one
teaming

part two
organizing to learn

part three
execution-as-learning

foreword

It gives me great pleasure to write a foreword for this very important and timely book. I have known Amy's work for more than a decade and am very pleased that she has now pulled together the main points that have emerged from her seminal research on the processes that underlie teamwork.

Let me comment first on why this work is *important* and why it is essential for leaders and managers in all kinds of organizations to absorb the lessons provided here. Even though our culture tends to accept groups and teams only when pragmatically necessary to win or to get a job done, teams and teamwork are at the very foundation of society and community. It is a tragedy of our organizational society that we joke about meetings being mostly a waste of time and groups being useless because they diffuse accountability. We have built all our incentive and promotion systems on individual performance to the point that even in team sports such as hockey, soccer, basketball, and football, it is the individual star on the team who gets the press and the big bucks. The result of this cultural bias is that most leaders are shockingly incompetent in running meetings or creating teams. Yet they are dependent on teamwork. This book's emphasis on "teaming," the processes that underlie effective collaboration, provides crucial insight and understanding on what is necessary for teamwork to work.

Why is this book *timely*? Because the world is becoming more complex and multicultural. Complexity is the result of the technological evolution of all the fields of science, engineering, management, and organization development. What this means is that to get anything accomplished in a technologically complex society requires the input of information and process sophistication from many fields. That, in turn, means that managers as individuals no longer know enough to make decisions and get things done. They are de facto increasingly dependent on all kinds of specialists. And that means they have to understand the processes of "teaming," of bringing these specialists together and enabling them to work. Nowhere is this more evident than in health care, where everything from running a hospital or community health care system to doing a complex cardiac operation requires high levels of teaming.

Along with complexity we see the world becoming multicultural. And I mean this both in the *ethnic* sense of many more nations contributing to the occupational pools of most organizations and in the *occupational* sense that the specialization referred to above also leads to strong occupational cultures. Some of these cultures have been around for a long time and bedevil teaming efforts, such as the gulf that exists between doctors and nurses. Other such gulfs have arisen between the culture of information technology that feeds the egalitarianism and openness of the new generations and the traditional management culture of hierarchy and control. How do you get collaboration between a young engineer bred on total transparency and a manager who "knows" that information is power and must, therefore, be tightly controlled?

Add to this the problems of different languages and thought worlds of the many national cultures and you have the need for what this book emphasizes above all—the ability to learn. Teaming in today's and tomorrow's world will be about learning. Old formulas for what a group should be, how it should be organized and run, will not work. One of these old formulas emphasizes group composition—find out what everyone's personal style and competence is and fit the parts together. The most obvious limitation to this formula is that the changing nature of complex tasks makes it difficult to decide ahead of time what personal style and competency set to measure. Secondarily, it will be more and more difficult to find and recruit whatever competence may be needed. What this book emphasizes so well is that the mindset of teaming has to be focused on how to get the job done with the team resources available, and that inevitably is a learning process.

Teaming and learning are here to stay. Enjoy learning about it.

Edgar H. Schein

For Larry Wilson,
who started me on this journey

introduction

M ost people recognize that the knowledge-based, twenty-first-century organization depends on cross-disciplinary collaboration, flattened hierarchies, and continuous innovation. One reason for this is that expertise has narrowed and many fields have splintered into subfields. Unfortunately, the problems that need solving in the world haven't narrowed accordingly. Instead, they've just become more complex. This means that many challenges must be approached by people working together across disciplines. Product design, patient care, strategy development, pharmaceutical research, and rescue operations are just a few of the activities that call for cross-disciplinary teamwork.

To succeed in a changing and competitive global economy, organizations must also be able to learn. Expertise in almost any field is a moving target. To keep up with developments in their field, people must become lifelong learners, and success will belong to those who can master new skills and envision novel possibilities. Employees must absorb, and sometimes create, new knowledge *while* executing. Because this process typically happens among individuals working together, collective learning—that is, learning in and by smaller groups—is regarded as the primary vehicle for organizational learning. Consequently, to excel in a complex and uncertain business environment, people need to both work *and* learn together. The implications of this new reality are enormous for leaders, professionals, and anyone working in an organization.

The recognition of this reality, however, doesn't always produce a new way of working. Many organizations still rely on the top-down, command-and-control approaches that fueled growth and profitability in the industrial era. Some of the most basic tenets of this management style—ensuring control, eliminating variance, and rewarding conformance—inhibit collaboration and organizational learning. The result is that great companies, led by great managers, can fail when they confront overly complex or dynamic contexts. Most business leaders agree that their employees are important and profess the value of hearing their feedback. Such leaders welcome employee opinions and understand the importance of meeting to discuss how to improve production or create more innovative products. Yet these well-intentioned leaders often fail to reshape how work is really done. *This book explores why this gap between recognition and practice persists and provides a leadership framework that can close it.*

Teaming to Collaborate and Learn

Teaming, coined deliberately to capture the *activity* of working together, presents a new, more flexible way for organizations to carry out interdependent tasks. Unlike the traditional concept of a team, *teaming* is an active process, not a static entity. Imagine a fluid network of interconnected individuals working in temporary teams on improvement, problem solving, and innovation. Teaming blends relating to people, listening to other points of view, coordinating actions, and making shared decisions. Effective teaming requires everyone to remain vigilantly aware of others' needs, roles, and perspectives. This entails learning to relate to others better and learning to make decisions based on the integration of different perspectives. Therefore, teaming calls for developing both affective (feeling) and cognitive (thinking) skills. Enabled by distributed leadership, the purpose of teaming is to expand knowledge and expertise so that organizations and their customers can capture the value.

Teaming: How Organizations Learn, Innovate, and Compete in the Knowledge Economy describes the basic activities and conditions that help organizations succeed through teaming. This includes how work gets done, how leaders help make it happen, and how a safe interpersonal environment frees up people to focus on innovation. The model and guidelines presented throughout the book provide readers with a supportive framework for understanding and responding to the dynamics of collective learning. I examine and describe the mindset required to successfully incorporate teaming within an organizational setting, provide a set of leadership practices that can help develop a team-based learning infrastructure, and supply specific strategies for successfully teaming across the most common boundaries that hinder collaboration. In addition, I examine group processes that systematically improve existing knowledge and explain how to effectively use this new collective knowledge to improve organizational routines.

Over the past twenty years, I've conducted a series of in-depth research studies on teaming and organizational learning in hospitals, factories, senior management teams, and on NASA's Space Shuttle Program. Additionally, I've written over a dozen case studies in which the themes of teaming and learning are explored in industries as varied as manufacturing, financial services, product design, telecommunications, government, and construction. Cumulatively, this research shows how organizational cultures inhibit or enable teaming, learning, and innovation. It also supports a new definition of what successful execution looks like in the knowledge economy and shows how the best organizations are able to learn quickly while maintaining high performance standards.

While studying organizational learning, I've met some extraordinary leaders who have found ways to make their organizations more responsive and competitive. You'll meet many of them in the chapters that follow. Not all of the leaders I've studied were CEOs or heads of major agencies. Many were what I call leaders in the middle: those individuals who make a difference in their organizations by leading projects, instigating improvement, and helping other employees grow. In the course of these studies, I've also met individuals, perhaps no less remarkable, in large and multinational organizations who were stymied in their genuine desire to make a difference. In some cases, these leaders were simply thinking about their roles in the wrong way. They thought they needed to provide answers, when instead they needed to ask the right questions.

Leaders and Learners

While contemplating flattened hierarchies and distributed leadership, readers might wonder if the need for strong leadership is fading. *In fact, as the book argues throughout, the opposite is true.* The activities of teaming—taking risks, confronting failure, and crossing boundaries—are anything but natural acts in large organizations. This means that leadership is now more needed than ever before in today's complex, constantly changing landscape. This leadership can take two forms: the first is formal leadership, which I call leadership with a large L. Large-L leadership generally includes high-level executives and involves decisions and activities that influence everyone in the organization. This role is critical to effective teaming and usually includes developing organizational culture, direction setting, and the creation of goals.

But much of the time, what's needed is what I call leadership with a small l. This type of leadership is exercised by people throughout the organization, not just at the top, and especially by those at the front lines where crucial work affecting customer experiences is carried out. This kind of leadership is about developing others' skills and shaping effective processes. In small-*l* leadership, those in the thick of collaborative activity help ensure that teaming occurs effectively. Sometimes these leaders have formal responsibility for a project or a department; at other times, they're simply the ones who see an opportunity to lead and act upon it. With teaming, the concept of leadership then becomes an activity that takes place both at the top ranks of the organization and at the front lines of operations.

As both a practical and research-based resource, *Teaming: How Organizations Learn, Innovate, and Compete in the Knowledge Economy* is tailored to a wide audience that includes leaders of all types and levels, as well as future leaders. Practitioners need approaches that they can readily apply to their work environment. To this end, I provide ideas, solutions, and strategies appropriate for all types of private and public organizations. These are intended to help leaders who wish to study or promote teaming in support of performance improvement. Leaders include executives, managers, team and project leaders, and supervisors searching for ways to create an environment that encourages and supports teaming. The book also is intended to help human resource professionals in aiding collaboration, training people to team, and implementing organizational learning.

In addition, academics and students of business administration and organizational behavior will find the book to be a useful resource for course curricula and research. In conceptualizing teaming, I incorporate relevant scholarly material and empirical evidence. I synthesize many of the findings from my research, previously found only in academic journals, so as to bring this work to the attention of a broader audience. I also draw heavily on the pedagogical tools I've developed over the years to deepen students' comprehension of business issues and to energize classroom discussion. In particular, students will find the three case studies presented in Chapter Eight useful in bridging the gap between theory and practical application.

Overview of the Book

The idea that an organization should be able to anticipate and respond to changes in its environment is as difficult to put into action as it is compelling. Many adults have to relearn how to learn, and everyone could use help learning how to team. For most individuals, truly engaging with others in a goal-oriented, open-minded, collaborative process requires letting go of some old habits. The human behaviors that make these valuable attributes possible must be painstakingly cultivated. This book explores these issues in three parts.

Part One focuses on teaming, describing the core activities that fuel teaming efforts and answering these questions: How does it work? What does it take for people to learn how to team? What do people do when teaming? How does teaming produce organizational learning? This section describes the challenges to teaming and shows what teaming looks like when it's done well. Chapter One opens by defining teaming and examining why it's so crucial in today's complex organizations, and then presents a new framework for understanding learning and knowledge. In Chapter Two, I describe the step-by-step teaming process in more detail, reveal how easily teaming breaks down, and establish four leadership actions that enable teaming and learning.

Part Two examines these four leadership actions in much greater detail. The emphasis here is on the human side of teaming, with an up-close look at how people work together in a wide variety of organizational contexts. More specifically, Chapter Three explores the power of framing and what leaders can do through framing to promote effective collaboration and learning. In Chapter Four, I look at how psychological safety promotes the attitudes, skills, and behaviors necessary for successful teaming. I detail just how much fear there is in today's workplace, despite rhetoric to the contrary, and how crippling this fear is for problem solving. Chapter Five shows why failure is an essential part of organizational learning and presents specific practices for overcoming the challenges that failure presents. Chapter Six follows with an examination of the importance, and challenge, of spanning boundaries between disciplines, departments, companies, or even countries—and shows what is possible when we do, starting with the story of the "impossible" rescue of 33 miners trapped under 2,000 feet of rock in the San Jose copper mine in Chile in 2010.

In Part Three, the emphasis shifts from individual and interpersonal behaviors to organizational implementation. Chapter Seven pulls together many of the lessons and strategies from the previous chapters to provide a new model for execution, which includes specific steps for diagnosing, designing, and implementing an iterative process that ensures continuous learning and improvement. I develop the characteristics and attributes of different contexts, based on the level of process knowledge, in more detail. A detailed case study reveals the risk of misdiagnosing process knowledge and the importance of experimentation. Chapter Eight offers three case studies that examine different potential learning outcomes, including process improvement, problem solving, and innovation. The first case study looks at leadership that inspires and empowers dramatic performance turnarounds in existing companies that have fallen behind. In the second case study, I describe leadership that engages people throughout an organization in working together to solve tough problems in complex operations. The third case study focuses on leadership that supports innovation, allowing the kind of teaming that gives rise to pioneering products and processes.

To help readers understand and use the ideas and frameworks, I've incorporated a number of special features throughout the book, including the following:

- Exhibits and bulleted lists containing critical strategies, definitions, and distinctions

- Tables outlining specific leadership strategies that reflect best practices assembled through decades of extensive research

- Sidebars that add context to salient ideas and provide additional resources

- Vignettes and real-world examples that help illustrate key lessons and stimulate reflection

- Chapter summary sections to help readers review critical concepts

Teaming: How Organizations Learn, Innovate, and Compete in the Knowledge Economy is intended as an accessible resource for anyone trying to increase collaboration and promote long-term success. It is designed so practitioners can easily navigate each chapter and locate specific topics or strategies. This means readers can shift from chapter to chapter and pull out what they need, when they need it. But there's also an advantage to reading the chapters in order: each chapter is clearly linked and the concepts presented build on each other to help readers develop a deeper understanding of the relationship between teaming, learning, and performance.

Regardless of how a reader chooses to use the book, however, my primary hope is that it will help improve organizational actions through the creation of a more optimistic, collective spirit. When leaders empower, rather than control; when they ask the right questions, rather than provide the right answers; and when they focus on flexibility, rather than insist on adherence, they move to a higher form of execution. When people know their ideas are welcome, they will offer innovative ways to lower costs and improve quality, thus laying a more solid foundation for meaningful work and organizational success.

part one

teaming

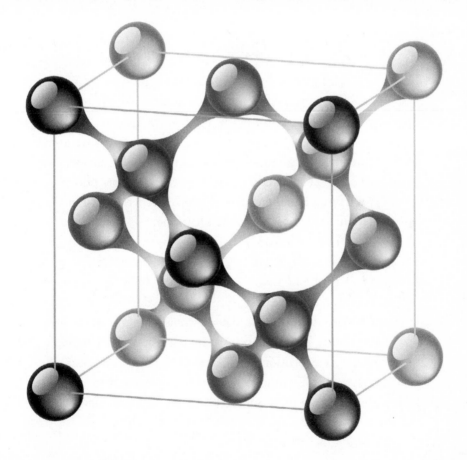

chapter one

a new way of working

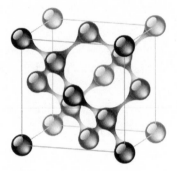

Say the word *team* and the first image that comes to mind is probably a sports team: football players huddled in the mud, basketball players swarming in a full-court press, or baseball players turning a game-saving double play. In sports, great teams consist of individuals who have learned to trust one another. Over time, they have discovered each other's strengths and weaknesses, enabling them to play as a coordinated whole. Similarly, musicians form bands, chamber groups, and orchestras that rely on interdependent talents. A symphony falls apart unless the string section coordinates with the woodwinds, brass, and percussionists. Even when a soloist is featured on stage, the orchestral score has a part for every musician. A successful performance is one in which the musicians complement one another and play in harmony. Like all good teams, they display synergy. The whole is greater than the sum of its parts. The players understand that they succeed or fail together—they win or lose as a team.

In today's complex and volatile business environment, corporations and organizations also win or lose by creating wholes that are greater than the sum of their parts. Intense competition, rampant unpredictability, and a constant need for innovation are giving rise to even greater interdependence and thus demand even greater levels of collaboration and communication than ever before. Teaming is essential to an organization's ability to respond to opportunities and to improve internal processes. This chapter aims to deepen your understanding of why teaming and the behaviors it requires are so crucial for organizational success in today's environment. To help illuminate the teaming process and its benefits, this chapter defines teaming, places it within a historical context, and presents a new framework for understanding organizational learning and process knowledge, and explains why these are important concepts for today's leaders.

Teaming Is a Verb

Sports teams and musical groups are both bounded, static collections of individuals. Like most work teams in the past, they are physically located in the same place while practicing or performing together. Members of these teams learn how to interact. They've developed trust and know each other's roles. Advocating stable boundaries, well-designed tasks, and thoughtfully composed membership, many seminal theories of organizational effectiveness explained how to design and manage just these types of static performance teams.[1]

Harvard psychologist Richard Hackman, a preeminent scholar of team effectiveness, established the power of team structures in enabling team performance. According to this influential perspective, well-designed teams are those with clear goals, well-thought-out tasks that are conducive to teamwork, team members with the right skills and experiences for the task, adequate resources, and access to coaching and support. Get the design right, the theory says, and the performance will take care of itself. This model focused on the team as an entity, looking largely within the well-defined bounds of a team to explain its performance. Other research, notably conducted by MIT professor Deborah Ancona, showed that how much a team's members interact with people outside the team boundaries was also an important factor in team performance.[2] Both perspectives worked well in guiding the design and management of effective teams, at least in contexts where managers had the lead time and the run time to invest in composing stable, well-designed teams.

In these prior treatments, team is a noun. A team is an established, fixed group of people cooperating in pursuit of a common goal. But what if a team disbands almost as quickly as it was assembled? For example, what if you work in an emergency services facility where the staffing changes every shift, and the team changes completely for every case or client? What if you're a member of a temporary project team formed to solve a unique production problem? Or you're part of a group of managers with a mix of individual and shared responsibilities? How do you create synergy when you lack the advantages offered by the frequent drilling and practice sessions of static performance teams like those in sports and music?

The answer lies in **teaming.**

Teaming is a verb. It is a dynamic activity, not a bounded, static entity. It is largely determined by the mindset and practices of teamwork, not by the design and structures of effective teams. Teaming is teamwork on the fly. It involves coordinating and collaborating without the benefit of stable team structures, because many operations, such as hospitals, power plants, and military installations, require a level of staffing flexibility that makes stable team composition rare.[3] In a growing number of organizations, the constantly shifting nature of work means that many teams disband almost as soon as they've formed. You could be working on one team right now, but in a few days, or even a few minutes, you may be on another team.

Fast-moving work environments need people who know *how to team*, people who have the skills and the flexibility to act in moments of potential collaboration when and where they appear. They must have the ability to move on, ready for the next such moments. Teaming still relies on old-fashioned teamwork skills such as recognizing and clarifying interdependence, establishing trust, and figuring out how to coordinate. But there usually isn't time to build a foundation of familiarity through the careful sharing of personal history and prior experience, nor is there time for developing shared experiences through practice working together. Instead, people need to develop and use new capabilities for sharing crucial knowledge quickly. They must learn to ask questions clearly and frequently. They must make the small adjustments through which different skills and knowledge are woven together into timely products and services.

Why should managers care about teaming? The answer is simple. Teaming is the engine of organizational learning.[4] By now, everyone knows that organizations need to learn—to thrive in a world of continuous change. But *how* organizations learn is not as well understood. As discussed later in this chapter, organizations are complex entities; many are globally distributed, most encompass multiple areas of expertise, and nearly all engage in a variety of activities. What does it mean for such a complex entity to "learn"? An organization cannot engage in a learning process in any meaningful sense—not in the way an individual can. Yet, when individuals learn, this does not always create change in the ways the organization delivers products and services to customers. This is a conundrum that has long fascinated academics.

This book offers a practical answer to the question of how organizational learning really happens: through teaming. Products and services are provided to customers by interdependent people and processes. Crucial learning activities must take place, within those smaller, focused units of action, for organizations to improve and innovate. In spite of the obvious need for change, most large enterprises are still managed according to a powerful mindset I call "organizing to execute."[5]

Organizing to Execute

If you stood on a main street in Detroit around 1900, you would have seen electric trolleys sharing the streets with horse-drawn carriages. A mere decade later, cars had arrived in force. Though inefficient and unreliable, these increasingly popular cars brought with them the promise of a new, exciting world. For a short time, however, both literal horse and mechanical horsepower tried to share the streets, sometimes with devastating consequences. Many people found the collision of old and new worlds difficult, especially when those streets became even more crowded with young men from the countryside drawn to the city by the promise of manufacturing jobs.

In this transitional period, it was not obvious to the average worker how much the new industrial era would disrupt the social order by calling for new forms of obedience, unprecedented conformity to routine, and a new mindset that revered systems of control. Self-sufficient farmers and shopkeepers, who had for generations confronted vicissitudes of weather and illness and found ways to survive, would subtly but inexorably be transformed into order-followers collecting paychecks from impersonal enterprises.

Organizing to execute found its seminal momentum in Henry Ford's invention of the assembly line: workers focused on fitting cog to component and component to cog. Emphasizing routine procedures, Ford's approach made the working life of employees menial and tedious. Reliable and predictable, Ford's assembly-line process was as much a novelty as its product. With the new century, age-old structures for self-reliance were being replaced with the small, repetitive steps that made mass production possible and brought about the modern world of products and services we know today. Ford's success was contingent upon a high level of managerial control over employee practices known today as command-and-control management, or top-down management. The practice of top-down management is one component of a broader organizational methodology known as scientific management.

Scientific Management

Ford's intellectual partner as a pioneer in mass production was management expert Frederick Winslow Taylor, who complemented Ford's assembly line with his efficiency methods and scientific measurement. Taylor and his followers devised ways to transform unpredictable and expensive customized work into efficient, economical systems of mass production. Long product life cycles allowed ample payback for the time invested in designing near-foolproof execution systems like the machine-paced assembly line. Periods of stability could be counted on. Products, processes, and even customers were mercifully uniform, minimizing the need for real-time improvisation to respond to unexpected problems, technological changes, or customer needs. Promoting the use of empirical methods, Taylor advocated his model of management and production in two influential monographs, *Shop Management* and *The Principles of Scientific Management*.[6]

As managers today well know, an advantage of these new small, repetitive tasks was their transparency. Small, repetitive tasks are easy to monitor. They make the performance of the individual worker easy to measure. The assumption that firm performance was the cumulative result of thousands and thousands of well-designed and well-executed individual tasks dominated managerial theory and matched the economic reality. Even today, when it comes to issues like efficiency and productivity, most managers and corporate leaders are driven by taken-for-granted beliefs that were first promulgated by Ford and Taylor. For example, many consider the ability to measure and reward the specific, differentiated performance of individuals crucial to good management—a belief that is inaccurate and unhelpful in certain settings.

Ford and Taylor's Legacy

Devotion to efficiency and productivity resulted in two major workplace changes. First, it spurred a demand for professional managers who could oversee a vast complex of work activity. Second, it instilled a basic distrust of the worker. To ensure that workers did their jobs according to specified procedures, objective measurements of individual performance were relatively easy for managers to develop and implement. And, for the most part, workers who tried harder performed better. In mass-production settings like the one designed by Ford, opportunities for worker decision making or creativity were nonexistent. With this transparency, fear worked reasonably well to motivate employees. Whether through a fear of supervisor sanction or loss of material rewards, managers were able to coerce and intimidate workers to ensure high productivity. If there were costs to this approach for the enterprise or corporation, they were not in plain view.

The primary problem this legacy creates for managers today is that these systems produced an overreliance on fear in management practice. As Taylorism gained a foothold in factories across the country, the corporate mood became dour. Taylorism was ruthless. The individual's worth was measured by his or her contribution to enterprise gains. A history of the United Auto Workers union described factory life in these early days as follows: "Every Ford worker is perfectly aware that he is under constant observation—that he will be admonished if he falls below the fast pace of the department."[7] Even in 1940, decades after the early days of the Ford miracle, a worker could be fired for smiling.[8]

For managers and owners, there were reasons to smile. The record time for assembling a car in 1908 was 12 hours and 28 minutes. After the process was Taylorized, the first moving assembly line in 1913 cut the time to 93 minutes. While it is true that workers felt fear during the day and resentment at night, it is equally true that Taylorism prepared the industrial world for new efficiencies and wealth creation that had never been experienced before.

Fear in the Modern Workplace

Unfortunately, draconian management practice is not relegated to the distant past. Consider the rash of employee suicides that brought Foxconn's factory conditions to the public eye in May 2010. Said one employee interviewed: "Every day, I repeat the same thing I did yesterday. We get yelled at all the time. It's very tough around here." Reports surfaced of twelve-hour standing shifts, having to ask permission to go to the bathroom, and relentless pressure to meet daily manufacturing quotas.

Source: http://www.bloomberg.com/news/2010-06-02/foxconn-workers-in-china-say-meaningless-life-monotony-spark-suicides.html.

Fear and routine have never been limited to blue-collar work. Ford's factory worker can be seen as the precursor to the 1950s "organization man," a term coined by sociologist William Whyte. Deindividuating labor was not all that different from deindividuating white-collar work. Much like the assembly-line worker, the office-bound "organization man" was bound by rules, processes, hierarchical structures, and fear. Moreover, the image of the organization man wasn't just promulgated by sociologists. Novelists and writers have portrayed work in large organizations as replete with both monotony and anxiety. American literature has long presented bankers and other managers as organization men, experiencing the same cog-in-the-machine dehumanization as their blue-collar counterparts. Notably, the works of John P. Marquand, Sinclair Lewis, and John Cheever depict men for whom the daily grind results in alienation from family and friends and requires release through fantasy or self-medication. The "man in the gray flannel suit" (the title of a 1955 novel by Sloan Wilson) was as bound by rules, processes, hierarchical structures, and fear as was his counterpart on the assembly line. The organization man is alive and well in contemporary culture—as the butt of satire, for example, in the hit TV series *The Office*, and in the somber portrait of skewed priorities in the 1950s business world, personified in *Madmen* advertising wunderkind Don Draper.

As a society, we are still largely inured to a fear-based work environment. We believe (most of the time, erroneously) that fear increases control. Control reinforces certainty and predictability. We don't immediately see the costs of fear, as explored in detail in Chapter Four. In fact, many managers believe that without fear people will not work hard enough.

Traditional models of organizing emphasize plans, details, roles, budgets, and schedules—tools of certainty and predictability. When we know a lot about what it will take to achieve the results we seek, these traditional models are superbly useful. And though this environment worked well for the assembly-line worker and the organization man, it is no longer a competitive advantage in today's knowledge-based economy. Just as people one hundred years ago underwent a profound change in how they thought about the way work gets done, today's turbulent work environment once again requires a new mindset—not just new slogans. It requires a new way of thinking and being.

The Learning Imperative

By nearly every measurement, General Motors (GM) has been one of the world's most successful enterprises. Founded in Flint, Michigan, in 1908, GM acquired more than twenty other fledgling automobile companies in its first decade of operation. During its remarkable ascension in the 1920s, GM passed Ford as the largest automaker in the United States. By 1931, GM had become the largest producer and seller of automobiles in the world. The company held this position for seventy-six consecutive years, throughout an era of remarkable economic growth and one in which both predictability and control dominated management thinking. GM's growth continued throughout the 1940s, as the practice of sharing components across different brands created incredible economies of scale. By the 1950s, GM had captured nearly 60 percent of the automotive market in the United States and produced the number-one selling brand in the world, Chevrolet. In 1955, GM topped the first of twenty consecutive Fortune 500 lists as the largest, most profitable company in the world. In 1970, GM was nearly twice the size of the next largest company, Exxon Mobil, and nearly three times the size of General Electric. By the 1980s, GM had 350,000 employees, operated 150 automobile assembly plants, and sold over 9.5 million cars per year.[9]

GM succeeded and grew to its dominant position in the automotive industry through successful execution. Along the way, it became a much-heralded model of how to organize and a venerated example of professional management. Confident of the wisdom of its approach, GM remained wedded to a well-developed competency in centralized control and high-volume execution for years. But as the world around the GM empire changed in dramatic ways, despite the firm's well-honed systems of execution, GM steadily lost ground at the turn of the twenty-first century. Sales deteriorated throughout the early 2000s, with GM finally losing its crown as "King of the Carmakers" to Toyota Motor Company in 2008. After years of decline, a stunned nation looked on in 2009 when the company filed for bankruptcy.

Uncertain and Unpredictable

Like many dominant companies in the industrial era, GM was slow to shift its routines and practices in ways that reflected the changing market. In any industry, success can be difficult to sustain. This difficulty is not due to the fact that people get tired of working hard. It is because the managerial mindset that enables efficient execution actually inhibits an organization's ability to learn and innovate. The narrow focus on getting things done inhibits the experimentation and reflection that are vital to sustainable success in an unpredictable and evolving business environment. A similar fate befell other industrial giants like U.S. Steel, Polaroid, RCA, Uniroyal, and Union Carbide.

Despite this history of failed giants, most executives still believe that consistent execution is a surefire path to customer satisfaction and financial results. Managers who let up on execution even briefly, the assumption goes, do so at their peril. Productivity must be maintained at all costs! This belief remains oddly alive in the popular management literature, as well as in business schools and MBA programs across the country. The penchant for execution manifests itself in the almost reverent focus on metrics and bottom lines inside and outside organizations. A belief that performance is a simple function of native ability plus effort expended—and can be easily measured as output—is often drilled into senior management, whose careers have spanned decades.

This mindset trickles down from the top into the ranks of most large organizations and works adequately when knowledge about how to produce the products and services customers want is well developed and unambiguous. But even the most exquisite plans and disciplined execution cannot guarantee success when knowledge about how to produce a desired result is either still developing or is in a state of dramatic flux. Under these circumstances, traditional models of organizing that stress execution falter. This has prompted a need to find new ways to organize that take into account dramatic changes in technology, globalization, expert knowledge of all kinds, and customer expectations.

Thriving in the Face of Uncertainty

As customer expectations continue to shift and competition becomes increasingly global, many companies struggle to succeed in a drastically changing landscape. Rapid developments in technology and changes in the legal environment greatly reduce the barriers to entry in a variety of industries, thus introducing new, nimble competitors. Now you see supermarkets, department stores, and funeral homes offering financial services formerly the exclusive purview of banks and banking institutions. Likewise, telephone companies offer television service, while television companies offer phone service. Heightened competitive pressure means that even in previously stable industries unexpected changes are occurring in a compressed period of time and creating new, unprecedented challenges.

Consequently, as management and system dynamics expert Peter Senge put it, "The organizations that will truly excel in the future will be the organizations that discover how to tap people's commitment and capacity to learn at all levels in an organization."[10] Learning new skills in an uncertain environment where knowledge is a moving target is now a competitive imperative in most industries. Consider the astonishing expansion of medical knowledge. If you were practicing medicine in 1960, you could subscribe to a few leading professional journals and most likely keep up with the literature in your field. In 1960, there were just a hundred articles published on randomized control trials, the gold standard for best practices in medicine. Today more than 10,000 articles reporting on randomized control trials are published annually.[11] An average engineer today sports a wristwatch with more computing power and memory than was available to the team of engineers working in the Apollo program at NASA in the 1960s.

Good-bye Taylor and Ford . . .
Hello Complex Adaptive Systems

The point is that knowledge in fields related to health care, technology, science, and engineering, as well as a host of others, is growing at such a pace that today's workplace is significantly different from that of the industrialized manufacturing era of Ford and Taylor. By now, most leaders and managers recognize that organizations that don't learn are left behind their more innovate and adaptive competitors. In this dynamic environment, successful organizations need to be managed as complex adaptive systems rather than as intricate controlled machines.

Academic interest in complexity science has grown over the past few decades. The term *complex adaptive system* describes systems that are dynamic and adaptable, much like those found in nature. A system is complex when it has many interacting parts. Feedback loops are a hallmark of complex systems. Feedback loops mean that part A has an impact on part B, which may then affect part C, which feeds back in turn to have an impact on part A. Taken together, these interactions create unpredictable dynamics. Trying to understand, much less predict, what happens in such systems when one is expecting linear, unidirectional relationships—where A influences B, which may influence C, and that is the end of the chain—will produce flawed results.

Complex adaptive systems self-regulate. Not always in preferred ways, mind you, but they change in response to both external and internal triggers. Examples of such systems range from an embryo to an ant colony to a hospital. What these systems have in common is that they encompass a number of similar elements (cells, ants, people) and they self-organize in reaction to external and internal disruptions (often called perturbations).[12]

Like their counterparts in nature, businesses and other organizations are complex adaptive systems. They may self-regulate, but they require thoughtful leadership to optimize their potential. As this book describes throughout, the spontaneous reactions of managers in organizations often ambush the requirements of the new, interconnected, knowledge-intensive world of work. Classic management theories, as we have seen, tended to overvalue control and treat organizations as mechanical systems.

The learning imperative requires relinquishing control as the ultimate goal. It requires embracing the creation of adaptive capabilities as a fundamental organizational competence. It requires flexibility and judgment. It requires a managerial approach that works when organizations face uncertainty created by new technologies, shifting customer preferences, or complex systems. Success requires a shift from *organizing to execute* to a new way of working that supports collaboration, innovation, and organizational learning.

Learning to Team, Teaming to Learn

Simply put, teaming is a way of working that brings people together to generate new ideas, find answers, and solve problems. But people have to learn to team; it doesn't come naturally in most organizations. Teaming is worth learning, because it is essential for improvement, problem solving, and innovation in a functioning enterprise. The complex interdependencies involved in learning and innovating require the interpersonal skills necessary to negotiate disagreements, overcome technical jargon, and revisit ideas or problems until solutions emerge—all activities supported by teaming. Learning in today's organizations involves what's called reciprocal interdependence, where back-and-forth communication and coordination are essential to getting the work done.

Although teaming can help any enterprise improve, it is absolutely critical to success when any of the following conditions are present:

- When the work requires people to juggle multiple objectives with minimal oversight.

- When people must be able to shift from one situation to another while maintaining high levels of communication and tight coordination. This situation literally defines the practice of teaming.

- When it is helpful to integrate perspectives from different disciplines.

- When collaborating across dispersed locations.

- When pre-planned coordination is impossible or unrealistic due to the changing nature of the work.

- When complex information must be processed, synthesized, and put to good use quickly.

Though teaming refers to a dynamic activity rather than to a traditional, bounded group structure, many of its purposes and benefits are grounded in basic principles of teams and teamwork. Among the benefits of teams is their ability to integrate diverse expertise as needed to accomplish many important tasks. Historically, the focus of team research and project implementation was on reorganizing production processes. Increasingly, however, teamwork extends beyond the factory floor. Management teams develop corporate strategies. Sales teams sell sophisticated services to complex, multinational customers. Product development teams create pathbreaking new technologies. Each of these examples involves people, often with very different backgrounds and expertise, working interdependently to accomplish a challenging goal. Their tasks may vary in terms of the degree of interdependence and the amount of collaboration required, but they all need to coordinate and cooperate.

Using teams to solve problems or shape new strategic directions has been popular in organizations for well over a decade. In 2003, the Manufacturing Performance Institute's (MPI) Census of Manufacturers reported that 70 percent of respondents used teams to accomplish their business goals. As Glenn Parker, consultant and author of several books on teams, noted that same year, generalism has replaced specialization, collaboration has replaced autonomy, empowerment has replaced power, and teamwork has replaced individualism.[13]

Yet all is not perfect with teams and teaming. Despite the fact that team use is steadily increasing, team effectiveness is not keeping up at the same pace. In the previously cited MPI report, only about 14 percent of organizations surveyed rated their teaming efforts as "highly effective," while just over half (50.4 percent) rated their teams as "somewhat effective." Thus, over a third of teams were rated as ineffective. This, in addition to scores of other reports and studies, indicates that although utilizing teams to get interdependent work done can be valuable, achieving the tremendous potential of teams is far more challenging than many expect—and successful teamwork is thus still elusive in many organizations. In the absence of a particular type of leadership, the right kinds of learning behaviors to deal with uncertainty and ambiguity tend not to occur. Teaming, it seems, requires a new type of leadership that supports speaking up, asking questions, and sharing ideas. In short, teaming requires a leadership mindset that cultivates an environment conducive to learning. I use the term "organizing to learn" to describe this leadership mindset and its accompanying practices.

Organizing to Learn

Staying competitive, as we have seen, requires learning. Organizing to learn is a way of leading that encourages critical teaming behaviors to promote collective learning. It supports the collaboration needed to solicit employees' knowledge, apply it to new situations or challenges, and to analyze outcomes. Organizing to learn is a way of moving forward in spite of uncertainty. Taking action without certainty can be a daunting prospect in organizations where stability and success are valued over variance and experimentation.

Learning, for individuals or groups, is an active process of gaining information, understanding, or capabilities. Learning is a process of action and reflection, in which action is taken, assessed, and modified to produce desired outcomes. Research in various settings has demonstrated significant performance benefits of individuals engaging in learning behaviors. Most work in organizations, however, requires coordinated action among multiple individuals. The knowledge required to conduct work successfully takes many forms and resides in many locations. To be successful, groups must access knowledge, develop a shared understanding of how best to apply it, and act in a coordinated manner that is reflective of new insights. This means work in groups frequently requires collective learning.

Collective learning includes such activities as collecting, sharing, or analyzing information; obtaining and reflecting on feedback from customers or others; and active experimentation. Individual learning behaviors within a collective learning experience include the following:

- Asking questions

- Sharing information

- Seeking help

- Experimenting with unproven actions

- Talking about mistakes

- Seeking feedback

These learning behaviors enable groups to obtain and process the data needed to adapt and improve. Through collective learning, organizations can detect changes in the environment, learn about customers' requirements, improve members' collective understanding of a situation, or discover the consequences of their previous actions. They require a willingness to take interpersonal risks such as discussing mistakes. This requires leaders who work to create environments that support and encourage sharing, experimenting, and learning.

The old mindset, organizing to execute, has been a century in the making, so it's no wonder that many leaders adopt it by force of habit and training. Organizing to execute has many strengths, especially in its emphasis on discipline and efficiency. However, it also has many risks, particularly when used in highly uncertain or complex contexts. In these settings, organizing to learn is critical to success. Table 1.1 highlights key differences between the approaches and identifies two distinct mindsets, and the corresponding management practices, that leaders can adopt when they are responsible for guiding people and organizations.

Organizing to execute makes sense when production processes are well understood and can be reliably used. In this case, managers

Table 1.1: Organizing to Execute Versus Organizing to Learn

Management Approach	Organizing to Execute	Organizing to Learn
Hiring	Conformers, rule followers.	Problem solvers, experimenters.
Training	Learning before doing.	Learning from doing.
Measuring performance	Did YOU do it right?	Did WE learn?
Structuring work	Separate expertise.	Integrate expertise.
Employee discretion allowed	Choose among options.	Experiment through trial and error.
Empowerment means	Employees can deviate from the script if special circumstances make it necessary.	There is no script. Improvise!
Process goal	Drive out variance.	Use variance to analyze and improve.
Watercooler conversation	About the weather	About the work
Business goal	Make money now.	Make money later.
Works when	Path forward is clear.	Path forward is not clear.

can hire people based on assessments of whether a candidate would be both willing and able to follow prescribed procedures. New hires typically go through a period of training to get them up to speed, and performance is then measured based on how well employees do what they've been asked to do. To make such measurement feasible, work is subdivided so it's easy to see who did what, and how well. In this type of context, jobs may require employees to successfully execute one of several options (such as giving the customer the right meal from a fast-food restaurant menu, or giving the right response to a particular billing query in a call center). Sometimes it is necessary to deviate a little further, if special circumstances require a customized response to a customer situation (for example, the call-center operator might gently ask a customer, "Is that a baby I hear crying in the background? Do you want me to call back later?"). At the watercooler, employees with routine tasks are likely to talk about their personal lives or the weather, not about their work. Organizing to execute is all about driving out unnecessary variance, so that the process is as efficient as possible—wasting as little employee time, material, and other valuable resources as possible. Efficiency is a crucial source of profitability. When organizing to execute is done well, processes hum along.

In contrast, when production processes are not yet developed, managers must organize to learn. As shown on the right in Table 1.1, they need to hire people willing to experiment, rather than to conform—that is, employees who will keep solving the many problems that inevitably surface when doing something new. Rather than receiving extensive training in existing processes to prepare for a new role, new employees instead are invited to get right to work helping to discover new processes. Performance is measured based on how well they do that—this includes making mistakes and learning from them. When facing an uncertain path forward, trying something that fails, then figuring out what works instead, is the very essence of good performance. Great performance, however, is trying something that fails, figuring out what works instead, *and* telling your colleagues all about it—about both the success and the failure. This discovery process usually requires people to integrate different areas of expertise to figure out new approaches to the work. A script simply isn't possible. People must improvise by trying out a variety of things, and they must use this variety as a source of learning. When this kind of collaborative learning is under way, employees at the watercooler are likely to talk about the work—problems they've encountered and solved, and, more important, those they still need help with. A colleague at the cooler is a resource!

In some respects, organizing to learn is not all that different from organizing to execute. There's the same discipline, respect for systems, and attention to detail. Look more closely, however, and it's a radically different organizational mindset that focuses less on ensuring a process is followed than on helping it evolve. When leaders adopt an organizing-to-learn approach, instead of focusing on making products more efficiently than the competition, they focus on learning faster than the competition. The goal is to find out what works and what doesn't. Most important, when an organizing-to-learn mindset is combined with teaming, the result is a manner of operating I call execution-as-learning.

Execution-as-Learning

Execution-as-learning is a way of operating as an organization that combines continuous learning with high performance. Simply stated, execution-as-learning means getting the work done while simultaneously working on how to do it better.[14] In a way, it folds the mindset and behaviors of learning into the discipline of execution, allowing workers, managers, and leaders to get as much done as possible. This partly depends on the state of process knowledge related to the work being done, as described next—while also driving improvement. Execution-as-learning usually requires teaming (as a way of working) and is enabled by the leadership practices of organizing to learn.

The defining attribute of execution-as-learning is its integration of constant, unremarkable, small-scale learning into day-to-day work. Execution-as-learning is akin to reflection-in-action, rather than reflection-after-action, a thinking habit embraced by skilled individual practitioners in fields ranging from architecture to medicine.[15] But execution-as-learning describes groups or organizations, not individual people. Instead of following long periods of action with weighty, time-consuming, after-action reviews or burdensome extra assignments in the form of lessons learned, some organizations have mastered the art of building learning processes into how work is executed. Figure 1.1 illustrates the relationship between teaming, organizing to learn, and execution-as-learning.

In Figure 1.1, teaming is the base. It includes the interpersonal actions and behaviors required to rapidly collaborate, adjust, and

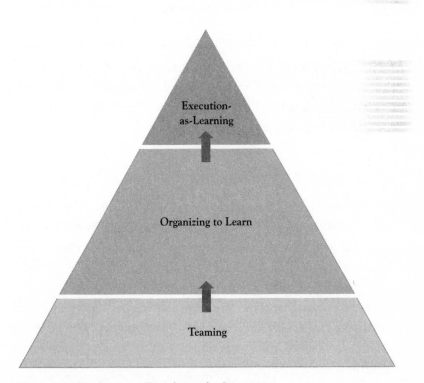

Figure 1.1. Teaming as a Foundation for Learning

learn. But promoting learning requires a type of leadership that encourages the interpersonal behaviors needed for teaming and collective learning. The next level of the pyramid presents this leadership framework. Organizing to learn helps leaders enable, focus, and apply organizational learning. At the peak of the pyramid, execution-as-learning represents a way of operating—as an organization—in which continuous, systematic learning occurs in tandem with product or service delivery. Execution-as-learning is thus a system of operating that builds learning into day-to-day work to meet ever-shifting needs and promote success over the long term.

As outlined in the introduction, this book has three parts that mirror the levels of the pyramid: Part One presents a way of working (teaming), Part Two explains a way of leading (organizing to learn), and Part Three describes a way of operating (execution-as-learning). Much like building a real pyramid, successfully implementing teaming starts with establishing the foundation. In this case, that foundation includes an understanding of what to expect from teaming efforts in various work contexts. Using such factors as knowledge maturity, work type, and uncertainty, the Process Knowledge Spectrum is an important tool for identifying work contexts and operational settings.

The Process Knowledge Spectrum

The obvious need for organizational learning in today's knowledge-driven workplace raises critical questions. What should be the focus of learning? What kind of learning—for example, continuous improvement of an essentially well-developed process, problem solving to fix a broken process, or innovation to create a new process—is most needed? The answers to these questions vary across companies, and divisions within companies, in accordance with where they are situated on the Process Knowledge Spectrum.

By process knowledge, I mean knowledge about how to produce a desired result, regardless of whether that result is an automobile, a hamburger, or a successful surgery. The more knowledge we have about how to achieve a desired result—for instance, how to manufacture an automobile or how to cure strep throat—the more mature the knowledge. The less knowledge we have about how something is done—for example, how to create an affordable car with no carbon footprint or how to cure amyotrophic lateral sclerosis (ALS)—the less mature the knowledge. When process knowledge is well developed or mature, as in a manufacturing setting, uncertainty is low. When employees follow a prescribed set of directions, they get a certain result. At the other end of the spectrum is innovation operations, where much of the sought-after knowledge is yet to be discovered. The Process Knowledge Spectrum, depicted in Figure 1.2, characterizes work according to the maturity of cause-effect relationships that translate goals into results.

At one end of the Process Knowledge Spectrum is high-volume repetitive work, such as one might see in fast-food restaurants, call centers, or assembly plants. At the other end is pioneering research and discovery, where little is known about how to obtain a particular desired result. This includes ambitious goals like curing a rare form of cancer or designing the next generation of green vehicles, along with smaller-scale ambitions like designing a new kitchen gadget, or implementing a new IT system. Because prior

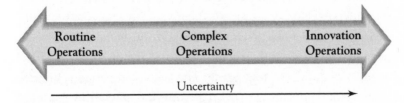

Figure 1.2. The Process Knowledge Spectrum

experience achieving the goal is limited, making progress requires risk taking and experimentation. In the middle are complex operations—exemplified by complex service organizations like a tertiary care hospital, where some knowledge is mature, such as the procedure for drawing blood, but much knowledge, such as how to treat a rare disease or the mix of patients to expect on any given day, is unknown or in flux. In these settings, teaming is not just challenging; it is invaluable.

How Process Knowledge Varies

Most of the workplaces I've studied can be characterized as complex or innovation operations. They sit in the middle or toward the right side of the Process Knowledge Spectrum. But I've also spent considerable time in factories that make products like cars and laptops, as well as those that mass-produce services of various kinds—fast food, billing services, and so forth. The contrasts between these different settings inspired the distinctions and categories depicted in Figure 1.2.

Routine operations. Laptops, toasters, or cars—every assembly plant relies on and applies well-developed and precisely codified process knowledge. There is no room for uncertainty. Learning, still valuable, is largely focused on improvement and making the existing process more accurate, less expensive, and less time-consuming. In short, success equals improved efficiency.

But even routine operations don't hum along forever. New machinery and new products often require temporary problem solving to develop new processes that will soon become standardized. Once the problems are solved and the bumps and hiccups removed, new standards and scripts can be devised. New products or services then become routine. The transition period is limited. Teaming and organizing to learn are thus integral to the process of organizing to execute.

Complex operations. Uncertainty about arrival times, customers' specific needs, and unpredictable interactions make complex operations challenging. Although knowledge of how to produce most of the specific results exists in a reasonably mature state for some situations, many can be difficult to predict. The combination of tasks is thus constantly shifting. Often, old and new tasks interact to produce novel, unexpected, or problematic results.

The most prominent form of learning in this context is problem solving. Most problems are what my Harvard colleague Anita Tucker and I call work process problems: disruptions that impede task completion, often due to shortages of material, skill, time, or to other sources of interference. But complex organizations also confront larger problems and more compelling challenges, such as safely operating a nuclear power plant or managing a space exploration program. Learning may involve collecting data to better understand patterns of customer arrival and need, increasing predictability, and designing less chaotic operations. Nonetheless, it is impossible to remove all uncertainty from complex operations. Perpetual problem solving is a way of life in these settings!

Innovation operations. In innovation operations, the primary purpose is to experiment and generate new possibilities. Success is found in novelty. The development of new, groundbreaking products is increasingly dependent upon collaborative teaming and presents a complex set of challenges. By definition, new product development means working without a blueprint. The challenge to develop a new product that is profitable in shorter and shorter time periods adds its own inherent stress on teaming.

Innovation operations often have vague, if ambitious, goals that require experimentation, trial and error, and collective brainstorming. Designers, engineers, marketers, and researchers actively and continually learn in order to come up with new products and services to help their companies remain competitive. The team boundaries may be porous. Individuals may join and leave the project at different points during the process, and roles for individual team members may shift as the project progresses. Many tasks must be defined, assigned, and improvised on-the-go. This is learning to create new possibilities, not to gain deep expertise in a narrow domain. Failure along the way is frequent and expected. Acceptable failure rates for research-based enterprises like biotechnology corporations may be well over 90 percent.

Matching Learning Activities to Process Knowledge

Where one's work, department, or entire organization sits along the spectrum has implications for achieving a match between the nature of the work and how learning can be optimized. When process knowledge is mature and uncertainty low, as in a routine production setting like an assembly plant, learning should focus on improvement, on the search for more efficient execution of known processes. When knowledge is very limited and uncertainty high, as in a pharmaceutical research lab seeking groundbreaking molecular compounds, teaming should focus on innovation and discovery.

But it's not that simple. Nearly every organization, and certainly every company of significant size, contains different departments or divisions that sit on different points along the spectrum. As a quick example, a company's mailroom may be a routine operation, while its IT department is a complex operation, and its research and development department is an innovation operation.

The Operational Diversity of Large Organizations

In fact, most organizations—certainly most large organizations—encompass all three types of operations within their boundaries. Consider Toyota. Its famously efficient assembly plants epitomize the activity most people associate with a car company—routine operations. Does that mean Toyota only plays in the routine operations space? Not even close. A large and successful global company like Toyota necessarily encompasses complex and innovation operations as well. Toyota has a large and vibrant R&D organization, one that developed the first widely available hybrid (electric and gasoline powered) vehicle, the Prius, giving Toyota an innovative, desirable "green" vehicle several years before competitors. Toyota's new product development process, like that of numerous other manufacturing companies, starts with cross-functional teaming to figure out what the product ultimately ought to be and to develop detailed specifications. Next, an interconnected set of smaller teams starts solving the problems these detailed specifications create. Ultimately, the proposed new design is handed off to manufacturing. To take a cutting-edge car from concept to market requires understanding customer preferences, designing new features to satisfy these, figuring out which existing components to keep, and teaming with parts suppliers to develop brand-new components, while also ensuring that both in-house and supplier components are integrated and tested. Add to this complexity a diversity of locations, cultures, and regulatory policies, and the magnitude of the innovation challenge is clear. It should also be clear that anyone working on a new car design is doing something he or she has not done exactly the same way before. Novelty dominates the process, requiring extensive brainstorming, communication, and many difficult decisions along the way, through a series of teaming encounters.

Managing innovation at an automotive company is clearly complex, but this is not what I mean by the term complex operations. As noted, complex operations comprise a mix of well-understood processes, novel situations, and unexpected events. At a company like Toyota, supply chain management perhaps best exemplifies a complex operation. Activities such as sourcing of parts and delivery of vehicles to dealers are well designed in advance, and assiduously monitored for adherence to expectations. Still, they are subject to numerous unplanned events and disruptions, related to weather, natural disasters, supplier problems, unexpected dealer requests, and so forth. An automotive supply chain is extraordinarily complex, with about 20,000 parts making up an average car, any one of which can prevent a car from being completed if unavailable. With several levels of suppliers, an automotive supply chain comprises thousands of suppliers in all.[16] As Japan's 2011 earthquake and tsunami illustrated all too vividly, a supply chain operation is highly vulnerable to disruption. Constant vigilance is needed to anticipate, detect, and respond to unexpected events, not unlike (on a very different scale) managing care delivery in an urban hospital emergency room.

Toyota is not unique in its diversity. Table 1.2 presents examples of how companies across industries comprise diverse operations that represent a range of working and learning contexts.

The approach a leader takes toward helping her organization learn must match the state of process knowledge. Management techniques and messages that work brilliantly in the factory would cripple the discovery process in the laboratory just as managing a factory like a lab might have disastrous results for productivity. Let's explore how leaders must shift their mindsets to help organizations learn, no matter where they sit on the Process Knowledge Spectrum.

A New Way of Leading

We've come a long way from the independent companies and isolated nations that dominated the twentieth-century landscape, a landscape itself the result of profound change. It's worth recalling the magnitude of the earlier transformation that took place over a century ago—shifting from craft-based, localized agricultural communities to industrialized multinational production systems. Former farmers and craftsmen took years to adjust cognitively and emotionally to mass production and hierarchical control. Today, letting go of taken-for-granted expectations that bosses should have answers, reward adherence to prescribed process, and forbid failure is equally challenging. In the industrial era, a mindset

Table 1.2: How Organizations Encompass Routine, Complex, and Innovation Operations

	Routine Operations	Complex Operations	Innovation Operations
Automotive Company	Assembly Plant	Supply Chain Management	Design and development of future cars
Computer Chip Maker	Fabrication Plant	Supply Chain Management	Design and development of next-generation chips
Personal Computer Company	Assembly Plant	Support and service for large business customers	Design and development of future computing devices
Fast Food Company	Restaurants	Supply Chain Management	Research and development of future products and services
University	Dormitory Management	Building Construction Project	Research labs Curriculum redesign group
Space Exploration Agency	Payroll Operations	Space Missions	Developing future programs
Airport	Security Food Services	Air Traffic Control	Future planning
Hospital	Phlebotomy	Emergency Room	EMR implementation

geared for maximizing the efficiency of production worked well. But a smaller and smaller portion of work in the knowledge-based economy is well served by that mindset. Does this mean it will simply fade away and cease to dominate managerial thinking? No. It's just not that easy.

What makes this transformation particularly difficult is that most of us carry elements of this outmoded mindset toward work, without thinking much about it. This frames how we interpret our own and others' actions, shapes our expectations for busyness, and often determines our response to failure. Despite rhetoric to the contrary, many of us still expect ourselves and others to get things right the first time. We view failures as unacceptable. We issue directives to those below, and look for direction from supervisors above. We prefer going along with the majority opinion rather than risk conflict or job loss if we truly speak out.

In many ways, the old mindset is comfortable and reassuring. Job duties are fixed. Goals are clearly stated. Targets are objective and immutable. Career progress can be mapped up a distinct, hierarchical ladder. Iconic industrialists such as Henry Ford amassed fortunes because they understood how to harness the power of the man at the top issuing direct orders to workers below. This made sense when work was primarily individually accomplished, and the knowledge base was stable. The best workers performed their tasks quickly and accurately, and individual performance could be accurately tied to individual workers—a rarity today. A manager's job was to supervise repetitive steps in a known process, and then reward and punish in accordance with performance.

Today's effective leaders differ from even the most successful managers in yesterday's routine-intensive organizations. The difference starts with a basic mindset about human beings. Whereas industrialization essentially infantilized workers, the knowledge-based economy only works well when it restores workers on all levels to self-respecting, self-determining adulthood. The classic industrial factory system took adults who raised children, voted public officials in and out of office, and owned their own homes—people who occupied positions of responsibility and were frequent decision makers—and then treated them as children inside the factory walls. At work, they were required to ask permission to go to the bathroom, punch in and out on a clock to verify hours worked, eat only when permitted, and do as they were told without asking questions.

Today, people engaging in teaming at work need to be responsible, accountable individuals who respect each other, understand the inevitability of conflict, and accept the responsibility to sort through such difficulties. To promote teaming, leaders must trust those they lead. A store manager who commands her employees to scan the parking lot every half hour for trash still holds the old mindset about work. In contrast, a store manager who understands the new way of working lets her employees know that they are responsible for keeping the parking lot trash-free, but trusts them to figure out how to best meet that goal. The latter approach, which may involve mistakes and missteps, also builds an environment of mutual respect. Trust and respect together make a workplace amenable to teaming and continuous learning.

Facing the many technological and geopolitical transformations reshaping the workplace, many leaders struggle to grasp the realities of teaming and continuous learning as a way of life. Letting go of outmoded, but taken-for-granted, concepts of authority and hierarchy takes effort. What are the mandates when workers work in factories on one continent while their corporate headquarters exist on another? With knowledge distributed at the speed of electrons, it cannot be handed down in a tidy, easily controlled manner. Instead, it's created and shared in disorderly ways. This calls for workers who know how to experiment, how to think on their feet, how to work in the absence of rules, and how to adapt quickly. Knowledge, changing quickly within disciplines, becomes even messier and more uncertain when integrated across disciplines, as it often must be, to get things done in the new workplace. Creating an appropriate environment for teaming and learning requires different management skills and expectations from those required in a repetitive task environment. Top-down management may have worked for Ford and Taylor. But today's managers need employees to be problem solvers and experimenters, not mere conformers.

Leadership Summary

The ability to learn is critical for organizations operating in today's fast-paced business environment. Relying on existing knowledge and skills succeeds only if you know exactly what should be done in a job and you expect the process to remain relatively fixed for a significant amount of time. In today's environment, that's the exception, not the rule.

Instead, what is needed are dynamic, flexible teams that combine employees' strengths, experience, and knowledge to achieve organizational goals. On-the-job teaming and learning is vital when the answers are still being discovered and when processes are still evolving. This type of teaming and learning requires leaders who have the imagination and courage to figure out how to proceed without answers—leaders who offer a clear direction, a tolerance for risk and failure, and an explicit invitation to work closely with others.

Leaders who work to create hospitable conditions for teaming and learning can build organizations that are better able to achieve and sustain success through continuous improvement, problem solving, and innovation. Throughout this book, you'll read stories about organizations and companies that have succeeded in teaming to create a productive and profitable learning environment. The next chapter focuses on the social, cognitive, and organizational barriers to teaming and describes the practices necessary to overcoming those barriers.

LESSONS AND ACTIONS

- Success in today's complex and volatile business environment requires flexibility, coordination, and collaboration.

- Teaming is a dynamic way of working that provides the necessary coordination and collaboration without the luxury (or rigidity) of stable team structures.

- Teaming and its associated interpersonal behaviors support organizational learning, and require the right leadership mindset to optimize outcomes. This way of working allows employees to grow personally and professionally, whereas traditional top-down and assembly-line models treated workers like children who must be told what to do.

- Organizing to learn represents this leadership mindset. Organizing to learn is a way of leading that encourages speaking up, asking questions, and sharing ideas so as to promote collective learning.

- Execution-as-learning is a way of operating that folds continuous learning into the day-by-day work process. Execution-as-learning usually happens in teams and is supported by the leadership practices of organizing to learn.

- The Process Knowledge Spectrum (Figure 1.2) is a useful tool for categorizing operational settings. Where one's work, department, or entire organization sits along the spectrum has implications for matching the work context to appropriate teaming and learning goals.

chapter two

teaming to learn, innovate, and compete

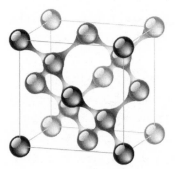

Friday afternoon in a major urban medical center: A patient's white blood cell count has suddenly spiked upward a few days after major surgery, indicating the possibility of a life-threatening infection. The patient's breathing is labored, and the color has all but drained from his face. To ascertain the infection's source, his physician orders a CT scan of the patient's abdomen and chest. The order is written just after noon.

What happens over the next four days illustrates how much can go wrong when the work is interdependent but teaming doesn't occur. Unfortunately, hospitals are settings in which teaming failures are frequent and can have life-or-death consequences.

A CT scan is a procedure that unfolds through a series of discrete steps, each carried out by a different specialist. These individuals may not see themselves as part of a team, but the procedure unfolds more smoothly and safely if they coordinate their actions as if they *were* members of a high-performing team rather than individual specialists completing a series of separate tasks. The procedure's execution involves the work of several individuals, each with a distinct area of competence and a distinct task to execute. First, for a post-surgical patient not yet able to eat, an expert technician carefully threads a nasogastric (NG) tube into the abdomen through the nose. Next, a different technician, armed with a portable x-ray machine, comes to the bedside to snap a quick image of the patient's chest and abdomen, as part of a process to ensure proper placement of the tube. This x-ray is then read by a licensed radiologist, who confirms the tube's placement before liquid is sent through it. Next, a nurse administers a contrast liquid, which must sit for at least an hour, and no more than six, before the patient can be transported to the giant CT scanner, located in its own specialized room. This sequence of tasks, when done well, results in images that help guide patient care.

In most hospitals, the process through which a CT scan procedure unfolds is barely recognized as teamwork. The team in question is a virtual one. Team members don't meet face-to-face, although each is aware of doing one step in a larger procedure that involves other specialists. A virtual team such as this is teaming when it carefully coordinates member-to-member actions to ensure that each task is done in a timely manner, with the patient's safety and the physician's diagnostic ease as its primary concerns.

In this situation, as is unfortunately often the case, coordination was left to chance. A couple of hours after the physician's request for a scan, the technician came to the bedside to insert the NG tube. Done quickly and expertly, the tube went in relatively smoothly, although not without causing discomfort. Almost an hour and a half later, the x-ray technician came by to produce images with which a radiologist could check the tube's placement.

At 5:00 PM, with the weekend fast approaching, the tube-placement x-ray had not yet been read by a radiologist. Watching and waiting, the patient's family asked the on-duty nurse when she would know the results of the x-ray and allow the patient to get her CT scan. The nurse responded with a mystified shrug. From her perspective, radiologists appeared to do things in their own time, not according to her schedule, or even to her patients' needs. But she agreed to look into it.

At 6:30, the x-ray was read, confirming the tube had been placed correctly some hours earlier and allowing the nurse to administer the contrast liquid. Almost three hours later, the patient, prepared and ready with the contrast dye, had yet to be taken to the scanner. The nurse reassured the family that even if radiology was gone for the weekend, a CT scanner in the emergency room could be used, so the patient would still get his scan. Another hour went by without the necessary specialist to execute this task, and just after 10:00 PM, the patient's blood pressure dropped precipitously, requiring the nurse to transfer him to the intensive care unit (ICU) for closer observation. At this point, hope of obtaining a CT scan that same day was lost, as the patient was too unstable to be taken to a scanner.

The next day at noon, the patient was sufficiently stable to be transferred out of the ICU and back to the floor where he had started. With the NG tube still in place, the contrast liquid had long since expired and would have to be re-administered for a scan to be completed. Unfortunately, it was now Saturday, and CT scans were done over the weekend only for emergencies.

At 3:00 PM, the nurse reminded the physician, by telephone, that the patient had now had an NG tube inserted for nearly 24 hours. The patient was having trouble breathing, and the tube appeared to exacerbate that difficulty, while also increasing the risk of infection. The surgeon recommended it be removed as soon as possible; after all, it could be reinserted later if a CT scan were to be attempted again. Despite the task's apparent simplicity, hospital policy required a physician to remove the tube, and so the nurse needed to find a resident physician to do it. Two hours later, a resident was located to remove the tube, which she did in a matter of seconds.

On Tuesday, four days after the original order was written, the entire CT scan procedure was undertaken again, this time successfully. Thus, four full days after the information was first needed, the source of the patient's infection was identified. Who or what is to blame for this inefficiency and additional risk to the patient? In fact, no one person is at fault. Each competently executed his or her task, and each in the midst of a day comprised of many such tasks for different patients and doctors. These individuals were, for practical purposes, unaware of being members of a temporary and virtual CT scan team, instead thinking of themselves as members of the radiology department or the unit-based nursing team.

Where did the individualistic concept of the work in this situation come from? The hospital, like most, was organized into departments that act as vertical silos and obscure horizontal relationships. Each silo is responsible for training and managing the expert execution of separate, specialized tasks, despite the fact that so many critical procedures involve people and tasks from multiple departments. Ideally, each person, aware of the others' role and input, would do his or her task at the best time and in the best way to support the entire procedure—this would qualify as teaming. But what more often happens (and what happened in this case), is that each person performs a task as efficiently as possible based on the needs of his or her specialized department. As a result, this CT scan, with direct labor amounting to far less than two hours, failed to be completed over a period of nearly 100 hours.

The silo-like structures that make up many hospitals fail to support the dynamic, real-time teaming needed to carry out many of the procedures through which care is delivered. The person who executes without judgment and acute sensitivity to data in a hospital may harm a patient who needs unique care. Although uncertainty is not exceedingly high, and consequential failure is certainly not routine, the possibility of failure lurks around every corner. This is the nature of complex operations. Everyone understands and seeks to avoid the danger created by interacting parts and the ever-present potential for system breakdowns. Increasingly, therefore, employees in the world's best hospitals actively engage in teaming. They employ such skills as ingenuity, judgment, intelligent experimentation, and resilience—skills that are difficult, if not impossible, for traditional management approaches to measure. Many organizations and companies recognize the necessity of teaming and continuous learning. Unfortunately, management mindsets and organizational structures have not always shifted accordingly, leaving people engaged in complex interdependent work *failing to recognize* that interdependence.

In the discussion that follows, I explore the processes and behavioral characteristics that enable teaming and also explain the social, cognitive, and organizational challenges that thwart teaming. Teaming requires awareness, communication, trust, cooperation, and a willingness to reflect. These are seemingly simple attributes, but ones that are too often thwarted by natural human characteristics. I explain the roots of these characteristics, drawing from psychological research, and describe how the teaming process works by overcoming. I end the chapter with four leadership actions that help overcome their effects, enable teaming, and promote organizational learning. Based on decades of data amassed from a range of organizations, with work spanning the Process Knowledge Spectrum, these four actions help cultivate an organizational environment that encourages the behaviors essential to successful teaming.

The Teaming Process

Teaming, by its nature, is a learning process. No sequence of events will unfold precisely the same way twice when people must interact to coordinate ideas or actions, and so participants in such a process are always in a position to learn. Learning in teams involves iterative cycles of communication, decision, action, and reflection; each new cycle is informed by the results of the previous cycles, and cycles continue until desired outcomes are achieved. As team members engage in this cycle, they surface and integrate their differential knowledge, and find ways to effectively use the new collective knowledge to improve organizational routines.

In addition to the essential role of learning, it's important to understand how teaming gets started and takes hold in settings where interdependent action is needed. Consider the aborted CT scan. This teaming failure occurred due to a lack of interprofessional and inter-task awareness on the part of the individuals involved in the work. Given the realities of different departments with different constraints and priorities, how can cross-functional teaming for both routine and novel tasks be enabled? Figure 2.1 depicts a sequence through which teaming unfolds in coordinated work.

It starts with recognition. Unless people are aware of their interdependence with others for accomplishing whole jobs, teaming cannot get underway. When people recognize the need for coordination, communication becomes natural, despite departmental silos. Individuals reach out and talk to those with whom they must interact to get their work done well, and this begins the conversation—often very brief—about how to coordinate their respective tasks. Next, the flow of interdependent action unfolds, followed by feedback and reflection that may simply acknowledge each other's contributions or may instead suggest changes to make things work better going forward. With practice, a teaming mindset

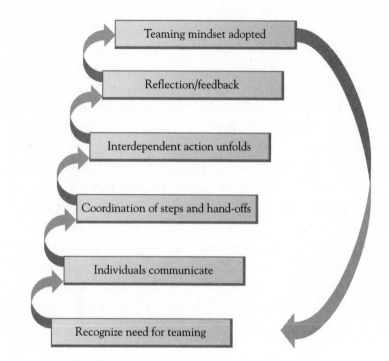

Figure 2.1. Teaming

becomes more or less second nature, and the recognition step that starts the flow of teaming becomes automatic.

Four Pillars of Effective Teaming

Teaming occurs when people apply and combine their expertise to perform complex tasks or develop solutions to novel problems. Often a fluid process, teaming may involve performing with others, disbanding, and joining another group right away. An episode of teaming ends once some or all of the work is complete, but teaming as a mindset—and approach to work—can continue indefinitely. Teaming is normal in the "temporary organizations" that characterize creative endeavors such as making a film, or in the coordination of complex events, such as producing a professional conference.

In such efforts, a mix of planned and spontaneous coordination often brings multiple players together to team.

Proficient teaming often requires integrating perspectives from a range of disciplines, communicating despite the different mental models that accompany different areas of expertise, *and* being able to manage the inevitable conflicts that arise when people work together. Fundamentally, this is a matter of developing interpersonal skills related to learning (inquiry, curiosity, listening) and teaching (communicating, connecting, clarifying). Teaming is thus both a mindset that accepts working together actively and a set of behaviors tailored to sharing and synthesizing knowledge. Sometimes teaming requires coordinating across distant locations, which both increases the potential for miscommunication and gives rise to new opportunities for innovation. One chemical company I studied used globally dispersed teams to innovate, overcoming various communication barriers to develop new products and processes that offered wider commercial value than those that could be developed in a single location. Whether face-to-face or mediated by communication technologies, successful teaming involves the four specific behaviors listed in Exhibit 2.1.

Exhibit 2.1: Behaviors Driving Teaming Success

- **Speaking Up:** Teaming depends on honest, direct conversation between individuals, including asking questions, seeking feedback, and discussing errors.

- **Collaboration:** Teaming requires a collaborative mindset and behaviors—both within and outside a given unit of teaming—to drive the process.

- **Experimentation:** Teaming involves a tentative, iterative approach to action that recognizes the novelty and uncertainty inherent in every interaction between individuals.

- **Reflection:** Teaming relies on the use of explicit observations, questions, and discussions of processes and outcomes. This must happen on a consistent basis that reflects the rhythm of the work, whether that calls for daily, weekly, or other project-specific timing.

Speaking Up

Candid communication allows teams to incorporate multiple perspectives and tap into individual knowledge. This includes asking questions; seeking feedback; talking about errors; asking for help; offering suggestions; and discussing problems, mistakes, and concerns. Speaking up is particularly crucial when confronting problems or failures of any kind. When people are willing to engage with each other directly and openly, they are better able to make sense of the larger shared work and more likely to generate ideas for improving work processes. Speaking up in this context refers to an interpersonal behavior that allows the development of shared insights from open conversation. It is essential for determining appropriate courses of action in any teaming encounter. Speaking up is also essential for helping people grasp new concepts and methods. Conversing about experiences, insights, and questions builds understanding of new practices and how to perform them. Although many people think of themselves as direct and straightforward, speaking up in the workplace is less common than you might think.

Speaking Up Is Less Common Than You Think

My research with Professor Jim Detert at Cornell University on voice and silence in the workplace shows that speaking up at work is less common than most people think. Through interviews with hundreds of executives, managers, and supervisors in a global high-tech company, we discovered that almost everyone could think of specific instances of not speaking up about a potentially important work-related issue. Most were well-educated, thoughtful people who spanned corporate departments, areas of expertise, and even country of origin. To explain why people frequently don't speak up, we analyzed hundreds of specific episodes and identified taken-for-granted beliefs about appropriate behavior in hierarchies that are far-reaching in their implications. Although most people we studied thought of themselves as pretty straightforward, rather than hesitant or fearful, they still held back potentially important ideas at work. In this study, and several that followed, we showed that there is a remarkable paucity of directness in the workplace. It appears that reluctance to speak up is overdetermined by human nature and by specific realities of the modern economy. From an evolutionary point of view, we're hard-wired to overestimate rather than underestimate certain types of risk: it was better for survival to "flee" from threats that weren't really there than to not flee when there was a real risk. And we appear to have inherited emotional and cognitive mechanisms that lead us to avoid perceived risks to our psychological and material well-being. In the workplace, fear of offending people above us in the hierarchy is both natural and widespread, and it means the speaking-up behavior upon which teaming depends must be cultivated rather than assumed to be present.

Collaboration

Collaboration is a way of working with colleagues that is characterized by cooperation, mutual respect, and shared goals. It involves sharing information, coordinating actions, discussing what's working and what's not, and perpetually seeking input and feedback. Teaming depends on collaborative behaviors within and between departments or organizations. Clearly, without collaboration, teaming easily breaks down. Plans are less well informed, and the execution of plans suffers from the kind of poor coordination illustrated in the hospital example at the start of this chapter. A collaborative attitude is also essential to shared reflection that may occur following coordinated action, because it allows full and thoughtful sharing of expertise and promotes the development of broader and deeper lessons from any experience. Imagine a product development team that doesn't collaborate with the marketing group and thereby fails to incorporate vital customer preferences or feedback!

Experimentation

Experimentation means expecting *not* to be right the first time. Borrowed from the literal experiments of scientists, experimentation behavior is a way of acting that centrally involves learning from the results of action. In teaming, experimentation behavior involves reaching out to others to assess the impact of one's actions on them, and also testing the implications of one's ideas with respect to what others are thinking. Experimentation is a vital aspect of teaming because of the uncertainty inherent in interdependent action. It's also a crucial part of learning, of course, as explored later in this chapter in a discussion of the teaming process.

Reflection

Reflection is the habit of critically examining the results of actions to assess results and uncover new ideas. Some teams engage in reflection on a daily basis. Others reflect at a natural break in the project, such as at halftime for sports teams, or when documenting aspects of a patient's care in a chart after a medical visit. Project teams may explicitly engage in a reflection exercise only when a project is completed. The "after action reviews" conducted by the U.S. Army following military exercises are explicit reflection sessions that use a rigorous structured approach to assess what occurred against what was planned or expected. Reflection does not necessarily mean extensive sessions to thoroughly analyze team process or performance, but rather is often quick and pragmatic. Reflection-in-action, for example, is the critical, real-time examination of a process so it can be adjusted based on new knowledge or, more often, in response to subtle feedback received from the work itself.[1] Reflection as a basis for effective teaming is more a behavioral tendency than a formal process. In one study of surgical teams, for example, I found no differences in outcomes for teams with formal reflection sessions, compared to those without such sessions; the teams that succeeded were those that were constantly reflecting aloud on what they were observing and thinking, as a way of figuring out how to work together more effectively.[2] For some types of teams, however, it may be more appropriate to wait for outcomes to be available before stopping to reflect on team process, in which case a more structured approach, such as a formal project review, is extremely valuable.

These four behaviors are the pillars of effective teaming. The challenges encountered on the factory floor, in the operating room, and around the glass-topped tables in corporate conference rooms differ significantly in look and feel, as well as in the nature of the work. Yet speaking up, collaboration, experimentation, and reflection are crucial behaviors across these disparate settings. In all of them, leaders who themselves embrace these behaviors make it easier for others to act in ways that support teaming. In addition to these behavioral tendencies, however, leaders must also understand the cyclical, recursive nature of the actual teaming process.

The Benefits of Teaming

One of the most successful product launches in history, Motorola's 2004 RAZR mobile phone, was the result of successful teaming. Battling fierce global competition in the mobile phone market in 2003, Motorola set out to create the thinnest phone ever released. Electrical engineer Roger Jellicoe was chosen to lead the team. In addition to designing the thinnest phone ever, Jellicoe's instructions were to create a thing of beauty, a device more like jewelry than a mere utilitarian object. To partner in leading the project, he chose mechanical engineer Gary Weiss, with whom he knew he could work well. Twenty Motorola engineers were invited to join the teaming effort with its ambitious deadline. They came from different groups and locations to collaborate in an otherwise unremarkable facility an hour from Chicago.

Speaking up and experimentation were critical to their success. Neither ideas nor criticisms were held back, as perpetual experimentation and debate led to possibilities and prototypes that were attempted, rejected, altered, tweaked, and refined. A core challenge was the integration of style and technology. Numerous tradeoffs, mostly between appearance and functionality, were considered, and the team resisted easy compromises, pushing instead for elegant solutions to the tough problems they confronted. By experimenting with different configurations, the team hit on the idea of putting the battery next to the circuit board (prior phones had them stacked) to reduce thickness. It worked, allowing the ultra-thin design that gave the phone its appeal and its name. The team's innovative solution ignored existing human factors experts who had strong views about how wide a cell phone could be to feel right in a person's hand. Experimenting with a wider mock-up of the phone, the team decided the experts were wrong.[3] Reflection was built into the teaming process from the beginning. Meeting every afternoon at 4:00 PM, the group discussed the day's progress, and reported on the status of such components as the antenna, speaker, keypad, or light source. Scheduled for an hour, the meetings frequently ran past 7:00 PM. These meetings were a primary mechanism for the team's focused conversation and debate. Reporting on failures as easily as successes and breakthroughs, everyone was engaged in the process of offering ideas and criticisms. Industrial designer Chris Arnholt, whose slim clamshell design was crucial to the team's success, had brought sketches to the meetings only to discover that his initial ideas for the style of the phone were neither practical nor easily understood by the engineers. In the teaming that ensued, Arnholt and the engineers jointly decided on a design that worked.

The project's biggest setback occurred when it missed its ambitious initial deadline, but the result, only a few months later and still within a fast time line, was worth waiting for: Motorola unveiled the RAZR, the thinnest phone ever produced, before the end of 2004, and went on to sell 50 million RAZR mobile phones within the next two years and 110 million over four years.[4]

The RAZR story showcases the positive relationship between a teaming mindset and behaviors and project performance. Team members, from multiple areas of expertise, jumped in wholeheartedly to work together to do something new, exciting, and remarkable. Many organizations rely on teaming to keep up with today's fast-paced, global environment. Consider how much of the work in today's organizations requires people to make decisions together, to reflect the different needs and different information each brings, in response to unforeseen or complex problems. Theoretical and empirical research has identified several benefits of teaming for organizations and their staff. These benefits largely fall into two categories: better organizational performance and more engaging and satisfying work environments.

Performance

Whether a new product development team made up of designers, marketers, and engineers, or a cardiac surgery team made up of surgeons, nurses, perfusionists, and anesthesiologists, the benefits of teaming for organizational learning and performance are significant. In particular, teaming helps organizations develop new routines and implement new technologies to meet the demands of a changing context. These kinds of organizational changes call for teaming because they require understanding and coordination across departments and disciplines. As Richard Hackman and I have argued, teams are an organization's best change agents.[5] Most models of change management call for a change leadership team or a change implementation team to promote better ideas and greater buy-in. But it shouldn't stop there. What really matters is not just the creation of a team, but how those selected work with each other and with other members of the organization to help create change in a dynamic, learning-oriented way. These change agents must listen, coordinate, and continually make adjustments in plans to accommodate each other's input. This naturally gives rise to uncertainty, and requires attention and sensitivity to feedback. The core behaviors of teaming thus drive organizational performance by facilitating the creation of new knowledge, new processes, and new products.

Performance improves when new knowledge is put to good use, also enabled by teaming. In a study of cardiac surgery teams, explored in greater detail in Chapter Three, my colleagues and I showed that teaming behaviors led to far more successful implementation of a new technology, compared to surgical teams with a more top-down control approach. Through teaming people were able to figure out what processes needed to be changed for the new procedure to work.[6] Similarly, I later studied dozens of quality improvement teams in 23 hospital ICUs and found that teaming and learning led to measurable improvement. Although going to the research literature to find the latest medical knowledge was important, the teams that best succeeded in implementing change were those who engaged in the interpersonal learning behaviors crucial to teaming. They communicated, coordinated, asked questions, listened, and experimented—both within and outside of the team's boundaries. This built knowledge and enthusiasm, which encouraged team members to make the behavior and process changes needed to improve patient care.[7] In both studies, we found that psychological safety, explored in detail in Chapter Four, enabled teaming and learning, and led to better performance. I have found similar results in work settings other than hospitals, including manufacturing, product development, and even the design and construction of buildings.

Engaged Employees

Teaming has a positive effect on people's experience at work. Interacting directly with people who have different knowledge and skills makes work more interesting, enriching, and meaningful. In organizations where teaming is common, employees learn from each other, enjoy a broader understanding of the work and how it gets done from start to finish, and can better see and act on opportunities for improvement. For example, Simmons Mattress Company, discussed in more detail in Chapter Eight, introduced team training to raise employee technical and interpersonal skills, which in turn led to greatly increased awareness of the contributions of other employees working in different parts of the manufacturing process. Once everyone began to understand what unseen colleagues did all day, why it was difficult, and how the combined tasks came together to make an entire mattress, not to mention an entire sales and distribution operation, they enjoyed the work more, and were also more productive.[8]

Teaming also benefits an organization by allowing people to combine their knowledge to create new products or implement new procedures. Teaming allows organizations to benefit from teams of experts working together to improve quality, reduce operating costs, and enhance customer satisfaction. Through teaming, diverse employees representing different attitudes, values, and beliefs perform in an environment of mutual respect, shared knowledge, and shared goals. Imagine all of this work occurring in iterative, self-regulating cycles of improvement and innovation that guarantee organizational success well into the future!

If only it were so easy.

Social and Cognitive Barriers to Teaming

I've spent an inordinate amount of time studying people in hospitals. People working in hospitals face some particularly challenging work environments. Demands for coordination are great, time is tight, and the stakes are high. As a result, the rest of us can learn a lot from understanding how the best hospitals manage these inherent challenges effectively. Medical knowledge and best-care practices, which are vast and constantly updated, must be consulted to inform high-stakes, cross-disciplinary communication and action, often under immense time pressure. And, unfortunately, even in a hospital—a setting that calls for nearly constant teaming—cooperation and trust face many challenges.

Consider a busy emergency room. At any moment, a patient with life-threatening, possibly unprecedented, symptoms might arrive by ambulance. Immediately, specialists from several departments—reception, nursing, medicine, laboratory, surgery, pharmacy—must coordinate their efforts if the patient is to receive effective care. These people must resolve conflicting priorities and opinions quickly. They may or may not have previously worked together as a team and most likely some are less experienced than others. Nonetheless, personalities must mesh rather than clash. And people must rely on their collective judgment and expertise, rather than on management direction, to decide what to do. It shouldn't surprise anyone that these busy clinicians sometimes make the wrong call. But the true problem is not just that they might sometimes get the medical diagnosis wrong. It's that they might do so by failing to work together effectively.

Serious Work Means Serious Tension

As Wynton Marsalis, artistic director for Jazz at Lincoln Center, says of his work with other jazz musicians: "There are *always* tensions that come up. Part of working is dealing with tensions. If there's no tension, then you're not serious about what you're doing."[9]

Certainly, teaming sometimes goes well in today's organizations. People recognize their interdependence and work effectively together. They offer their ideas freely, carrying out their part of the collective work and responding thoughtfully to others' ideas and actions. At other times, however, teaming breaks down and coordination fails. Signals get crossed or conflicting opinions derail the conversation. Many teaming efforts—whether in routine, complex, or innovation operations—start with high hopes, only to falter. What are some of the obstacles to effective teaming?

People Don't Always Get Along

Teaming requires participants to productively manage the inevitable conflicts that arise when people work together in serious endeavors. Well-functioning teams are powerful, but rarely static. They are as hard to create as to sustain. Many tasks are technically complex to begin with and present interdependencies that make them even more so. Personality, leadership, resource allocation, differences in knowledge and background—any problems encountered in these areas can give rise to misunderstanding or dysfunction. Fear is a major barrier to teaming, as discussed in Chapter Four. Similarly, lacking a clear, shared objective also inhibits the effortful behaviors that comprise teaming. Organizational factors, such as bureaucracy, layers of management, or contradictory incentive systems, also get in the way. Teaming is as difficult as it is necessary.

It's far easier for an individual to have a clear and well-bounded task to do over and over again than to figure out how to carry out more complex and interdependent work with others. Interdependent work requires coordination through back-and-forth communication to do it well. When we are interdependent, it necessarily means we cannot do everything that must be done alone. This is a rather humbling realization, and many shy away from embracing it. It can be hard for people to muster both the humility and the genuine curiosity that is needed to really learn from others. It turns out that cognitive, interpersonal, and organizational factors all get in the way of effective learning in teams. It's a cruel irony—our success depends upon effective collaboration and learning, the essence of teaming, but these don't come naturally either for individuals or the social systems we create. The following sections examine the cognitive and structural factors that inhibit teaming.

Silence Is Easier Than Speaking Up

When leaders fall into a default "do it my way" management style, it silences nearly everyone except the person with the loudest

voice or the largest office. But silence in today's economic environment is deadly. Silence means good ideas and possibilities don't
bubble up, and problems don't get addressed. Silence stymies
teaming. Most people feel a need to manage what I call interpersonal risk—a risk that others will think less of them—so as to
minimize harm to their image, especially in the workplace, and
especially in the presence of bosses and others who hold formal
power. One way to minimize risk to one's image is simply to avoid
speaking up unless you're sure you're right, avoid admitting mistakes, and, of course, never ask questions or raise tentative ideas
that you're not sure have merit. Although this approach may work
for individuals—protecting them from being seen by others in an
unfavorable light—it is clearly problematic for organizations and
their customers.

Shhhh, Here Comes the Boss

Research shows that hierarchy, by its very nature, dramatically
reduces speaking up by those lower in the pecking order. We are
hard-wired, and then socialized, to be acutely sensitive to power,
and to work to avoid being seen as deficient in any way by those
in power. Most of this behavior is unconscious. As a result, in most
organizations, even if leaders at the top of the hierarchy say they
welcome employee feedback, and even if people have the knowledge and training to say something of importance, they still may
remain silent out of fear of negative consequences.[10]

Research does show, however, that leaders can promote speaking up through particular behaviors and actions.[11] Most important,
when leaders explicitly communicate that they respect employees,
it makes it easier for employees to volunteer their knowledge. More
specifically, by acknowledging the need for the knowledge and
skills that others bring, leaders issue a credible invitation for people
to speak up. Mistakes, in particular, require active encouragement
if they are to be reported or discussed. In sum, speaking up is not
natural in organizations, but it can and does happen, particularly

when leaders actively model, invite, and reward candor and openness. In contrast, inaccessibility or a failure to acknowledge vulnerability can contribute to a reluctance to incur the interpersonal risks of teaming behavior.

Disagreement

Speaking up brings challenges, too. As soon as people speak up and communicate freely with one another, there is bound to be disagreement and sometimes seemingly irresolvable conflict. The problem with disagreement is not that it occurs; the problem is the sensemaking in which people spontaneously engage when disagreement occurs. All of us have at one point or another spontaneously attributed unflattering motives, traits, or abilities to those who disagree with our strongly held view. In such cases, we might say something like "She doesn't get it" or "He's just out for himself."

Our own views seem so right that others' disagreement seems irrational, or worse, deliberately unhelpful. This is why, as research on social cognition helps explain, conflict can be a roadblock to effective teaming. But it doesn't have to be. Rather than wasting precious time and eroding personal relationships, conflict can be an opportunity for building new understanding, respect, and trust. It helps to consider two common cognitive errors identified by psychologists, *naïve realism* and the *fundamental attribution error*.[12]

Naïve Realism We are all prone to naïve realism, a term coined by psychologist Lee Ross, which is a person's "unshakable conviction that he or she is somehow privy to an invariant, knowable, objective reality—a reality that others will also perceive faithfully, provided that they are reasonable and rational."[13] So, when others misperceive our "reality," we conclude that it must be because they are unreasonable or irrational and "view the world through a prism of self-interest, ideological bias, or personal perversity."[14] And therein lies the trouble.

One outcome of naïve realism is that people tend to see their own views as more common than they really are, leading them to falsely assume that others share their views. For example, someone might say, "We need to dramatically curb carbon emissions to prevent further global warming." Or, "Everyone knows we have the best medical system in the world." Social psychologists call this the false consensus effect. And such assumptions usually go unnoticed—until unexpectedly refuted when someone disagrees. This means, if someone replies, "I don't think human activity is contributing to climate change. Temperature fluctuations have gone on for millennia," the original speaker may spontaneously conclude that the responder is closed-minded, wrong-headed, or worse. Similarly, someone might respond to the second statement, "If we have the best medical care, why do we rank 36th in the world for life expectancy?" while privately viewing the original speaker as ignorant or misguided. For most people, finding out that a friend or colleague disagrees with us on something we care about is usually an unpleasant surprise.

The Fundamental Attribution Error The second cognitive error that makes it hard to cope with conflict productively was dubbed the "fundamental attribution error" by Lee Ross.[15] The term describes our failure to recognize situational causes of events and our tendency instead to overattribute individuals' personality or ability as likely causes. An outgrowth of this cognitive error is that we tend to explain others' shortcomings as related to their ability or attitude, rather than to the circumstances they face. That is, we blame the *people* for things that go wrong—not the situation. Every parent of more than one child has heard, "Don't blame me, it's his fault." In the workplace, the same thing happens, even if the words are less direct and unambiguous.

It's almost amusing to realize that we do exactly the opposite in explaining our own failures. That is, we spontaneously attribute them to external factors. For example, if we show up late for a meeting, we may blame circumstances outside our control, like rush-hour traffic. If a subordinate is late for a meeting, however, we think he is not committed to the project, or that he's disorganized. On both sides of the attribution coin, we make judgments effortlessly—remaining largely unaware that there was an alternative cause to consider. As natural and sometimes humorous as this asymmetry is, it creates a couple of problems for teaming. First, when we blame others for things that go wrong, productive discussion of the issues is less likely to occur. Worse, we tend to believe we have sized up the situation and its causes accurately. Second, we begin to think less of others, and then may be less motivated to engage wholeheartedly in teaming with them.

This error is called "fundamental" because it's essentially universal. All of us do it, and we do it without thinking. In fact, it takes cognitive effort to override it and think, "I wonder if she ran into unexpected traffic on the way to this meeting?" This means remaining open—deliberately interrupting the attributional process. If we really paused to think about it more often, we'd probably laugh at ourselves for so quickly jumping to unkind conclusions. But when people don't stop to challenge the unflattering causal attributions they make about others' ability or intentions, teaming obviously suffers.

Tension and Conflict

The fundamental problem with disagreements, and the cognitive structures that exacerbate them, is that they create tensions in a group. Tensions are to be expected when teaming. Although rarely fun, tensions are not always bad. They can evoke creativity, sharpen ideas, and refine analyses. But there's a catch: patience, wisdom, and skill are needed to transform tensions into positive results. This is because most of us naturally resist tensions and the conflict they invariably bring.

When Conflict Heats Up

Nobody likes pushback. We naturally prefer others to agree with us. When we resist conflicting points of view or don't have the skills necessary to transform tensions into creativity and excellence, it's easy to fall back into the old, top-down mindset. Collective action is always easier when there is someone clearly in charge to settle differences, quash disagreement, and defuse conflict. When the stakes are high and conflicting opinions meet uncertainty, trying to remain cool and logical can seem like a losing game. Frank conversations must occur for teaming to succeed. Understanding the cognitions, behaviors, and reactions that underpin conflict is vital to supporting teaming.

Hot and Cool Cognition

Research by cognitive psychologists Janet Metcalfe and Walter Mischel showed that we each have two distinct cognitive systems through which we process events.[16] Trying to understand the mechanisms that allow people to delay gratification—a crucial ability for everything from goal achievement to weight control—Metcalfe and Mischel identified two types of human cognition, which they called "hot" and "cool," as shown in Table 2.1. The hot system, when engaged, triggers people to respond emotionally and quickly. In this case they are often said to speak or act in the heat of the moment. The cool system, in contrast, is deliberate and careful. When using our cool system, we can slow down and gather our thoughts. The cool system is the basis for self-regulation and self-control. Consequently, it is a necessary tool for teaming effectively when (not if) conflict occurs.

Spontaneous Reactions

Teaming breaks down when conflict heats up; rather than triggering new creative thinking, it works instead to slow progress. Often,

Table 2.1: Hot Versus Cool Systems

Hot System	Cool System
Emotional	"Know"
"Go"	Complex
Reflexive	Reflective
Fast	Slow
Develops Early	Develops Late
Accentuated by Stress	Attenuated by Stress
Stimulus Control	Self-Control

Source: Metcalfe, J., and Mischel, W. "A Hot/Cool System of Delay of Gratification: Dynamics of Willpower," *Psychological Review* 106, no. 1 (1999). Reprinted with permission of the American Psychological Association.

individuals will go back and forth, repeating the same points over and over again. As summarized in Table 2.2, conflicts typically heat up when three conditions are present: controversial or limited data that are subject to differing interpretations, high uncertainty, and high stakes. Conversations can get especially heated when people hold different values or belief systems, or have different interests and incentives. This can make aspects of the conflict hard to discuss productively, because people often hesitate to mention the personal gain they anticipate from one of the potential decision outcomes.

These conditions were present in the senior management team of a company I'll refer to as Elite Manufacturing to protect confidentiality. I studied eight senior managers at Elite over several months as they met to diagnose and design corporate strategy.[17] Ian McAlister, the head of Elite's struggling core business, and Frank Adams, the president of a small, successful subsidiary with less expensive product lines, became embroiled in a conflict that quickly turned personal.

Table 2.2: Contrasting Cool and Hot Topics

	Cool Topics	Hot Topics
Data	Accessible, relatively objective, conducive to testing of different interpretations	Controversial and/or inaccessible, interpretation is highly subjective, different interpretations hard to test
Level of Certainty	High*	Moderate to Low
Stakes	Low to Moderate	High
Goals	Largely shared	Differ based on deeply-held beliefs, values, or interests
Discussion	Reasonable, fact-based collegial	Often emotional, lack of agreement about which facts matter and what they mean, veiled personal attacks likely

*High certainty situations involve present actualities or near-term possibilities that can be illuminated relatively easily through facts and analyses.
Source: Edmondson, A. C., and Smith, D. M. "Too Hot to Handle? How to Manage Relationship Conflict," California Management Review 49, no. 1 (2006): 6–31.
© 2006 by the Regents of the University of California. Reprinted by permission of University of California Press.

Adams spoke first. Looking directly at McAlister, he told the group that future industry growth was in low-end inexpensive products. This meant that investing in the core business run by McAlister was a losing venture. McAlister, who naturally felt attacked by Adams's proposal, countered that his own data suggested just the opposite: the company needed to invest more in the core business to regain appeal and brand recognition for the majority of customers who valued quality and design. Already, the conflict was heating up.

As often happens, especially in ambiguous situations, conflicting interpretations of the same facts were used to fuel conflicting truths. To Adams, the data plainly showed that the core business was fundamentally flawed; obviously, only the lower end of the market was growing. McAlister, however, rejected Adams's conclusion. In McAlister's view, the data indicated that smart, attractive products were needed to expand market share in the lucrative high end of the market, consistent with Elite's long (and mostly successful) history. According to McAlister, it was only a matter of time and commitment. Looking at the same "reality," the two executives had arrived at very different conclusions about how to deal with an uncertain future full of risk. As the meeting wore on, Adams and McAlister continued to argue, fanning the flames of conflict still higher, neither budging from his original position until they found themselves at a standoff.

When conflicts reach an impasse, the discussion often starts to get personal. Adams believed that McAlister's wrongheaded view was merely a façade for increasing his own power in the company. Unsurprisingly, McAlister had reached the same conclusion about Adams. Both had fallen victim to the fundamental attribution error. More generally, whether blaming each other's motives, character, or abilities, people in the midst of a tough conflict like this one often silently blame someone else for the lack of progress on their shared task.

How can managers seeking to learn from different perspectives overcome the teaming challenges encountered by Elite's executives? In other words, how do we cool hot topics in fast-paced conversations about important topics? Exhibit 2.2 lists four strategies for mitigating conflict and ensuring the cooperative effort needed to successfully team.

Identifying Task and Relationship Conflict

Management researchers who study conflict in teams have concluded that conflict is productive, as long as teams stay away from the personal and emotional aspects of conflict. Task conflict—a difference of opinion about the product design—is useful. Relationship conflict—personal friction or emotionality—is counter-

---

Exhibit 2.2: How Leaders Can Cool Conflict

- **Identify the Nature of Conflict:** Though a difference of opinion about a product design or a work process is useful, personal friction and personality clashes are counterproductive. Understanding the differences between types of conflict allows leaders to better manage contentious exchanges.

- **Model Good Communication:** Good communication when confronting conflict, especially heated conflict, combines thoughtful statements with thoughtful questions, so as to allow people to understand the true basis of a disagreement and to identify the rationale behind each position.

- **Identify Shared Goals:** By identifying and also embracing shared goals, teams are able to overcome the fundamental attribution errors that erode respect and instead develop an environment of trust.

- **Encourage Difficult Conversations:** Through good communication, as just defined, it's useful to engage in authentic conversations that help build resilient relationships and put aside ideological and personal differences.

---

productive and should be avoided.[18] These researchers assert that task conflict improves the quality of decisions by engaging different points of view, while relationship conflict harms group dynamics and working relations.

This, of course, sounds like great advice. The problem is, it's too simple. First, as we just saw at Elite, it's far easier said than done. Adams and McAlister were trying to stay away from emotions and avoid personal friction. Neither one brought past grudges or suspicions to the table deliberately. They wanted to focus on the facts, and they intended to be guided by logic and analysis in arriving at a sensible team decision. Despite these intentions, they still ended up with raised voices, frustration, and concerns about each other's motives. Why does this so often happen in well-meaning attempts at teamwork?

Many conflicts arise from personal differences in values or interests but are presented as professional differences in opinion.

For example, if some executives believe that good design sells products (as McAlister did) while others believe that customers are primarily motivated by price (as Adams did), a conflict that pits design against price is a conflict of values. Values are beliefs we hold dear, and when our values are dismissed by others, even inadvertently, we react with strong emotions. Adams was proud of his subsidiary's rising sales. McAlister was proud of the parent company's design heritage. Each believed that other reasonable people would share their values—naïve realism at work—and each was disappointed to find he was wrong. Similarly, when personal interests are involved—one department may become the target of layoffs—emotions are hard to curb.

In contrast, calm and cool resolution of differences is easy when the problem is pure task conflict. In such cases, disagreement readily submits to resolution through facts and reasoning. Differences of opinion can be adjudicated through calculations or analyses that unambiguously assess the different options under consideration. In these situations, the advice to steer clear of relationship conflict and focus on task conflict is both feasible and sensible. However, when conflicts pit values against each other, it can be not only necessary but also fruitful to engage in thoughtful discussions of the emotions, values, and personal struggles behind the conflicts. When done skillfully, this kind of conversation allows meaningful progress on important challenges and debates, some that lie at the heart of a company's strategy.[19]

Good Communication and Shared Goals

Teaming, by its very nature, brings people from different backgrounds together to solve problems, coordinate processes, come up with new ideas, and deliver innovations. Interpersonal interactions can be engaging and intense. It is not surprising, given this intensity, that relationship conflict shows up uninvited despite leaders' best efforts to avoid it. It shows up in the midst of seemingly task-focused discussions. At Elite, the problem to be addressed was whether growth could be achieved by raising the quality of design or lowering product prices. What happened next took deliberate leadership.

With help from my colleague, skilled interventionist and author Diana Smith, the team at Elite Manufacturing switched gears. These senior executives were able to work together to learn and practice the skills for managing conflict effectively. First, McAlister and Adams each honestly examined to what degree their positions reflected what they believed best for the company and how much self-interest was involved. They also considered how their personal values influenced their views. Adams, a relative newcomer to Elite, was able to listen to McAlister, an "old-timer," speak about the company's long-term value of integrity in design. McAlister was proud of Elite's history. Several other managers who had been at Elite for many years chimed in with stories of Elite's having successfully weathered prior crises and times of slow growth. They also spoke of iconic designs that had made the company great.

After listening thoughtfully, Adams expressed appreciation for Elite's history and reputation. That was why he'd wanted to come to Elite in the first place. Adams said he understood why the core business was so important to McAlister. But he wanted McAlister and the others to understand his experience at a previous company, where lean operations and streamlined management structures had produced phenomenal results.

Now it was McAlister's turn to listen. After Adams had shared the role he'd taken in growing a division at his previous company, McAlister expressed renewed respect for Adams's track record and strategic agility. That's why the entire leadership team had wanted to bring him on board. The tension leaving the room was like air escaping from a balloon. By sharing the personal experiences and deeper rationales behind their respective positions, McAlister and Adams began to build respect and trust. Each man found that he could in fact be curious about what motivated the other to take his position. Another executive, who had not spoken up until that moment, pointed out that Elite was in tricky territory that differed in some fundamental ways from the challenges faced in the past. Another suggested listing crucial topics: How will we compete? How will we reduce costs? Do we need to redefine Elite's core mission?

The managers learned how to reflect on and challenge their spontaneous emotional reactions to disagreement. They became willing to experiment with reframing the situation, which meant looking at the issue from a different perspective. Reflecting and reframing are effective ways to cool a hot conflict. When practiced, they help to build a cooling system that's able to interrupt emotional hijackings before they erupt and bring a team's progress to a halt.

Encourage Difficult Conversations

Engaging conflict productively cannot be accomplished by avoiding emotions and personal differences. Openness is required.[20] This is a teaming skill that starts with willingness to explore rather than shy away from different beliefs and values. It requires acknowledging emotional reactions openly and exploring what led to them, rather than pretending they don't exist. It requires recognizing the inseparability of task and relationship conflicts in knowledge-intensive work in uncertain contexts. Team members must understand that "winning" the argument does not usually produce the best solution. Instead, the best solutions usually involve some integration and synthesis of differences. When people put their heads together, truly intent on learning from one another, they can almost always come up with a solution that is better than anyone could have come up with alone. This is teaming at its best.

Authentic communication about how we think or what makes us tick helps to build the genuine, resilient relationships that are crucial to effective teaming. Once McAlister and Adams realized that neither of their views had the corner on truth, they were willing to put aside ideological and personal differences, at least temporarily, to think about a new range of issues with their colleagues. But this took guidance and leadership skill.

Leaders who do not fully grasp the concept that conflict of some sort is necessary and even desirable to teaming are destined to fail in all but the most routine of work environments. To close the gap between how we want to lead and how we actually do lead, more of us need to learn the leadership skills to engage conflict directly and effectively. This takes commitment, patience, a willingness to make mistakes, self-awareness, and, of course, a sense of humor. At the very least, it involves a willingness to examine one's own role in a situation, even in a heated disagreement, and to wonder: "How am I contributing to the problem here?"

Leadership Actions That Promote Teaming

Teaming and learning do not happen automatically. Instead, they require coordination and some structure to ensure that insights are gained from members' collective experience and used to guide subsequent action. As research demonstrates across varied cases and settings, teaming and learning both depend on the deliberate exercise of leadership. It takes leadership to understand and resolve conflict and to instigate thoughtful conversations about errors. It takes leadership to adhere to process discipline and to help people remember to explore and experiment. In short, leadership is needed to help groups build shared understanding and coordinate action.

In nearly two decades of research, I've discovered that successful teaming efforts have followed strikingly similar paths, even across very different settings. Though the organizations I've examined operate in a range of environments and include enterprises in varied locations on the Process Knowledge Spectrum, many experienced similar failures when attempting to facilitate a significant transition or implement a novel technology. To help

Exhibit 2.3: Leadership Actions for Organizing to Learn

- Action 1: Frame the situation for learning.
- Action 2: Make it psychologically safe to team.
- Action 3: Learn to learn from failure.
- Action 4: Span occupational and cultural boundaries.

organizational leaders, I've synthesized both the positive and negative lessons I've learned from my research into four leadership actions. Presented in Exhibit 2.3, these actions form the basis of a way of leading I call organizing to learn. As explained in Chapter One, organizing to learn is a framework for creating an organizational environment conducive to teaming and learning activities, such as accessing collective knowledge, integrating diverse expertise, and analyzing uncertain outcomes.

These four actions, outlined in the following sections and discussed in much greater detail throughout Part Two, are not solely practices intended for teaming and learning. In fact, these individual practices translate directly to improved leadership and performance under nearly any circumstance. Taken together, however, they form the foundation for leading a successful teaming effort and provide a path forward for integrating learning into everyday execution.

Framing for Learning

Framing is crucial for leading the kind of change necessary to engage people as active learners. Leaders seeking to facilitate teaming and produce organizational learning must frame their project in a way that motivates others to collaborate. Researchers agree, however, that many of our spontaneous frames at work are inherently about self-protection.[21] These self-protective frames dramatically inhibit opportunities to collaborate, learn, and improve. However, people can learn to reframe and shift from spontaneous, self-protective frames to reflective, learning-oriented frames. Doing so involves interdependent team leaders, empowered teams, and an aspirational purpose. Chapter Three explores the process of framing and provides a number of practical framing tactics to help leaders seeking to facilitate teaming and promote collective learning.

Making It Psychologically Safe

An environment of psychological safety is an essential element of organizations that succeed in today's complex and uncertain world. The term *psychological safety* describes a climate in which people feel free to express relevant thoughts and feelings without fear of being penalized. Although it sounds simple, the ability to ask questions, seek help, and tolerate mistakes while colleagues watch can be unexpectedly difficult. Because coordinating and integrating complex tasks requires people to ask questions, share thoughts openly, and act without excessive concern about what others think of them, teaming flourishes with psychological safety and diminishes without it. Chapter Four includes information on how team leaders can shape and strengthen the teaming and collective learning processes by fostering an environment of psychological safety.

Learning to Learn From Failure

An essential, if difficult, teaming activity is learning from failure. Failure, broadly defined, encompasses both the small and large events in organizations that don't go as planned. Examples include a defect occurring in an assembly process, a new drug failing in clinical trials, or a strategy meeting breaking down. Learning from failures of all kinds is as vital as it is difficult. No one wants to look bad in front of his or her peers, and few of us want to admit failure. Yet failure is a necessary aspect of both teaming and organizational learning. As Chapter Five explains, failures of many kinds offer the chance to gain new insights into how to improve a process or product. The secret for organizations is to figure out how to gather and act on, rather than ignore or suppress, this potentially valuable information.

Spanning Knowledge Boundaries

Teams that succeed today don't merely work well around a shared conference table; they also have the ability to collaborate across boundaries and reach people who have the knowledge and information to help them apply resources effectively. Rapid developments in technology and the greater emphasis on globalization have dramatically increased the significance of boundary spanning in today's work environment. The information technology that has allowed us to communicate instantaneously across continents, however, sometimes leaves us with a false sense of confidence that productive teamwork is merely a click away. Education and other socializing processes lead people to favor their own group, discipline, location, or department. Ignoring such boundaries can easily blindside even the most well-intentioned teaming efforts. Chapter Six explores the various kinds of boundaries that people must span when teaming and how they can learn to collaborate despite different points of view, skill sets, and locations.

Leadership Summary

For teaming to work, participants must be willing to ask questions, offer suggestions, and voice concerns. This often includes coordinating across dispersed locations and communicating across different areas of expertise. Though seemingly simple, such collaborative efforts are often tested by many of our natural characteristics. Cognitive, interpersonal, and organizational factors get in the way of effective teaming. Psychological biases and errors that reduce the accuracy of human perception, estimation, and attribution create group tensions and interpersonal conflict. Conflict, however, is a natural part of teaming.

Productively engaging the conflict that teaming creates is done not by avoiding emotions and personal differences, but rather by developing a willingness to explore different beliefs and values. Leaders hoping to employ teaming, and to promote the learning that accompanies it, need to develop the leadership skills necessary to engage conflict effectively. Doing so has very real consequences for the way teaming occurs, or fails to occur, in work teams of all kinds. Fostering an atmosphere in which trust and respect thrive, and flexibility and innovation flourish, pays off even in the most deadline-driven work settings.

These leadership skills, challenging and rare as they may be, are crucial for such teaming activities as accessing collective knowledge, integrating diverse expertise, and analyzing uncertain outcomes. The four leadership actions presented at the end of this chapter, and explained in depth in Part Two, help cultivate an organizational environment that encourages the behaviors essential to successful teaming and organizational learning. These actions form the foundation of a way of leading I call *organizing to learn*. Organizing to learn is a leadership framework that optimizes teaming and ensures the cooperative learning needed for improvement and innovation.

LESSONS AND ACTIONS

- Although teaming is imperative in today's organizations, neither teams nor organizations naturally do it well.

- Successful teaming requires four behaviors: speaking up, collaboration, experimentation, and reflection.

- These behaviors are enacted in iterative cycles. Each new cycle is informed by the results of the previous cycle. Cycles continue until desired outcomes are achieved.

- There are several benefits to teaming. These benefits fall into two categories: better organizational performance and more engaging and satisfying work environments.

- The collaborative behaviors required by teaming, however, create group tensions and conflict. Leaders who do not grasp the concept that conflict is desirable to teaming and who do not learn the skills necessary to confront conflict are destined to fail.

- To moderate conflict, leaders should identify the nature of the conflict, model good communication, identify shared goals, and encourage difficult conversations.

- Due to the challenges of teaming, particular attention should be paid to the role of leadership. The mindset and practices of organizing to learn enable both teaming and learning.

- Successfully implementing an organizing-to-learn mindset involves four actions: framing for learning, making it psychologically safe, learning to learn from failure, and spanning occupational and cultural boundaries.

part two
organizing to learn

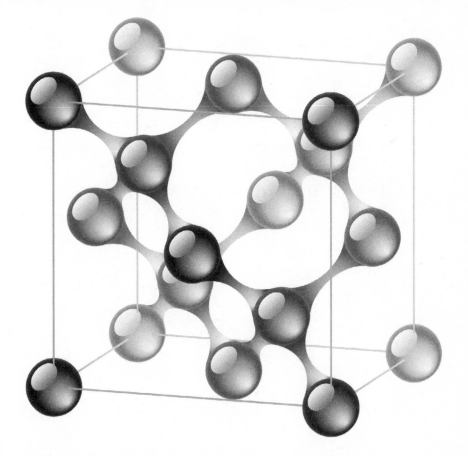

chapter three

the power
of framing

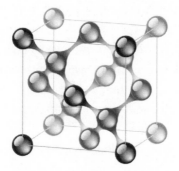

Teaming behavior is often at odds with the demands of formal organizational structures, which divide people by specialty and focus more of their attention on bosses than on peers. Natural cognitive biases can get in the way, too; for many kinds of knowledge work, effective teaming requires suspension of the spontaneous assumption that one's own perspective is more accurate than those of others. In many workplaces, therefore, engaging in teaming may feel like an unnatural act; thus, leadership is needed to create an environment conducive to teaming.

Framing is a crucial leadership action for enrolling people in any substantial behavior change. It is especially important for promoting teaming and learning. Framing helps people interpret the ambiguous signals that accompany change in a positive and productive light, and facilitates understanding of new performance expectations. This chapter explores what leaders can do to frame a new initiative or project in a way that supports successful teaming and engages people in the learning and problem-solving challenges that lie ahead.[1]

Leaders seeking to facilitate teaming as an essential activity in organizational learning must frame the work in a way that motivates people to collaborate. Although the need for collaboration may seem obvious in some settings—from patient care to new product development—it cannot be overstated that people tend to focus on their own tasks, failing to give adequate attention to how their tasks fit into the larger picture of the collective enterprise. Leaders cannot assume that everyone understands the work in the same way, and therefore must actively frame it for them. Eschewing a top-down, authoritative management style that characterizes organizing to execute, leaders must help people recognize their interdependence and then encourage and provide resources for the teaming and learning that follow. The key dimensions of situation-specific frames include assumptions about participants' roles and the purpose of the teaming effort. Leaders can facilitate teaming and accelerate learning by explicitly promoting team roles that support curiosity, responsiveness, and cooperation. Likewise, leaders must connect a new teaming effort, and its likely struggles, to a larger purpose that inspires and unites team members. An essential first step in establishing these elements involves understanding cognitive frames—their prevalence and their power.

Cognitive Frames

A frame is a set of assumptions or beliefs about a situation. Most of the time, framing occurs automatically. We rarely recognize the power of the automatic frames we've superimposed on situations, because we take them for granted. Frames nearly always exist, shaped by past experiences. Without our realizing it, these prior experiences affect how we think and feel about the current situation. Framing is neither bad nor good; it is simply inevitable. We interpret what is going on around us through an invisible lens shaped by our personal history and social context. The problem is that we tend to assume that our framing represents the truth, rather than merely presenting a subjective "map." In truth, however, each frame offers its own image of reality.

Tacit Interpretations

In complex situations, such as a busy hospital ward, an improvement project, or a strategy session, people interpret ambiguous cues and draw conclusions about what is happening. Cognitive research shows that many of these effortlessly drawn interpretations are tacit (taken for granted, not explicitly recognized), yet extremely powerful.[2] Once we interpret a situation, we think we know its true meaning. In addition, when we work closely with others, we develop shared interpretations, and these are also taken for granted.[3] As a result, people in a particular workplace often look at what's going on through tacit, shared frames. In studies of workplace conversation, in particular, researchers have identified frames that shape how we talk to each other. These frames feel natural, but make it difficult for people to learn much from each other, especially when they have conflicting points of view.[4] In a conflict, most people have a tacit goal of winning (few of us enter a conflict with a goal of learning as much as we can about the merits of the other person's point of view). Within this frame, conflict is viewed as a competition to be won rather than a problem to be understood and solved.

Others have used the term "mental model"[5] or "taken-for-granted assumption"[6] to convey a similar idea, but the terminology of framing applies particularly well to understanding teaming behavior. The terms *frame* and *framing* suggest the idea of looking through something at something else. A frame directs attention to features of the object of interest in a subtle way. Although our focus is on the painting, its frame can enhance or diminish our appreciation of the painting's colors and shapes without our conscious attention. Similarly, leaders and managers can use cognitive frames to highlight or encourage specific traits that help promote behaviors necessary for teaming and learning.

In a well-known example of the power of framing, Viktor Frankl, a Nazi concentration camp survivor, endured Auschwitz by imagining himself sharing the stories of courage he saw around him to friends and family on the outside. Frankl, a psychiatrist, later described the moment of transformation that allowed him to persevere in these worst of conditions: it was when he recognized the opportunity to reframe his experience from one of minute-to-minute suffering and fear to one of future-oriented visioning and hope.[7] It's an extreme example, but Frankl's remarkable story of courage and resilience illustrates the potential consequences of reframing—seeing the same situation one way rather than another, very different way.

Reframing for Learning

Psychologists and behavioral scientists have established the power of a variety of alternative cognitive frames. For instance, when people frame a task as a "performance situation" they are more risk averse and less willing to persist through obstacles than when the same task is framed as a "learning situation."[8] Not only do people adopting a learning frame persist longer in unfamiliar, challenging tasks, but they ultimately learn more as a result. In addition, people with a performance frame engage in less experimentation and innovation and are less likely to formulate new strategies in difficult situations. Instead, they're more likely to fall back on ineffective strategies they have used previously. Similarly, other research distinguishes between a "promotion" and a "prevention" orientation in approaching a task or challenge. A promotion orientation is characterized by ideals, goals, and eagerness to attain them. It reflects a tendency to frame new situations in terms of what can be gained. Conversely, a prevention orientation is characterized by a sense of obligation and by vigilance against loss. It indicates an inclination for framing new situations as opportunities to lose ground.[9]

Fortunately, frames can be changed. Behavioral scientists and therapists have studied the process of reframing to help people change their tacit frames and obtain better results in their lives. One approach, rational behavioral therapy, teaches people to try out more productive, learning-oriented ways of framing themselves.[10] Managerial research has also explored the process of framing, how it works, and how powerful it can be for improving results. Notably, Chris Argyris, one of the seminal scholars of organizational learning, conducted research over many years with managers to identify and challenge the tacit frames that shaped how they interacted with each other in difficult, confrontational conversations.[11] Similarly, Donald Schön, another pioneering researcher and a longtime colleague of Argyris, showed that how people framed their roles shaped their behavior and, correspondingly, helped determine the results they achieved.[12]

Selected References for Research on Framing

To learn more about framing, the following articles and books are classics on the topic from social psychology, linguistics, sociology, and organizational behavior.

Argyris, C. *On Organizational Learning.* Malden, MA: Blackwell Business, 1999.

Benford, R. D., and Snow, D. A. "Framing Processes and Social Movements: An Overview and Assessment." *Annual Review of Sociology* 26 (2000): 611–39.

Entman, M. R. "Framing: Toward Clarification of a Fractured Paradigm." *Journal of Communication* 43 (1993): 51–58.

Feldman, J., and Lakoff, G. I. *Framing the Debate: Famous Presidential Speeches and How Progressives Can Use Them to Change the Conversation (and Win Elections).* Brooklyn, NY: Ig, 2007.

Goffman, E. *Frame Analysis: An Essay on the Organization of Experience.* Cambridge, MA: Harvard University Press, 1974.

Hammond, S. (1998). *The Thin Book of Appreciative Inquiry.* Bend, OR.

Lakoff, G. *Simple Framing: An Introduction to Framing and Its Uses in Politics.* Berkeley, CA: Rockridge Institute, 2006.

Tversky, A. "The Framing of Decisions and the Psychology of Choice." *Science* 30 (1981): 453–458.

Most models of framing in psychological research consist of two contrasting alternatives: learning versus performing, goal achieving versus self-protecting, or health enhancing versus health limiting. Building on this, a given project, or any collaborative work, can be framed as a learning opportunity or as mere execution. A learning opportunity is the right frame if the work will involve solving new problems. An execution frame applies well if the tasks ahead are completely routine and the coordination entirely programmed.

Leaders exert the primary influence on which frame is adopted. Cognitive psychologists have identified habitual difference across individuals in framing. Behavioral therapists have described ways to help individuals reframe to improve their health. Similarly, organizational researchers have shown that leaders can frame, or reframe, a situation in ways that powerfully influence how others respond to, or engage in, the situation. The following example emphasizes the power of leaders to influence how colleagues view the purpose of a project and understand their roles in achieving that purpose.

Framing a Change Project

Cardiac surgery is performed to treat age-related or genetic problems with the heart. The operation unites multiple professions and an array of specialized equipment in a carefully choreographed routine. Surgeons carry out the actual repair of diseased tissue, supported by scrub and circulating nurses, an anesthesiologist, and a technician called a perfusionist. The nurses assist the surgeon both before and during the procedure, the anesthesiologist controls the delivery of anesthesia to the patient, and the perfusionist runs the heart-lung bypass machine.

A typical cardiac surgery department does hundreds of open-heart operations a year, and an operating room team's sequence of individual tasks constitutes a well-defined routine. This routine, perhaps more than any other in hospitals, had remained stable over a long time and was also strikingly similar across different hospitals. In the face of this consistency, a new technology, which I'll refer to as Minimally Invasive Cardiac Surgery (MICS), was introduced by a medical company a few years ago. MICS enabled surgical teams to perform the surgery less invasively and thus had the potential to offer a competitive advantage for the hospitals that adopted it. Using the technology, however, required a profound change in how the operating room (OR) team worked together.

Conventional open-heart surgery has saved countless lives, but the operation's invasiveness resulted in a painful, lengthy recovery. The standard cardiac operation consisted of cutting open the chest, splitting the breastbone, stopping the heart, repairing the damaged parts of the heart, and closing the chest wound. MICS provided a less invasive way to access the heart through a small incision between the ribs. This small incision forced surgeons to operate in a severely restricted space. Tubes for the heart-lung bypass machine had to be threaded through an artery instead of the incision, and a balloon had to be inserted and inflated in the aorta to act as an internal clamp. These changes required much greater coordination. As one nurse noted, "When I read the training manual, I couldn't believe it. It was so different from standard cases." Not surprisingly, adopting the new technology was much more difficult than expected.

Four Teams: Two Results

To better understand the challenges to implementing new technology, I examined cardiac surgery departments in 16 different hospitals attempting to adopt MICS. I didn't set out to study leaders' framing, but by the time the research was over it turned out to be the single most powerful factor explaining success. The following sections summarize the study findings by highlighting four of the 16 cases. Consistent with past research on innovation, the study deliberately varied factors previously associated with successful outcomes. These included the hospitals' innovation history, resources, management support, and the organizational status of the project leader. Three of the hospitals had senior surgeons in charge of the project (two were chiefs of their respective departments), and one had a new, more junior surgeon leading the transition. Two were academic medical centers; two were community hospitals. Two had more senior management support; two had less. As Table 3.1 shows, none of these factors explained the difference in implementation success.

Two of the four hospitals succeeded in their efforts to adopt MICS; two ultimately abandoned the effort. The difference between success and failure was not determined by management support, resources, project leader status, or expertise. Surprisingly, the difference wasn't determined even by whether the hospital was academic, or by its prior history of innovation. Instead, differences in how the project was framed by each project leader gave rise to different attitudes about the technology and the need for teamwork. During the study, three dimensions emerged in how MICS was framed. Exhibit 3.1 outlines these dimensions.

Table 3.1: Background Summary and Implicit Frames for MICS Implementation

	Hospital #1	Hospital #2	Hospital #3	Hospital #4
Hospital Type	Academic	Community	Academic	Community
History of Innovation	Extensive	Limited	Extensive	Limited
Management Support	Management opposed	Management neutral	Extensive support	Extensive support
Project Resources	Somewhat constrained	Adequate	Adequate	Adequate
Status of Adopting Surgeon	Chief of Department	Junior surgeon	Chief of Department	Chief of Department
View of the Leader's Role in Project	Skilled senior surgeon who communicated a rationale for and confidence in the technology and a need for help from his highly skilled team.	Junior surgeon who communicated excitement about the challenge and emphasized the critical role of other team members.	Skilled senior surgeon who had considerable past experience with the technology and would make it work single-handedly.	Skilled senior surgeon who minimized the degree of challenge and change posed by the new technology.

(Continued)

Table 3.1 *(Continued)*

	Hospital #1	Hospital #2	Hospital #3	Hospital #4
View of Team's Role in Project	Hand-selected professionals and highly valued subordinates whose skills were vital to success.	Critical members of the team, without which the project would fail.	Executors of the surgeon's new technology project.	Nonsurgeon team members were seen as playing a relatively unimportant role.
View of Project Purpose	To help patients.	To empower the team and thereby accomplish ambitious goals for the department.	To demonstrate leading-edge capability.	To stay competitive with other hospitals.
Members' Perceptions of Their Ability to Speak Up in Action	"I am very comfortable speaking up." —Nurse	"There's a free and open environment with input from everybody." —Nurse	"If you observe something that might be a problem you are obligated to speak up, but you pick your time." —Nurse	"[People] are afraid to speak out." —Nurse
Project Outcome	Successful implementation	Successful implementation	Eventually abandoned	Abandoned early

Exhibit 3.1: Critical Dimensions for Successfully Framing Implementation

- **The leaders' role:** whether the surgeon, as the team leader, framed himself as an interdependent team leader or an individual expert
- **The team's role:** whether the team's role was framed as empowered partners or skilled support staff
- **The project purpose:** whether the project purpose was communicated as aspirational or defensive

More than anything else, these three aspects of framing determined which cardiac teams succeeded and which failed. In addition, these three aspects were vital in understanding the way leadership actions guide organizational members toward a team-based, collaborative interpretation of reality.

The Leader's Role

In general, leaders are visible spokespeople. They can create a shared awareness of a crucial performance gap and are in a position to articulate the potential opportunity represented by a new direction or initiative. People pay particular attention to what leaders say and do compared to what peers and others say and do.[13] Therefore, in engaging others in the uncertain path forward of a new initiative, leaders can deliberately use framing to help focus attention and motivate action. By deliberate use, I mean leaders should present themselves in a way that encourages teamwork and fosters mutual respect, which is crucial to helping others share information, ask questions, and experiment with the variety of new behaviors or tasks that may be involved.

Interdependent Team Leader or Individual Expert

In the successful instances of MICS implementation, the cardiac surgeons explicitly communicated that they were interdependent with others in making the new technology work. In particular, they each emphasized their own fallibility and need for others' input. Without working together as a team, the minimally invasive routine would be nearly impossible to choreograph, these leaders explained.

It's important to recognize that in the world of cardiac surgery, surgeons occupy a venerated, even exalted, position. While performing the traditional cardiac procedure, the surgeon maintains absolute control over the OR team, the patient, and the process. By and large, this top-down approach has worked well in that setting. The problem was that minimally invasive surgery didn't unfold in the same way. It required more collaboration and interaction. Because the surgeon lacked the same full access to the visual data of the heart as when the sternum was split apart, he needed others on the team to guide some of his actions by reporting on data from various monitors and images. Without conveying any loss of expertise or status, these successful leaders simply recognized and communicated that in doing MICS they were dependent on others.

In hospital #1, the team leader, who was head of the department, emphasized that he had hand-picked great people for the project. The team leader in hospital #2, a young surgeon, went a step further and treated implementation of MICS as a project that needed to be both structured and led. His leadership took two forms: managing a project and empowering a well-selected team. He recognized that MICS represented a paradigm shift for himself and the rest of the OR team:

> The ability of the surgeon to allow himself to become a partner, not a dictator, is critical. For example, you really do have to change what you're doing based on a suggestion from someone else on the team. This is a complete restructuring of the OR and how it works. You still need someone in charge, but it is so different.

He further explained that his own role had to shift from order-giver to team member and that he hoped to empower and inspire others on the team to put in the effort it took to change. He paid attention to operating room dynamics. "The whole model of surgeons barking orders down from on high is gone," he said. "There is a whole new wave of interaction."

In contrast, hospital #3's surgeon team leader presented MICS as a change that should be driven forward by a surgeon and emphasized its technical features. A nationally renowned surgeon with significant prior experience with MICS, he explained in an interview that he did not see the new technology as particularly challenging. Instead, he considered the implementation process as simply "a matter of training the team." He didn't alter his approach to communicating with others on the OR team, whom he believed should know their jobs, and did little to guide team members through the transition. As one team member noted, the surgeon simply expected that "we know what is going on."

Similarly, in hospital #4 the team leader did little coaching and was difficult to approach. One nurse described his leadership style as "very regimented." She added, "Proper decorum in the room is his big thing. We were told in two different interviews that the surgeon was the 'captain of the ship' and in one that 'he's the chairman and that's how he runs the show.'" Unfortunately, both leaders of hospitals #3 and #4 failed to create an interdependent, collaborative environment. Their attitudes and actions communicated that other team members were not playing a significant role in implementing the new technology.

Ask, Listen, and Learn

As this study showed, a command-and-control approach fails to produce the teaming and learning necessary to successfully develop the new routines that are required by a novel technology or service. Instead, leaders must explicitly convey their own sense of interdependence with others for a successful outcome, express their own fallibility, and communicate a need for collaboration. For many leaders, however, this requires adjusting the concept of leadership. To succeed in implementing change or transforming the way work is accomplished, leaders must frame their role in the project in ways that invite others to participate fully. They need to alter the existing hierarchical relationship, ask for help, listen, and acknowledge their own limitations. Doing so helps to create a more open environment with input from all team members. Moreover, this difference in how leaders present their roles has direct and obvious implications for how others view their roles.

Team Members' Roles

When temporary teams form, it's natural for people to assume roles according to position, expertise, or personality. Due to this inevitability, thoughtfully framing the roles that different people should play in a joint effort is important to building a cohesive team and an effective process. In particular, in a setting where jobs have traditionally been highly segmented—such that task interdependence is managed in advance by clear role boundaries—making a shift to a way of working characterized by back-and-forth communication can be extremely challenging. Getting people to start teaming requires a new frame.

Empowered Team or Skilled Support Staff

Members of the cardiac surgery teams for hospitals #3 and #4 struggled with the changes that the new technology required, particularly in the face of the surgeons' lack of acknowledgment of significant change. Instead of considering themselves as valuable colleagues and pioneering learners, they saw themselves as mere doers. A sense of true teamwork and collegiality was missing. At hospital #3, the surgeon's position as an expert excluded others from seeing a way to make genuine contributions beyond performing their own specific, predetermined tasks. His expertise was not the problem. The problem was the framing of his expertise: colleagues were led to think their input didn't matter. However, the roles that others needed to play did not require surgical expertise so much as constant communication to assess and guide placement of surgical components during the surgery. This unsuccessful framing was further hampered by the fact that the surgeon played no role in configuring the team, which was composed by default according to seniority. The approaches of hospitals #3 and #4 can be summarized as follows:

- The overarching view of the project was that implementing the new technology was "not that different" from normal OR situations.

- During an operation, the understood goal was to "do your job."

- The expectation of each individual during the project was to know his or her job and to know how to interact with others' jobs.

- Other participants besides the lead surgeon were viewed as subordinates.

In contrast, at hospitals #1 and #2 all of the operating room team members felt a profound sense of ownership of the project's processes and believed they had critical roles to play in its success. Nonsurgeon team members felt comfortable voicing their observations and concerns in the operating room and they were included in meaningful reflection and discussions to assess the technology and the team process. With team members seen as playing an essential role in implementation success, the approaches of hospitals #1 and #2 can be summarized as follows:

- The overarching view of the project was that implementing the new technology was a challenging opportunity to try new techniques, and was full of unknowns.

- During an operation, the understood goal was to learn as much as possible while ensuring that the patient was safe.

- The expectation for an individual during the project was to communicate and act interdependently in getting the work done and overcome any challenges that arose.

- Other participants besides the lead surgeon were viewed as partners, valued teammates, and essential resources for overcoming new challenges.

The first step of the team leader at hospital #1 was to put together a special OR team. After selecting a second surgeon to manage data collection, he deferred to leaders in each of the other three disciplines to select the remaining team members. Each disciplinary group selected thoughtfully. For example, the head of cardiac surgical nursing selected herself and another highly experienced nurse to participate because of the challenge of the new procedure. The second nurse reported being selected because "the surgeons recognize how important our knowledge is."

This reframing extended beyond the operating room. Perfusionists and nurses began to reframe their own roles—from skilled technicians who supported surgeons' work to involved thinkers who read the medical literature. As a perfusionist at hospital #2 reported, "If an unusual case is coming up, I ask surgeons about it, look at the literature, and talk with the surgeons beforehand. The surgeons are open to me bugging them on that level. It used to be viewed skeptically, but they have grown to expect that interaction from me."

Intellectual and Emotional Commitment

A critical part of framing people's roles in a temporary team project is to communicate that they are being selected for the

project for a reason. This builds intellectual and emotional commitment to the implementation process and acts as an invitation
to others to participate in shaping the specifics of the effort, in
addition to helping execute. It also represents an implicit awareness
that new technology imposes a need for change, that change is
hard, and that everyone affects whether or not the change succeeds.
When leaders emphasize that they have hand-picked great people
for a project, it builds intellectual and emotional commitment.

In contrast, when leaders fail to convey that others play vital
roles in the project, team members may not believe they can or
will make genuine contributions to its success. This compromises
their ability to envision and help shape how a new technology or
process can transform the work to help the organization or its
customers. Framing powerfully influences commitment and motivates people to exert the effort and take the risks that change
requires. These observations point to a simple but incontrovertible
fact: teaming works when everyone makes it work. Learning
happens when individuals commit to cooperating in a unified
effort to overcome the inevitable setbacks that accompany innovation and implementation. Deliberate, positive reframing motivates
team members to communicate more intensively, thus lessening
the confines of hierarchy. Individual motives become more closely
aligned with the purpose of the project.

The Project Purpose

Even when individual employees are aware of problems, a collective effort focused on solving them is unlikely to occur when
people do not understand and care about a common purpose.
Therefore, effectively framing a task involves providing a compelling answer to the question of why a particular project exists. What
purpose does it serve? What value does the project offer to employees, customers, or society? The leader's job is to articulate and help
people cohere around this shared purpose. Whether or not the
effort to create a sense of purpose is effective hinges on the leader's

ability to connect the teaming effort to goals and objectives that motivate people to persist during a novel, uncertain endeavor. Just as individuals have a promotion or prevention orientation, projects are often framed in either an aspirational or a defensive way.

Aspirational or Defensive Purpose

Although each of the four hospitals profiled here followed a unique journey in implementing MICS, they fell into two groups in terms of team beliefs—explicit or inferred—about the reason for implementing the new technology. Members of the successful teams shared a sense of purpose that can be described as aspirational— driven by a desire to accomplish compelling goals for patients or for the hospital. Hospital #1 emphasized patient benefits; hospital #2 was motivated by testing boundaries and reaching new frontiers in cardiac surgery. In contrast, the two unsuccessful teams' goals were fundamentally preventative and reactive. They both viewed the technology as a necessary burden to be endured. These teams were driven by concerns about competition and encumbered by the anxiety of coping with technological change. This latter belief seemed to be the default state, in the absence of leadership effort to impose a new, inspiring belief, as occurred in hospitals #1 and #2.

Despite both being in academic hospitals, which are all but required to innovate to remain leading-edge medical centers, the teams in hospitals #1 and #3 had a fundamentally different view of the MICS project because of the way the two surgeons framed the purpose of the new technology. Hospital #3's highly experienced leader, seeing the change imposed by the new technology as relatively insignificant, did not explicitly frame the journey or feel a need to motivate others in the OR team to learn the new procedure. Team members were left to infer a rationale for implementing MICS, and in the vacuum no one identified a compelling purpose for the change. Instead, they saw each novel procedure as a burden to be dreaded. The absence of an explicit purpose for change left the team assuming that it benefited the surgeon to be on the leading edge of technology while feeling no ownership of this goal themselves.

Compare that to team members at hospital #1. Each person I interviewed separately noted a sense of excitement in doing something new that helped patients recuperate more quickly from surgery. Nurses reported being glad they were picked for the project and inspired by the challenge. By focusing on patient benefits, hospital #1's lead surgeon motivated the team to accept the hardship that learning MICS entailed. He frequently communicated his growing confidence in the technology, and team members shared a belief that patients benefited greatly from the procedure. One nurse enthused, "Every time we're going to do a [MICS] procedure, I feel like I've been enlightened. I can see these patients doing so well. It is such a rewarding experience. I am so grateful I was picked."

The two community hospitals, cases #2 and #4, displayed a similar split. In hospital #4, team members communicated a belief that the reason for doing MICS was to "keep up with the Joneses" and to avoid being compromised by competitive pressures in the future. The chief of cardiac surgery decided to adopt MICS because, as he explained, "We'd like everyone to know we can do it. It is a marketing thing." Others believed his reason for doing MICS was solely for image. As a nurse explained, "He wanted to be competitive with other institutions." In contrast, team members at hospital #2 expressed their conviction that MICS was an exciting opportunity to test the possibilities not only for cardiac patients, but also for an OR team. As the perfusionist at hospital #2 saw it, MICS implementation was "about what a group of people can do."

Communicating a Clear and Compelling Purpose

Engaging others' willing contribution is a core leadership task. This means that leaders in uncertain, dynamic contexts have to stimulate and guide a collective learning process. To do so, leaders must communicate a clear and compelling purpose that resonates with all members of the team. The type of purpose that motivates teaming generally has meaning beyond making money or self-preservation, providing a clear, aspirational goal that energizes others and encourages a focus on collective responsibility for teaming and learning. An aspirational purpose encapsulates the excitement of doing something that aids others and helps team members endure the hardships of learning. By explicitly communicating growing confidence in a new process or technology, leaders ensure that team members recognize that they are making progress toward achieving the purpose.

Together, these three dimensions of framing—establishing the leader's role, others' roles, and a shared purpose—play a crucial part in determining success or failure in a substantial change effort. By helping shape others' perceptions of roles and objectives, deliberate framing can make the difference between the creation of an environment that supports collaboration and encourages persistence, or a defensive environment that implicitly presents change as a burden to be endured. The framing makes all the difference between individuals who see themselves as embarking on a valued learning journey and those who are merely trying to get the work done.

A Learning Frame Versus an Execution Frame

Leaders who frame themselves as interdependent with others in accomplishing important changes, view others as crucial partners, and put forward an aspirational purpose are employing a learning frame. Two of the hospital teams discussed earlier had a learning frame. In contrast, in those sites with defensive goals, leaders who presented themselves as experts who were more important than others in completing the journey ahead, and saw others as supporting actors, can be characterized as having an execution frame. Table 3.2 directly contrasts the three dimensions of a learning frame with those of an execution frame.

Table 3.2: Learning Frame Versus Execution Frame

Project Dimension	Learning Frame	Execution Frame
Leader's view of self in carrying out the project	Important and interdependent in overcoming the challenges ahead.	Knows what to do and in a position to tell others what to do.
Leader's view of others in carrying out the project	Valued partners with essential input for overcoming the challenges ahead.	Coactors or subordinates.
Overall view of the situation created by the project and corresponding tacit goal for the project	Challenging, full of unknowns, and an opportunity to try out new concepts and techniques. The tacit goal is to learn as much as possible so as to figure out what to do next.	Same as, or "not that different from," normal situation. The tacit goal is to get the job done.

The learning frame involved a more inclusive, inquiry-oriented leadership style, in which surgeons acted as interdependent members of the team. The other practitioners in the operating room experienced themselves as full-fledged team members vital to the success of a meaningful enterprise. In contrast, teams with an execution frame had apparently adopted defensive goals for the projects by default—avoiding loss of market share to nearby hospitals, for example—with leaders positioned as technical experts, and others as supporting actors. In addition, in hospitals #1 and #2, but not in hospitals #3 and #4, nonsurgeon team members felt competently comfortable voicing their observations in the operating room. Likewise, team members were included in meaningful reflection sessions to discuss how MICS was progressing, further confirming their essential roles in project success.

When managing a project in which risk and uncertainty are high, leaders who employ and communicate a learning frame help launch a rewarding collaborative effort that promotes learning and innovation. In contrast, when, by design or by default, work is framed as an opportunity to "get it right" on the first try, people are less able to learn during the process and ultimately get it right. Any implementation process that involves uncertainty is most successful when participants are open to change, eager to find the best fit, and recognize that other people may have different perspectives. When people are very aware that others may have observed or interpreted something in a different way, they are more likely to be curious and to engage each other in relevant discussions about what to try. This is the very essence of a learning frame. To even consider this possibility, however, requires either an innate or trained habit of being self-aware, collaborative, and curious. Unfortunately, these traits and their corresponding cognitive frame rarely appear spontaneously in corporate and other organizational settings.

Changing Frames

In general, researchers agree that many of the spontaneous frames we bring to work are inherently about self-protection. Unfortunately, protection comes at a cost. Self-protective frames dramatically inhibit the opportunity to learn and improve. Research shows that people can learn to reframe and shift from spontaneous self-protective frames to reflective or learning-oriented frames. When this happens, the new frames are no longer tacit—at least not at first—but rather explicitly imposed on a situation or project in an effort to be effective.[14] Following are steps for developing and reinforcing a learning frame, along with specific tactics to help individuals embrace a new way of interpreting their roles.

Establishing a Learning Frame

In those hospitals that adopted learning frames and successfully implemented MICS, the collective learning process consisted of four tightly coupled, recurring steps. The first step was enrollment of carefully selected team members by the leader, followed by team preparation, and then by multiple cycles of trial and reflection. Table 3.3 summarizes these steps and shows specific activities that successful implementers of the new technology had in common. It also suggests underlying cognitions supportive of these activities.

Enrollment. A critical feature of enrollment is communicating to others that they are being specifically selected for a project or role. This builds intellectual and emotional commitment to the work. Enrollment is also about building awareness that a new technology imposes change, that change is challenging, and that everyone involved will affect whether or not the change succeeds. Enrollment, which is a fundamental leadership action, sets the tone of the journey that follows. It may be the first communication about a proposed change, allowing team members to form first impressions about what lies ahead for them and for the organization. When first impressions contain excitement or confidence that one's participation matters to outcomes, this can have a lasting effect.

Preparation. Preparation may involve attendance at an off-site training, or in-house team practice sessions, or it may be a quick team-building meeting to get to know others' strengths, weaknesses, hopes, and fears. Depending on the nature of the project, preparation sessions should include discussion of how existing routines may need to be altered, in order to collect ideas for getting this to happen. More important, having an explicit practice session reduces the real and perceived risks of trying new things in "real" situations where customers or other outsiders could be harmed or receive a negative impression. Practice also allows team members to refine their own skills and integrate their actions with those of other participants. Other activities that should take place during the preparation phase include the establishment of team norms, a

Table 3.3: Activities and Cognitive Frames for Successful Implementation

Step	Activities	Frames (Implicit Cognitions)	Effects
Enrollment	Communicate deliberateness in project team selection. Communicate purpose of project.	The project will create significant change in this organization or in people's jobs. Others play an important role in whether or not it succeeds.	Participants feel part of a team, have a shared sense of purpose, and feel committed to the project.
Preparation	Offline sessions to safely explore implications of the new technology or other change. Practice with new behaviors.	We need to learn how to work together and to anticipate problems, if the project is going to succeed.	Participants develop an increasing willingness to take interpersonal risks in the project team and are motivated to expend effort on novel and uncertain actions.
Trial	Try out new concepts, processes, and tools. Pay close attention to what happens.	Actions at this stage of implementation are experiments. It's not about getting it right the first time. I feel a sense of curiosity about what will happen.	Every event, every action is seen as an opportunity to learn; people pay attention and are alert for possible changes that could be made.
Reflection	Discuss trial results.	It will help me/us to learn from the past trials. I wonder what others may have seen that I missed.	Participants discuss what they did and what happened. Then they analyze what it means and brainstorm alternatives, if needed.

thorough discussion of how the team should work together, how to encourage speaking up with concerns and observations, and how power relations might affect the group.

Trial. The next step in the team learning process is a first, real trial of the new technology, or other change. This means doing actual work while actively framing that work as an experiment from which much may be learned. In the trial step, people will begin to envision and enact how the new process or technology transforms the way work is done in the organization. The goal here is not to execute perfectly on the first try, but rather to quickly identify what adjustments or changes may be necessary for future success. Trials work well when those involved are curious and inquisitive.

Reflection. Paired with the previous step, reflection constitutes an opportunity to learn from what worked and what failed. Salient observations should then be used to make potential improvements after each round of trials. Together, these last two steps, trial and reflection, are the basis of a learning cycle that fuels successful implementation or innovation. Until such time as a new process or technology is completely routine, each use of it is an experiment, and each may be subtly different from prior use. Such differences are only useful if they are noticed, analyzed for their impact, and considered in the design of the next trial. In this way, the design of subsequent action continuously benefits from the knowledge gained in the prior cycle. Change happens through iteration.

Reinforcing a Learning Frame

One factor that facilitates deeper acceptance of a learning frame is making its use public rather than practicing it privately. Whether leading or participating in implementation projects, individuals seeking to follow the tactics for reframing can be open with others

---

Exhibit 3.2: Leadership Tactics for Reinforcing a Learning Frame

- Use verbal and visual discourse to promote the learning frame.
- Reinforce this framing by explaining and modeling the desired interpersonal and collaborative behaviors.
- Explain these desired behaviors in practical terms, such as "Speak up if you see something wrong" or "Just pick up the phone and ask if you have a question."
- Initiate activities, for example, a kick-off meeting, a meeting to identify personal goals within the teaming or learning effort, and training on how to efficiently deal with interpersonal conflict. These can facilitate new processes or routines and help team members build confidence.
- Use artifacts such as a prominent sign in the project work area to visually reinforce the learning frame.

---

about what they are trying to do—allowing others to understand, provide feedback about, and even experiment with the learning frame themselves. Note that this is not the typical way leaders act; more often, they keep their strategy for engaging others (even when noble) to themselves. Exhibit 3.2 offers five leadership tactics for reinforcing a learning frame.

The Ideal Employee?

This chapter has emphasized the use of deliberate framing. But it's the unconscious frames that may exert the strongest influence on learning in an organization. Many managers have a taken-for-granted concept of an ideal employee. Consider the following: an ideal employee can handle with ease any problem that comes along (without bothering managers, of course), quietly corrects errors (her own and others') without making a fuss, performs flawlessly, and is deeply committed to the organization and its processes. I often pose this hypothetical person to managers, and I ask, "What's wrong with this employee?" They nearly always respond, "She doesn't exist!" My response is, no, that's not the problem. She exists. Every large organization has a few of these tireless and unassuming souls. But that's not the real problem. What's wrong with this so-called ideal employee is that she is making it more difficult for the organization to learn.

In the learning organization, problems and errors must be reported so everyone can learn. Flawless performance means not stretching enough. And the organization's processes need to be challenged, not blindly followed and enforced. In reflecting on our study explaining why hospitals don't learn from failures, Anita Tucker and I suggested, provocatively, that managers who want to build a learning organization must reframe the ideal employee in their own minds—and get ready to celebrate *the disruptive questioner who simply won't leave well enough alone*.[15] This organizational-learning enabler is constantly questioning and improving, not accepting and using, current practices.

Tactics for Individual Reframing

Until this point, framing has been discussed as a leaders' job. Indeed, framing is one of the most important ways leaders can positively influence others and shape outcomes. However, anyone involved in a change initiative, in any role, can exert leadership in the form of helping to establish or reinforce a learning frame. Facing significant change, formal leaders should not be the only ones to actively frame the work ahead as a collaborative learning journey. General participation in cocreating a learning mindset not only ensures that it is widely shared, but it also helps others build their own leadership skills.

The most challenging part of shifting one's frame is recognizing the taken-for-granted frame that underlies one's current perceptions of a situation. Making a decision to reframe is comparatively easy, as outlined here in Exhibit 3.3. Yet another important challenge must be mentioned: Quite often people are attached to viewing their situation or the work ahead as burdensome; coping with an inherently difficult situation can become part of their self-image and may even lower their sense of responsibility for achieving great results. By thinking, for example, "The situation is impossible and it's not my fault if things don't go well . . . " people defend themselves against feelings of inadequacy or against others blaming them when things go wrong. For some, this mindset is deeply held and difficult to shift. For others, recognizing the existence of a tacit, and unhelpful, frame can be liberating. Experimenting with a new, empowering frame becomes a welcome opportunity for personal growth and development. Exhibit 3.3 presents four tactics that anyone confronted with the challenge of teaming, learning, implementing new technology, or driving organizational change can use to help adjust an existing cognitive frame.

These reframing steps, when practiced diligently, are more powerful than they appear. There is broad agreement in the therapeutic literature that it is difficult to change behavior to obtain different results without changing the underlying cognitions that give rise

---

Exhibit 3.3: Four Tactics for Individual Reframing

To achieve better results with any teaming or organizational learning project, experiment with the following four tactics for reframing:

- Tell yourself that the project is different from anything you've done before and presents an exciting opportunity to try out new approaches and learn from them.

- See yourself as critical to a successful outcome and yet as unable to achieve success without the willing participation of others.

- Tell yourself that others are vitally important to a successful outcome and may provide key knowledge or suggestions that you can't anticipate in advance.

- Communicate with others exactly as you would if the above three statements were true.

to and support the desired behaviors.[16] And so, the four tactics for individual reframing must be brought to bear on new situations repeatedly before they can become second nature.

Leadership Summary

In promoting teaming and learning, framing is a good place to start. How we think shapes our behavior, which in turn influences how effectively we obtain desired results. This basic causal relationship has been identified in different research traditions, including cognitive psychology, behavioral therapy, and organizational learning. Just as cognitive psychologists have identified habitual differences across individuals in framing, and behavioral therapists have described ways to help individuals reframe to improve their emotional and psychological health, this chapter emphasizes the power of leaders. Leaders of teams that are responsible for new initiatives are uniquely placed to influence how others see the project, especially how they view its purpose, and how they see their own role in achieving that purpose.

Developing a learning frame occurs when a leader, at any level in an organization, recognizes the important contributions of others, especially subordinates, and adopts a different stance with respect to hierarchical structure. In particular, project leaders need to foster a shared understanding of the goal, the purpose, and desired behaviors. They should emphasize that team members were hand-picked for the project. Then, to take it one step further, leaders should emphasize the high level of interdependence they share with others on the team in achieving a successful outcome. This should be accompanied by explicitly communicating an aspirational purpose that energizes team members. This purpose should be both compelling and challenging, but not so challenging as to evoke feelings of doubt or helplessness.

Taken together, these three dimensions of framing—the leader's role, others' roles, and the project purpose—have profound implications for how people work together and create a shared understanding of the task at hand. Learning-oriented cognitive frames and their corresponding behaviors are uncommon in most traditional professional settings. Fortunately, people's cognitive frames can be changed. The last section of the chapter offers strategies for establishing and reinforcing a new, more interdependent frame that encourages collaboration and persistence. These strategies are designed to help leaders frame a project as a learning endeavor. They will help leaders to communicate the fact that they are greatly in need of everyone's best ideas and most perceptive questions. They are designed to help everyone communicate openly, which in turn begins the process of building an environment of psychological safety, the topic of the next chapter.

LESSONS AND ACTIONS

- Frames are interpretations that individuals rely on to sense and understand their environment. Most of the time, framing occurs automatically.

- Reframing is a powerful leadership tool for shifting behaviors and enrolling people in change.

- How people working in an organization, especially those in leadership positions, frame a project can determine the difference between success and failure.

- Successfully framing a new initiative that calls for both teaming and learning is about roles and goals: the leader's role, team members' roles, and the teaming effort's goal or purpose.

- In framing their role, leaders must explicitly communicate their interdependence and express both their own fallibility and the need for collaboration.

- In defining team members' roles, leaders need to emphasize that they have picked skilled people who are vital to the success of the project.

- To inspire and unite team members, leaders must communicate a clear and compelling purpose.

- Establishing a learning frame involves four iterative steps: enrollment, preparation, trial, and reflection.

- To reinforce a learning frame: use verbal and visual discourse; explain desired interpersonal and collaborative behaviors in practical terms; initiate activities that facilitate new routines and help build confidence; and use artifacts to visually reinforce elements of the frame.

- To achieve better teaming or learning results, experiment with the following individual tactics: tell yourself that the project presents an exciting opportunity; see yourself as critical to a successful outcome; tell yourself that others are important to a successful outcome; and communicate with others as if the preceding three points are true.

chapter four

making it safe
to team

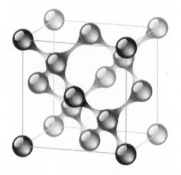

On January 16, 2003, the space shuttle *Columbia* was successfully launched from the Kennedy Space Center on a sixteen-day research mission. The next day, shuttle engineer Rodney Rocha reviewed a video of the launch and became deeply concerned about the size and position of a chunk of insulating foam that appeared to have fallen off the shuttle's external tank and struck its left wing. The video images were grainy, and it was impossible to be sure what had happened. To determine whether damage had occurred, Rocha hoped to obtain photographic images of the shuttle's wing from spy satellites. Although the photos would have to be authorized by the Air Force, the request would require neither a technical nor financial miracle. It did mean that NASA would have to ask for help from the Department of Defense.

Rocha initially expressed the need for the satellite images in an e-mail to his immediate superior, emphasizing the urgency by using bold-faced type. When he learned that his request was unlikely to be honored, Rocha wrote a scathing e-mail: "Remember the NASA safety poster everywhere around, stating, 'If it's not safe, say so?' Yes, it's that serious." He didn't send the e-mail to the Mission Manager, however, only shared it with fellow engineers.[1] Later, he explained that "engineers were often told not to send messages much higher than their own rung in the ladder."[2]

Discouraged by his early efforts to call attention to the foam-strike issue and convinced that voicing concerns was career limiting at NASA, Rocha refrained from sharing his anxiety in a critical mission management team meeting, eight days into the flight. He fervently hoped others with more clout might offer their concerns. The opportunity passed, however, and the issue was never formally revisited in a mission management team meeting. Just eight days after this lost opportunity to speak up, the shuttle burned up upon reentry into the Earth's atmosphere, resulting in the death of all seven astronauts. Much later, asked in a television interview with ABC News Anchor Charlie Gibson why he didn't voice his doubts about the safety of the shuttle in that mission management team meeting, Rocha replied, "I just couldn't do it. I'm too low down . . . and she [Mission Management Team Leader Linda Ham] is way up here," gesturing with his hand held above his head.[3]

The 2003 *Columbia* space shuttle tragedy reflects an unusually dramatic consequence of not speaking up in the workplace—especially with tentative concerns or unproven ideas—an all-too-common organizational dynamic. Instances where people are reluctant to voice concerns or engage in behaviors that could threaten their image occur within a wide spectrum of industries and organizations. Although it's understandable to keep silent about mistakes when not much is at stake, in many situations errors can be deadly. Consider a nurse momentarily pondering, but then immediately dismissing, the possibility that the medication dosage for a hospital patient seems high. As the thought crosses her mind to call the doctor, by then fast asleep at home, she recalls his disparaging comments the last time she called. In that brief moment of opportunity to voice concern, her brain exaggerates the importance of the doctor's scorn and minimizes the chance of harm to the patient.

Far from the urban hospital, a young pilot in a military training flight notices that the senior pilot may have made a crucial misjudgment, but lets the moment go by without pointing out the error. The young pilot is not only of lower rank, but is also formally evaluated on every flight. The prospect of speaking up to the superior officer brings significant emotional costs, even though the pilots are interdependent members of a cockpit team. Unlike the nurse, the pilot may actually be choosing silence over preservation of his own life. Here again, his mind, against reason, discounts the chances that not speaking up will lead to a fatal crash and exaggerates the importance of his discomfort at being chastised or ignored.

Even those at the top of the hierarchy are not exempt from the fear of speaking up. Consider the following example: a senior executive, recently hired by a successful consumer products company, has grave reservations about a planned takeover. New to the top management team, and conscious of his status as an outsider, he remains silent because other executives seem uniformly enthusiastic. Many months later, when the takeover has failed, the team gathers to review what happened. Aided by a consultant, each executive muses on what he or she might have done to contribute to or avert the failure. The silent executive, now less of an outsider, reveals his prior concerns. Openly apologetic about his past silence, he explains that the others' enthusiasm left him afraid to be "the skunk at the picnic."

What all of these vignettes have in common is the degree to which interpersonal fear can dominate modern work life and thwart the collaboration that is desperately needed in the knowledge-intensive organizations that dominate today's economy. Interpersonal fear—the fear associated with personal interaction and social risks—is at the root of many of these failures. The problem is widespread. In corporations, hospitals, and government agencies, my research has found that interpersonal fear frequently gives rise to poor decisions and incomplete execution. Fortunately, effective leadership and practice with new ways of thinking and working can create an environment of psychological safety that mitigates this problem.

The term *psychological safety* describes a climate in which people feel free to express relevant thoughts and feelings. Although it sounds simple, the ability to seek help and tolerate mistakes while colleagues watch can be unexpectedly difficult. Yet, frank conversations and public missteps must occur if teaming is to realize the promise of collaboration across differences.

This chapter explains the construct of psychological safety and examines methods and behaviors for developing a psychologically safe environment. Drawing from extensive research, I begin by defining psychological safety and exploring its fundamental attributes. I then describe the seven ways that psychological safety contributes to successful teaming and organizational learning, and examine the corrosive effect hierarchy can have on psychological safety. I end the chapter with a detailed explanation of how to cultivate psychological safety, including how a team leader can shape and strengthen the collective learning process both directly and indirectly by fostering an open, safe environment.

Trust and Respect

Simply put, psychological safety makes it possible to give tough feedback and have difficult conversations without the need to tiptoe around the truth. In psychologically safe environments, people believe that if they make a mistake others will not penalize or think less of them for it. They also believe that others will not resent or humiliate them when they ask for help or information. This belief comes about when people both trust and respect each other, and it produces a sense of confidence that the group won't embarrass, reject, or punish someone for speaking up. Thus psychological safety is a taken-for-granted belief about how others will respond when you ask a question, seek feedback, admit a mistake, or propose a possibly wacky idea. Most people feel a need to "manage" interpersonal risk to retain a good image, especially at work, and especially in the presence of those who formally evaluate them. This need is both instrumental (promotions and rewards may depend on impressions held by bosses and others) and socio-emotional (we simply prefer approval over disapproval).

Psychological safety does not imply a cozy situation in which people are necessarily close friends. Nor does it suggest an absence of pressure or problems. Psychological safety does not mean a group has to be cohesive or in agreement about things. As research has shown, group cohesiveness can reduce people's willingness to disagree with or challenge each other. The term *groupthink* refers to this problem. Specifically, in many cohesive groups, people are reluctant to disturb the feeling of harmony created by the group's apparent agreement about an important issue. This leads them to hold back or fail to admit to holding a different view, and thus contributes to poor decision making. Yale professor Irving Janis attributed President Kennedy's ill-fated plan to send Cuban exiles to invade the Bay of Pigs in 1961 to groupthink.[4] In contrast, psychological safety describes a climate in which raising a dissenting view is expected and welcomed. A tolerance of dissent allows productive discussion and early detection of problems.

I have found that many people are genuinely pained and frustrated by keeping silent at work. For the most part, the people I've studied aren't failing to provide ideas or input because they've "checked out" or don't care, but because of a subtle but pervasive fear of what others, particularly those in power, might think of them. As most people intuitively recognize, each of us engages in a tacit "calculus" in which we assess the risk associated with a given interpersonal behavior, quickly and effortlessly, as we face a micro-behavior decision point. To illustrate what I mean by a micro-behavior decision point, imagine that while you are in a conversation with your boss, you consider fleetingly, "Should I say something about this?" In this almost imperceptible thinking process, you weigh the potential gain against the potential loss. You wonder, "If I do this, will I be hurt, embarrassed, or criticized?" If you quickly conclude that the answer is no, then you have a sense of psychological safety, and you proceed to voice your thoughts. (If you believe that the answer might be that you could be hurt but you speak anyway, then you are demonstrating courage.) Typically, proceeding means being authentic. It means expressing the work-relevant thoughts and feelings on your mind without excessive self-censorship.

Consider the fact that admitting a mistake or asking for help may be unthinkable in one work setting and yet readily accepted, even valued, in another setting. The difference between the two situations is what psychological safety is all about.

The easy solution to minimizing image risk at work is to avoid doing or saying anything unless you're absolutely sure you're right. This is obviously a facetious solution. Not only does it limit creativity, stifle innovation, and preclude authentic relationships, it also creates important risks of another kind—risks to performance and safety. This is especially true in dangerous industries such as nuclear power, where admitting errors and asking for help may be critical for avoiding catastrophe.[5] The human tendency to favor silence over voicing concerns is also particularly troubling in organizations where lives are at stake, such as in hospitals. Extensive research on hospitals and other high-risk organizations has shown that rules and required procedures are not enough to eradicate errors that were not caught or corrected due to a lack of psychological safety. This isn't because people deliberately break rules, but rather because of the subtle ways in which we make sense of uncertainty and view each other at work.

Interpersonal Risks in Work Environments

Whether frequently or infrequently, overtly or implicitly, most people in organizations are being evaluated in an ongoing way. The presence of others with more power or status makes the threat associated with being evaluated especially powerful, but it by no means disappears in the presence of peers and subordinates. In Exhibit 4.1, I have identified four specific risks to image that people face at work.

Exhibit 4.1: Image Risks at Work

The four following concerns powerfully shape our willingness to speak up:

- **Being seen as ignorant:** When individuals ask questions or seek information, they run the risk of being seen as ignorant. Most of us can think of a time when we hesitated to ask a question because it seemed that no one else was asking, or perhaps we believed the information was something we were already expected to know.

- **Being seen as incompetent:** When admitting mistakes, asking for help, or accepting the high probability of failure that comes with experimenting, people risk being seen as incompetent. For example, if you admit that something you tried didn't work as expected, it could possibly signal to others that you're not skilled or smart enough to reliably perform your job.

- **Being seen as negative:** To learn and improve, it's essential to critically evaluate current and past activities and performance. The risk of being seen as negative, however, often stops people from providing critical assessments. People often believe that critiquing others' performance will make them appear overly critical or hard to work with. In addition, it is well known that bad news rarely travels well up the hierarchy.

- **Being seen as disruptive:** Fearful of disrupting or imposing upon others' time, people avoid seeking feedback, information, or help.[6] In particular, individuals are often reluctant to seek feedback about their performance, despite the personal gains that can be obtained from feedback. Although this reluctance can be attributed to the possibility of hearing something negative, it also stems from a wish not to be seen as intrusive or lacking in self-sufficiency.

When we speak up about concerns or ask questions at work, we risk being seen as ignorant. Right or wrong, people may expect us to already know the answer or understand the situation. Similarly, most people intuitively believe that speaking up about mistakes or seeking help will lead people to conclude that they're incompetent. And when someone speaks up about problems or errors, he or she also risks being seen as negative. Because most people also believe themselves to be working to the best of their abilities, when others give them negative feedback, it can be seen as inaccurate, and so the messenger can be seen as a troublemaker. Finally, in speaking up about something, we might risk giving an impression of being disruptive. This is particularly true in busy organizations where it's often hard to accomplish the day's tasks within normal business hours, and so interruption can seem more disruptive than helpful.

Good Interruptions

Interestingly, research by University of Minnesota professor Mary Zellmer-Bruhn shows that interruptions benefit learning. A study of 90 teams working in the pharmaceutical and medical products industry found that interruptions increased the transfer of knowledge and the acquisition of new routines.[7] Despite such benefits of speaking up, however, organizational silence is prevalent due to the inherent risks and associated fear of speaking up. In one study, over 85 percent of the managers and staff interviewed admitted to remaining silent about a concern.[8]

A Brief History of Psychological Safety Research

The construct of psychological safety has its roots in early research on organizational change. In 1965, MIT professors Edgar Schein and Warren Bennis (later a professor at the University of Southern

California), discussed the need to create psychological safety to make people feel secure and capable of changing.[9] Schein, in a later paper, argued that psychological safety helps people overcome the defensiveness, or "learning anxiety," that occurs when they are presented with data that contradicts their expectations or hopes.[10] With psychological safety, he reasoned, individuals are free to focus on collective goals and problem prevention rather than on self-protection.

Since that time, several other researchers have explored psychological safety in work settings. In an influential 1990 paper, Boston University professor William Kahn argued that psychological safety enables personal engagement at work.[11] He studied how psychological safety affects individuals' willingness to engage in an organizational setting; that is, to "employ or express themselves physically, cognitively, and emotionally during role performances," rather than disengage, or "withdraw and defend their personal selves."[12] Further, Kahn argued that people would be more likely to believe they would be given the benefit of the doubt—a defining characteristic of psychological safety—when relationships within a given group were characterized by trust and respect.

In 1999, I introduced the term *team psychological safety* as a group-level construct. My research shows that psychological safety typically characterizes a team as a unit rather than being an attribute of individual employees. In a series of studies, across many organizations and several industries, I found that perceptions of psychological safety were similar among people who work closely together, such as several members of the same team or teaming effort. This is because people working together tend to have the same set of contextual influences and their perceptions develop out of important shared experiences.[13] For example, people will conclude that making a mistake doesn't lead to scorn or ridicule when they've had experiences in which appreciation and interest were expressed when discussing mistakes. In addition, my research has found that levels of psychological safety vary from department to department and from work group to work group. This means that psychological safety is not a personality difference, but rather a feature of the workplace that leaders can and must work to build.

Psychological Safety Characterizes Small Groups Within Organizations

In almost any company or organization, even one with a strong culture, psychological safety typically differs across departments. This is true, for example, across floors in a hospital, divisions in a company, or restaurants in a chain. In a given district's public school system, psychological safety may vary dramatically between schools, and even from classroom to classroom within a school. Because it's a local phenomenon, psychological safety is not something that can be changed by mandate or decree from the top. Instead, it's a pervasive aspect of the climate that takes shape as a consequence of two factors—the frames and behaviors of local leaders and the daily behaviors and interactions among peers working together.

Informal relationships play a major role in psychological safety. Chances are that if you feel psychologically safe in a working environment, so do your coworkers. You may be an extrovert working with introverts, or the other way around. Psychological safety is unrelated to gregariousness; it's about the perceived consequences of being yourself and being straightforward, even when the news is not good. On production lines or kitchen queues, how people feel about one another has a great deal to do with how efficiently they perform. Research has documented that people typically prioritize warmth, trustworthiness, and morality over competence. Presumably, this is because, from an evolutionary perspective, another person's intent matters more to our survival than the person's ability. If people perceive an associate as not warm or trustworthy, they will be less likely to ask questions or interact in ways necessary for collaborative teaming and learning, even if the associate is perceived as competent.[14]

Psychological Safety for Teaming and Learning

In psychologically safe environments, people are willing to offer ideas, questions, and concerns. They are even willing to fail, and when they do, they learn. The need for psychological safety is based on the premise that no one can perform perfectly in every situation when knowledge and best practices are in flux. Mutual recognition of this fact in a particular workplace helps build psychological safety. But when uncertainty clouds our thoughts and views, especially views that appear to be at odds with those of others, we often take the path of reduced interpersonal resistance. It happens when much is at stake (a patient's health, an aircraft's safety, a costly takeover) and when not much is at stake (a small improvement idea not communicated to an individual or team who could act on it). In either case, the silence inhibits teaming in organizations that depend upon learning for their ongoing viability and survival.

Therefore, psychological safety is crucial in organizations where knowledge keeps changing or workers need to collaborate. In examining the connection between environmental factors, organizational learning, and team performance, research reveals seven specific benefits provided by psychological safety in the workplace. Exhibit 4.2 lists these benefits.

Speak Up!

The most important reason to care about psychological safety in the workplace is that it encourages speaking up. This includes increasing the chances of learning behaviors, such as seeking help, experimentation, and discussion of error. For the most part, people are unaware of psychological safety as a specific attribute of the work environment: it just feels risky to speak up with what they know or with questions they'd like to ask, or else it doesn't. How and why it either does or doesn't feel risky is not something most people spend a lot of time thinking about, but I have found that

---

Exhibit 4.2: The Benefits of Psychological Safety

- **Encourages speaking up:** Psychological safety alleviates concern about others' reaction to behaviors or actions that have the potential for embarrassment.

- **Enables clarity of thought:** When the brain is activated by fear, it has less neural processing power for exploration, design, or analysis.

- **Supports productive conflict:** Psychological safety allows self-expression, productive discussion, and the thoughtful handling of conflict.

- **Mitigates failure:** A climate of psychological safety makes it easier, and therefore more common, to report and discuss errors.

- **Promotes innovation:** Removing the fear of speaking up allows people to suggest the novel ideas and possibilities that are integral to developing innovative products and services.

- **Removes obstacles to pursuing goals for achieving performance:** With psychological safety, individuals can focus on achieving motivating goals rather than on self-protection.

- **Increases accountability:** Rather than supporting a permissive atmosphere, psychological safety creates a climate that supports people in taking the interpersonal risks necessary to pursue high standards and achieve challenging goals.

---

when probed, most people are easily able to characterize their work environment in these terms. People intuitively understand that their workplace is psychologically safe or unsafe.

Enable Clarity of Thought

Neuroeconomist Gregory Berns, a researcher and professor at Emory University, has performed brain-imaging experiments demonstrating that when the parts of the brain that normally process pain become activated by fear, the brain has less neural processing power for exploratory activity.[15] Low-intensity fear leads to changes in perception, cognition, and behavior that include the narrowing of attention to focus on potential threats.[16] Similarly, high-intensity fear triggers a fight-or-flight reaction in the brain, which reduces effective cognition still further. This means that when fear is neurologically activated, employees are less capable of the kind of analysis, innovation, or communication that is needed for optimal performance. A psychologically safe climate, however, allows the brain to maximize its neural processing power for clarity of thought and creative expression.

Support Productive Conflict

As discussed in Chapter Two, conflict is inevitable when teaming. Psychological safety does not ensure conflict-free teaming. In truth, psychological safety may lead to more conflict and disagreement than would happen in a less safe environment. In a psychologically safe climate, teachers with conflicting beliefs about pedagogical methods will express them; nurses will challenge the use of specific procedures; and members of a project team might express resentment about differing levels of responsibility. Termed "creative abrasion" by Harvard Business School professor Dorothy Leonard-Barton, this type of conflict must be moderated by psychological safety to enable a learning climate of discussion and innovation.[17] Otherwise, such conflict is destructive and characterized by aggression and the possibility of humiliation. Those organizations where self-expression and productive discussion are welcome can be pretty tough places in the sense that people are direct. They say what they think and they're willing to be proven wrong.

Mitigate Failure

Nowhere is the issue of psychological safety more important than when people have to confront failure. I discovered the relationship between psychological safety and failure by accident. When I first began to study teamwork, my goal was to show that better teamwork led to fewer errors. In a study of how teaming may help administer medications accurately, I anticipated finding a positive relationship between teamwork and the measured rates of errors.

Instead, when the statistical analyses were run, the data strongly suggested that well-led teams with good relationships were making more mistakes, not fewer.[18] This presented a puzzle: Did better-led teams really make more mistakes? Eventually, after more research, I was able to show instead that in well-led teams, a climate of psychological safety makes it easier, and therefore more common, to report and discuss errors, compared with teams with punitive leaders.

Promote Innovation

Research has also found that psychological safety is critical to innovation. Removing the fear of speaking up allows people to suggest novel or unorthodox ideas, which are integral to developing innovative products and services. Social psychologists Michael West and Neil Anderson studied top management teams in British hospitals and found that organizational support for speaking up enabled participation, which led to proposing more innovations.[19] In a similar vein, experimental social psychologists Leslie Janes and James Olson showed that people exposed to others being ridiculed (even by simply watching a video of the ridicule in progress) became more afraid of failure, as well as less creative and more likely to conform, compared with people exposed to humor that did not involve the ridicule of others.[20] Similarly, in the study of cardiac surgery teams discussed in Chapter Three, teams with greater psychological safety were better able to engage in innovation. This was a critical factor in the successful implementation of new technology in their hospitals.[21]

Remove Obstacles to Pursuing Goals for Achieving Performance

Extensive research in social psychology documents the benefits of clear, challenging goals in motivating effort and achievement in groups and teams. However, interpersonal fear can get in the way—blocking the motivating effects of a compelling goal on performance achievement. Why? Because people who are worried about others' impressions may be reluctant to engage in the kinds of behaviors necessary to cooperate and accomplish shared goals. Such behaviors are unscripted; they require improvisation. Successful improvisation requires accepting the possibility of being wrong or foolish or simply unhelpful. Further, when people working in a group don't trust each other, and when psychological safety is low, they tend to focus more on achieving their own goals rather than cooperative goals. In contrast, psychological safety, which is characterized by mutual trust and respect, promotes cooperative behavior and increases the sharing and use of each other's expertise. Even with a strong desire to design a better production process or implement a new technology, unless people experience some degree of psychological safety, the risks of engaging wholeheartedly in the necessary collaboration and inquiry to accomplish these types of goals are simply too great, and goal achievement is hampered.

Increase Accountability

Some might argue that fostering psychological safety in the workplace would make it difficult to hold people accountable. Certainly, if employees feel too friendly or close to one another, slipping into behaviors more appropriate for the break room than the conference room, performance might slip. But developing psychological safety doesn't mean creating a permissive, lax, or undisciplined organizational atmosphere. It means creating a climate that allows people to feel safe while taking the risks necessary to improve and innovate. Psychological safety is one component of a group's interpersonal climate, whereas accountability is another. Accountability defines the degree to which people are expected to adhere to high standards and pursue challenging goals. Psychological safety and accountability are not two ends of a continuum, but rather two distinct attributes of a work environment. To help clarify this relationship, Figure 4.1 depicts four organizational archetypes. Few

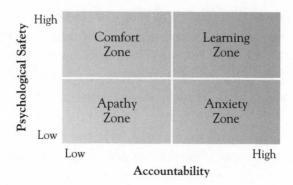

Figure 4.1. Psychological Safety and Accountability

Source: Edmondson, A. C. "The Competitive Imperative of Learning," HBS Centennial Issue. Harvard Business Review 86, nos. 7/8 (2008): 60–67. Reprinted with permission of Harvard Business Review.

workplaces are pure forms, but considering the nature of these four archetypes helps build intuition about the connection between psychological safety and high accountability.

In work groups low in both psychological safety and accountability (lower left), employees tend to be apathetic about their work. Discretionary effort might be spent jockeying for position rather than accomplishing shared goals. Organizations most vulnerable to having people fall into this quadrant are large, top-heavy bureaucracies where people can and do figure out how to perform their jobs with a minimum of effort. In workplaces characterized by high psychological safety but low accountability (upper left), people enjoy working with one another, are genuinely convivial, but rarely feel challenged. Thus, they seldom work very hard. Some, though certainly not all, family businesses and government agencies fall into this quadrant. When employees are comfortable being themselves but don't see a compelling reason to seek additional challenge, it is difficult to foster learning and innovation. This is sometimes called the *comfort zone*.

Next, organizations with high performance standards but low psychological safety (lower right) are far too common in today's fast-paced work environment. They are breeding grounds for anxiety. Managers in these organizations have unfortunately confused setting high standards with good management. High standards in a setting characterized by uncertainty and inter-dependence, combined with a lack of psychological safety, is a recipe for suboptimal performance. Following the mistaken, though often well-intentioned, belief that intense performance pressure is the best way to ensure excellent results, managers inadvertently create an environment in which employees are afraid to offer ideas, try new processes, or ask for help. This can work—as long as the work is both clear-cut and individualistic. When there's uncertainty or a need for collaboration, the result is more anxiety than success.

Finally, when both accountability and psychological safety are high (upper right in Figure 4.1), people can easily collaborate, learn from each other, and get the job done. Some of the most successful organizations today have worked hard to build work environments characterized by both high accountability and high psychological safety. To do so, however, these organizations have figured out how to manage the tension between hierarchy and psychological safety.

The Effect of Hierarchy on Psychological Safety

As discussed in Chapter Two, we are both hard-wired and social-ized to be acutely sensitive to power and hierarchy. This means most people are well aware of where they fall in the power hierar-chies at work. In addition, their position shapes their perceptions of how safe it is to take interpersonal risks within their team or group. Unfortunately, research shows that those with lower status in a group or department generally feel less psychologically safe than those with higher status. This makes them less likely to check with others when they are unsure about something, more fearful that mistakes will be held against them, less able to bring up tough problems, and less certain that others value their skills.[22] This might not be a problem if people on the front lines of the organization are ignorant or lack ideas or, conversely, if they always know exactly the right thing to do or say. But in most organizations, that is simply not the case. Those lower in the hierarchy frequently encounter opportunities to ask questions or to offer ideas. Leaders must ensure that they are able to do both. Though leaders often preach empowerment, they may be unaware of the fear created by differences in rank or status and, therefore, may not do enough to ensure that a message of empowerment is delivered in a psychologically safe environment.

Hierarchy and Fear

The role of fear in hierarchy is ages old. Fear has long been used as a tool for maintaining control. If people lower in the hierarchy are afraid of those who have power, it stands to reason that they will do what they are supposed to do. But fear as a motivator has profound limits, especially for knowledge work, as this chapter explores.

The problem is that hierarchically embedded fear is not so easy to shrug off or replace with psychological safety just because it is a good idea. You might say we're all working against thousands of years of genetic training and social development. In nature, the alpha dominates, and the subordinates who occupy lower hierarchical rungs learn that self-protection equals survival. Similarly, humans' biological response in a situation deemed dangerous—the rapid heartbeat, rushing adrenaline, racing brain, and desire to flee—is experienced as necessary to ensure basic existence, even though its utility is long expired in the modern workplace. Contemporary mind-body medical practitioners such as Harold Benson, whose research includes helping people relieve physiological stress, find that when we hear a fire engine's clanging bell, for example, our bodies respond as if we are experiencing a charging lion.[23] Other research suggests that fear, on an individual or organizational level, impedes collective learning. Fear in those with subordinate roles leads to a tendency to conceal one's tentative thoughts. Not surprisingly, this desire to figuratively fade into the background hinders the process of teaming. Consider some common euphemisms for speaking up: "sticking one's neck out" and "rocking the boat." Small wonder that our overriding tendency is not to speak up.

When Hierarchy Inhibits Voice

Let's briefly reconsider the space shuttle tragedy presented at the beginning of the chapter. Why did an engineer, whose job was to use his expertise to team with others with different expertise, feel unsafe speaking up about his concerns? Part of the explanation comes from the hierarchical culture of NASA. Another reason lies in the way the team's leader handled meetings. In Mission Management Team (MMT) meetings, team leader Linda Ham often authoritatively stated her opinion early in the meeting, including the specific belief that the mission was not in danger from possible foam strikes. This raised the bar for speaking up.

When people in power speak authoritatively and speak first, it often results in greater self-censorship by others, even if this was not the original intention. Likewise, without meaning to, managers often reduce willingness to engage in meaningful dissent by seeking endorsement, rather than an honest questioning, of their views. Ham did precisely this when she requested the opinion of Calvin Schomburg, a very senior and very respected engineer, at several critical points in an MMT meeting to bolster her belief that foam strikes did not present a problem. When asked, Schomburg, a thirty-eight-year NASA veteran, expressed strong doubts that foam strikes presented a risk to the mission. Tragically, Ham did not consider that Schomburg's specific expertise was in other aspects of the shuttle's surface hardware. Schomburg's statements made it that much more difficult for other, more informed engineers to speak up and contradict the prevailing opinion.

Low Psychological Safety

If asked whether they prefer to work in a psychologically safe place or not, it's safe to guess that most individuals would respond in the affirmative. Who wouldn't want to work in places where the interpersonal risks are low, learning behaviors are appreciated, and individual and collective performance are high? Yet, one study found a median rating of workplace psychological safety of 76 out of 100 across a variety of industries in numerous countries.[24] This suggests that a significant percentage of the global workforce is employed in organizations where psychological safety is lower than is optimal for teamwork and organizational learning.

While acknowledging the lack of psychological safety in NASA's shuttle program, some have argued that individual dissenters were at fault for lacking the courage to speak up. Former astronaut Jim Bagian put it this way: "Should have, would have, could have doesn't matter. You were asked that day and you buckled. You buckled, you own it. Don't make other people own it. Nobody put a gun to your head."[25] But Sheila Widnall, former U.S. Secretary of the Air Force, suggested instead that leaders need to own the inquiry, rather than waiting for others to come forward with dissent. The job of leaders is to draw others out. As she explained:

> I always say to engineers "Don't just give me a list of everything you're worried about. Express your concerns in actionable form. Try to be as precise as possible about your concern and try to be quantitative about it. . . . Tell me what you want me to do about it. What data do you want, what test do you want, what analysis do you want?" In this case [the *Columbia* mission], the engineers *did* express their concerns in actionable form.

They said they wanted pictures. That's an action. It was based on a sound judgment about the potential for risk, about something that had actually happened that had been observed. It satisfies my criteria for the proper behavior of engineers dealing with very complex systems.[26]

In psychologically safe environments, engaging in meaningful dialogue requires neither profound courage nor extraordinary encouragement. I argue that leaders, especially those leading complex operations, have a responsibility to work hard to create a climate where voice is welcomed. There are many challenges to overcome in creating this type of environment. Psychological safety is a set of intangible, interpersonal beliefs that cannot be changed with a simple managerial lever. There are actions that leaders can take to build psychological safety, as discussed in the following section, but the fact is that a new, more open environment cannot simply be authorized or mandated. This helps explain the gap between leaders' espoused beliefs and the reality of their workplaces. Intellectually, leaders may endorse psychological safety or the voice and participation it enables, but it's not always easy to forgo the raised voices or angry expressions that signify dominance in a hierarchical system. And for others, it's not easy to stop, stand one's ground, and speak up. Instead, it's easier and more natural to flee into the safety of silence.

Cultivating Psychological Safety

How do leaders raise the level of psychological safety in an organization? This is the question that Arthur Ryan, CEO of Prudential, asked himself after taking the hundred-year-old insurance and investment company public. Ryan looked around at the increasingly complex and competitive financial services industry and concluded that the Prudential culture—dubbed "Pru-polite" by employees for its cautious feel—would have to change to succeed. In particular, Ryan believed that operating successfully as a public company would require direct, honest communication among employees. This meant creating a psychologically safe environment that enabled them to openly debate issues and analyze customer needs.

In an effort to increase levels of psychological safety, Ryan asked a team from the human resources department to create a program focused on encouraging employees to speak up and share their thoughts. Calling the program the "Safe-to-Say" initiative, the team worked energetically to design and implement a series of integrated training programs and recurring staff meetings that would make the work climate more psychologically safe. Many at Prudential, including senior managers and front-line representatives, spoke positively of the efforts, but substantial change in the culture was slow. An internal survey revealed remarkably stable scores on items relevant to the ability to speak up. The primary lesson here: you cannot metaphorically snap your fingers with short-term initiatives, no matter how well intentioned, and expect psychologically safety to suddenly exist.

Studying this effort, I observed that many employees applauded the goal but did not understand exactly how the value of openness, as manifested in the "Safe-to-Say" initiative, related directly to improved performance. I concluded that focusing directly and explicitly on producing psychological safety was the wrong way to produce the change that was needed. What if Ryan had instead invited managers throughout the organization to help employees see how the tasks in financial services were changing? For example, they might have emphasized the growing importance of sharing expertise, inquiry, early detection of developing threats in financial markets, or the role of relationship management in increasing customer satisfaction and producing financial returns. With this approach, the emphasis is on the work, how it's changing, and what's needed to do it well, rather than on psychological safety.

The change team at Prudential was perhaps overly constrained by its focus on creating safety for speaking up. Ryan's mandate or the team's myopia (a focus on its own area of expertise) limited their ability to focus on the needs of the evolving business environment. Instead, they presented the need for culture change as an end in itself. This mistake likely hindered the process for altering Prudential's work environment. It also highlights the powerful effect leaders have on psychological safety.

The Role of Leaders in Creating Psychological Safety

Leaders—at all levels, but particularly those in the middle of an organization—play crucial roles in creating a psychologically safe organization. The impact of leaders on organizational culture is well established by research.[27] Studies have shown that leaders' responses to events influence other members' perceptions of appropriate and safe behavior.[28] It's clear that signals sent by people in power are critical to shaping others' ability and willingness to offer their ideas and observations. When a leader of a team is supportive, coaching oriented, and nondefensive in response to questions and challenges, team members are likely to feel that the team constitutes a safe environment. In contrast, team leaders who act authoritarian or punitive reduce others' psychological safety and, as a consequence, hinder their ability to contribute everything they can to the collective effort.

The most important influence on psychological safety is the nearest manager, supervisor, or boss. These authority figures, in subtle and not so subtle ways, shape the tone of interactions in a team or group. Therefore, they also must be engaged as the primary drivers in establishing a more open work environment. They must take practical steps to make the workplace psychologically safe. That is the key phrase: take practical steps. Psychological safety is a shared sense developed through shared experience. Leaders at all levels and in all types of organizations may make statements like, "I want you to come to me with issues" or "I have an open-door policy." But in the majority of cases, this type of vague stance fails to initiate significant change. As the Prudential example demonstrates, a psychologically safe environment can't be created with directives, guidelines, and slogans. To institute practices and conditions where psychological safety can thrive, leaders must act.

Leadership Actions to Cultivate Psychological Safety

Research clearly indicates that leaders can create more effective teaming and learning environments by acting in ways that promote psychological safety. Research also reveals a number of behaviors and actions that stimulate speaking up and encourage interpersonal risk. Leaders must communicate that they respect employees, in particular by acknowledging the expertise and skills the employees bring. They need to actively encourage speaking up and reporting mistakes. By inviting others in this way, leaders trigger and support an environment of psychological safety. In contrast, leaders' autocratic behavior, inaccessibility, or failure to acknowledge their own vulnerability all can contribute to team members' reluctance to share ideas or examine mistakes.[29] Exhibit 4.3 presents a number of simple, if not always intuitive, behaviors and actions that make an enormous difference in leading an effort to establish an environment that values asking questions and offering input.

Be Accessible and Approachable

Leaders encourage team members to learn together by being accessible and personally involved. In one of the cardiac surgery teams presented in Chapter Three, an operating room nurse made this association by describing the surgeon leading her team as "very accessible. He's in his office, always just two seconds away. He can always take five minutes to explain something, and he never makes you feel stupid." In striking contrast, the surgeon in one of the less successful teams requested that nonphysician team members go through his residents (junior physicians who are still in training)

Exhibit 4.3: Leadership Behaviors for Cultivating Psychological Safety

To develop a high-performance, psychologically safe environment for teaming and learning, do the following:

- **Be accessible and approachable:** Leaders encourage team members to learn together by being accessible and personally involved.

- **Acknowledge the limits of current knowledge:** When leaders admit that they don't know something, their genuine display of humility encourages other team members to follow suit.

- **Be willing to display fallibility:** To create psychological safety, team leaders must demonstrate a tolerance of failure by acknowledging their own fallibility.

- **Invite participation:** When people believe their leaders value their input, they're more engaged and responsive.

- **Highlight failures as learning opportunities:** Instead of punishing people for well-intentioned risks that backfire, leaders encourage team members to embrace error and deal with failure in a productive manner.

- **Use direct language:** Using direct, actionable language instigates the type of straightforward, blunt discussion that enables learning.

- **Set boundaries:** When leaders are as clear as possible about what is acceptable, people feel more psychologically safe than when boundaries are vague or unpredictable.

- **Hold people accountable for transgressions:** When people cross boundaries set in advance and fail to perform up to set standards, leaders must hold them accountable in a fair and consistent way.

if they had something to say, rather than speak to him directly. Through their behaviors, these two surgeons conveyed very different messages to their teams: the first surgeon increased the likelihood that people would speak up openly both in and outside of the operating room when they had concerns and questions, whereas the second surgeon obviously made the process of communication more difficult.

Acknowledge the Limits of Current Knowledge

Explicitly acknowledge the lack of answers to the tough problems your group or team faces. Strange as it may seem, many leaders are unwilling to publicly express the fact that they don't have the answers to every issue or challenge. It's not that they don't recognize the imperfect state of knowledge; they just fail to mention it. Acknowledging uncertainty may seem like a weakness, but in fact it's usually an intelligent and accurate diagnosis of a murky situation. Moreover, it creates an implied invitation to offer information or expertise.

Display Fallibility

To create psychological safety, team leaders must demonstrate a tolerance of failure by acknowledging their own fallibility. Self-disclosure by team leaders is an effective way to reveal one's limitations.[30] For instance, one cardiac surgeon team leader in the previously mentioned study repeatedly told his team: "I need to hear from you because I'm likely to miss things." The repetition of the phrase was as important as its meaning. People tend not to hear or believe a message that contradicts old norms or stances when they hear it only once. Acknowledging one's fallibility and the need for feedback suggests to others that their opinion is respected and contributes to establishing a norm of active participation. Moreover, when managers and supervisors admit that they don't know something or made a mistake, their genuine display of humility encourages others to do the same.

Invite Participation

A logical extension of acknowledging limits and modeling fallibility is inviting others to offer observations and ideas. This means explicitly requesting input from other people on a team or in the organization more broadly. Team and organizational-level learning both depend on gaining access to a valuable, untapped body of individually held knowledge.[31] Leaders must seek out this individual, internal knowledge, especially from lower-status team members who might otherwise be reluctant to speak. Team leaders can play a role in drawing out members' thoughts by setting up reflective sessions where job and time pressures are temporarily removed. In these types of sessions, ask questions. But be sure to ask real questions, not leading or rhetorical ones. When people believe leaders and managers want to hear from them and value their input, they're more responsive.

Signs That a Workplace Is Psychologically Safe

A leader or manager knows that psychological safety is present when:

- People on a team say such things as:
  - "We all respect each other."
  - "When something bugs me, we're able to confront each other."
  - "Everyone in our group takes responsibility for what we do."
  - "I don't have to wear a mask at work. I can be myself."
- People talk about mistakes and problems, not just successes.
- The workplace appears to be conducive to humor and laughter.

Highlight Failures as Learning Opportunities

By avoiding punishing others for having taken well-intentioned risks that backfired, leaders inspire people to embrace error and failure and deal with them in a productive manner. Chapter Five explores the topic of failure in more detail, but vivid examples of purposefully refraining from penalizing failure exist throughout management literature. Apocryphal stories prevalent in many organizations capture the ways in which senior management can powerfully influence views of psychological safety in the organization as a whole. One such story involves Tom Watson Jr. at IBM and a field executive responsible for a ten-million-dollar mistake. Called into the chairman's office, the executive was understandably anxious. As retold by Paul Carroll, "Watson asked, 'Do you know why I've asked you here?' The man replied, 'I assume I'm here so you can fire me.' Watson looked surprised. 'Fire you?' he asked. 'Of course not. I just spent $10 million educating you.' He then reassured the executive and suggested he keep taking chances."[32]

Truth or myth, such stories have lasting effects in an organization. The sent message is that failure is inevitable and the point is to learn, to share the learning, and to try again. As espoused by Watson, "You really aren't committed to innovation unless you're willing to fail. . . . The fastest way to succeed is to double your failure rate."[33] One of the best-known examples is the story of 3M's wildly successful Post-it product. As nearly everyone has heard by now, the adhesive used in Post-it notes came from a botched attempt to create a super-strong adhesive. Similarly, a well-known public relations firm has a ritual of opening monthly meetings by recognizing the "Mistake of the Month." This is a lighthearted way to both build a sense of community and acknowledge the value of learning from mistakes.[34]

Use Direct Language

In knowledge work, people can't afford to avoid critiques due to a fear of sounding negative, criticizing the boss, or making the company appear fallible. Strategy teams, new product development, and other project teams often face crucial decisions that require evaluating the current situation and suggesting difficult changes. A major challenge in these discussions is to be objective and blunt. Often, however, the language is anything but direct.

For example, the top management team of a manufacturing company that I studied engaged in a series of meetings to develop a new strategy. In these conversations, I observed a persistent pattern of using metaphors, rather than direct language, to describe the company's strategic options. As one executive commented during one meeting:

> Listening to Bob talk about the ship, I'd like to explore the difference between the metaphor of the ship and how the rudder gets turned and when, in contrast to a flotilla, where there's lots of little rudders and we're trying to orchestrate the flotilla. I think this contrast is important. At one level, we talk about this ship and all the complexities of trying to determine not only its direction but also how to operationalize the ship in total to get to a certain place, versus allowing a certain degree of freedom that the flotilla analogy evokes.

Although metaphors can provoke new ideas and elicit creativity, they can sometimes obscure the real issues and preclude direct or contentious discussion. In this team, members rarely asked for clarification of each other's words or tried to identify areas of disagreement. Instead, the team continued to discuss the company and its situation abstractly, avoiding disagreement and postponing resolution. By the end of six months of regular meetings, little progress had been made; the team's abstract ruminations had failed to translate into any sort of action.[35]

Set Boundaries

Paradoxically, when leaders are as clear as possible about what constitutes blameworthy acts, people feel more psychologically safe than when boundaries of acceptable action are subject to guesswork. This means leaders must establish and clarify boundaries at the outset of a teaming or learning effort. In a financial institution, this may mean never exceeding a particular investment limit without approval. In a hospital setting, it may mean never failing to ask for help when there is any doubt about a patient's condition or medication. For the RAZR team at Motorola, it meant never violating the code of secrecy about the project, until the product was publicly unveiled. Establishing this clear restriction helped promote a sense of freedom and expression within the delineated boundaries, including the willingness to ignore the recommendations of human factors experts about the phone's width. Regardless of the situation, by setting clear boundaries for action and behavior within the team, leaders contribute to building an environment of psychological safety.

Hold People Accountable

It's the job of leaders to help people understand that unacceptable behaviors do occur and must be equitably addressed. When leaders take the difficult step of punishing or even firing someone, they must clearly explain what happened and why, while observing rules for confidentiality as appropriate. Providing the justification behind such difficult actions helps protect other people against fear that the actions were arbitrary and could happen to them, without warning. In most cases, people understand both the rationale and the need for sanctions to preserve the team or organization's integrity, so that it can effectively fulfill its purpose. Although it is more about avoiding the destruction of psychological safety than about creating it in the first place, holding people accountable builds fairness and responsibility, which removes the fear of leader arbitrariness. This is why psychological safety and accountability are both essential to a "just culture," an increasingly central concept in health care and other high-risk operations. The idea of a just culture was developed to acknowledge that "competent professionals make mistakes and . . . even develop unhealthy norms (shortcuts, 'routine rule violations')" while maintaining "zero tolerance for reckless behavior."[36] In short, psychological safety is not created through lax standards or permissiveness, but rather through sober recognition that any workplace presents both challenges and constraints that must be discussed openly if progress is to be made.

Setting boundaries and holding people accountable are critical for a leader hoping to cultivate an environment of psychological safety. It may seem counterintuitive, but think of these two actions as being like guardrails on a bridge. If the guardrails are missing, you're likely to drive as close to the center line as possible. It's obviously frightening to drive near the bridge's edge without rails in place. When teaming and learning, the equivalent is sticking to safe, tractable behaviors that shield you from possible punishment, while avoiding behaviors with interpersonal risk, like admitting mistakes, that may be interpreted as "outside the lines." But when the guardrails are in place, there's less risk in venturing to the outside lanes and gaining a broader, more informed perspective. With clear boundaries and the structures that enforce them, you're more likely to test the limits of current processes and knowledge. In doing so, team members and teams greatly increase their ability to collaborate, learn, and innovate.

Leadership Summary

Psychological safety is a social construct that describes a work climate characterized by interpersonal trust and mutual respect. Beliefs about how others will respond if you say something potentially threatening, such as pointing out someone else's error, or embarrassing, such as reporting your own error, determine how psychologically safe you feel. Psychological safety allows self-expression, productive discussion, and, when needed, thoughtful handling of conflict. Because coordinating and integrating complex tasks requires people to share thoughts openly and act without excessive concern about what others think, teaming flourishes with psychological safety and diminishes without it.

Research has shown, however, that most people feel the need to manage their image in front of others, especially at work, unless efforts have been made to counteract this natural tendency by establishing a learning environment. All of us are likely to hold back in the workplace, failing to share ideas, questions, and concerns. In many companies, organizational hierarchy and the fear it creates have a powerful influence on teaming and learning behaviors. Because of this fear, people are often reluctant to engage in behaviors that could threaten their image. In many cases, speaking up the hierarchical ladder can feel nearly impossible to those on a lower rung. In some situations, this may not be harmful. But when teaming is needed and learning expected—when people with diverse ideas and important expertise have to integrate what they know and do—a lack of psychological safety can be crippling.

Fortunately, research also indicates that skilled team leaders can reward excellence, sanction poor performance, and still embrace the inevitable errors that accompany teaming and learning. In other words, it's possible to have both high psychological safety and high accountability. To do so, leaders must communicate clear expectations about performance and accountability without communicating a resistance to hearing bad news.

Psychological safety means no one will be punished or humiliated for errors or questions in the service of reaching ambitious performance goals. The following lessons and actions provide team leaders with a framework for cultivating a climate of psychological safety and creating an environment conducive to learning from failure.

LESSONS AND ACTIONS

- Psychological safety describes individuals' perceptions regarding the consequences of interpersonal risks in their work environment.

- Four specific image risks that people face at work are being seen as ignorant, incompetent, negative, or disruptive.

- In psychologically safe environments, characterized by both trust and respect, people believe that if they make a mistake or ask for help, others will not penalize them.

- Because psychological safety encourages self-expression and productive discussion, it's essential to teaming and organizational learning.

- Psychological safety is not about being nice or about lowering performance standards. Instead, psychological safety allows groups to set high goals and work toward them through collaboration and collective learning.

- Research reveals seven specific benefits provided by psychological safety: it encourages speaking up, enables clarity of thought, supports productive conflict, mitigates failure, promotes innovation, moderates the relationship between goals and performance, and increases employee accountability.

- Hierarchy and the fear it creates negatively affect psychological safety. Research shows that lower-status team members generally feel less safe than higher-status members.

- Leaders play crucial roles in promoting a psychologically safe organization. But psychological safety cannot be simply authorized or mandated. Instead, it requires specific leadership actions.

- In attempting to establish an environment of psychological safety, the emphasis should be on the group's tasks, how they're changing, and what's needed to do them well. This makes the need for psychological safety a conclusion that people can discover for themselves.

- To cultivate a psychologically safe environment, leaders should be accessible and approachable, acknowledge the limits of current knowledge, be willing to display fallibility, invite participation, refrain from penalizing failure, use direct language, set boundaries, and hold people accountable.

chapter five

failing better to succeed faster

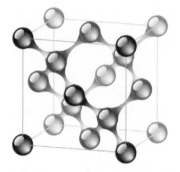

Teaming rarely unfolds perfectly, without any bumps, glitches, or failures. This means that the ability to learn from failure is an essential teaming skill. And although most leaders say they understand the importance of failure to the learning process, not many truly embrace it. In my research, I've found that even companies that have invested significant money and effort into becoming learning organizations struggle when it comes to the day-to-day mindset and activities of learning from failure. Managers in these companies were highly motivated to help their organizations learn in order to avoid recurring failures and mistakes. In some cases, they and their teams had devoted many hours to after-action reviews and post-mortems. Even these types of painstaking efforts fall short, however, if managers or leaders think about failure the wrong way.

Most executives I've talked to believe that failure is bad. They also believe that if failure does occur, learning from it is pretty straightforward: simply ask people to reflect on what they did wrong and instruct them to avoid similar actions in the future. Or, better yet, assign a team to review what happened and develop a report to distribute. Unfortunately, these widely held beliefs are misguided. Here's the simple truth about failure: it is sometimes bad, sometimes good, and often inevitable. Good, bad, inevitable—learning from organizational failures is anything but straightforward.

To learn from mistakes and missteps, organizations must employ new and better ways to go beyond lessons that are superficial (procedures weren't followed) or self-serving (the market just wasn't ready for our great new product). This requires jettisoning old cultural beliefs and stereotypical notions of success and replacing them with a new paradigm that recognizes that some failures are inevitable in today's complex work organizations and that successful organizations will be those that catch, correct, and learn from failures quickly. This chapter examines the inevitability of failure while teaming and highlights the importance of learning from small, seemingly insignificant failures. It then explains the cognitive and social barriers to learning from failure and demonstrates how failures vary across the Process Knowledge Spectrum. Finally, the chapter closes by providing practical strategies for developing a learning approach to failure.

The Inevitability of Failure

Workplace failure is never fun. From the small disappointment (a suggestion falls flat in a meeting) to the large blunder (a design for a new product is rejected by a focus group after months of work), failure is emotionally unpleasant and can erode confidence.[1] Even when engaged in a process explicitly designed to be trial-and-error, most of us would still prefer not to fail. But failure is a fact of life.

There is no such thing as perfection, especially in teaming. When bringing together people with different perspectives and skills to collaborate, failure is inevitable for two primary reasons. First, there are the technical challenges. New equipment, technological advances, and process changes all contain unexpected features and require new knowledge and skills. That's why individuals or groups faced with new or complex problems or procedures rarely get things right the first time.

The second reason that failures occur while teaming are the interpersonal challenges that people face. These challenges are less tangible than the technical puzzles, but are often far more difficult to understand and resolve.[2] One person may fail to report crucial information, provoking resentment from others in the group. Another person may struggle with learning how to implement a new technology. A team of people who are unfamiliar with one another's strengths and weaknesses may encounter flaws in how they interact. These flaws include assigning detail-oriented tasks to a person whose strength is working with the "big picture," or scheduling a shift with two people who are inexperienced with a new procedure rather than pairing a less experienced team member with a more experienced mentor. These challenges are compounded by a tendency shared by many high achievers to think of colleagues as an audience—that is, as people who expect a great performance—rather than thinking of them as colearners and coworkers. Add up these interpersonal variables, and any new teaming effort will experience failures on a social level that might not arise in the same way in a bounded, long-term team. Of course, this doesn't mean failures should be avoided. It means they need to be as small as possible and they must produce as much learning as possible.

The Importance of Small Failures

Large, well-publicized organizational failures make people sit up and take notice. But many of these "headline failures," such as the

Columbia and *Challenger* shuttle tragedies, the massive BP oil leak in the Gulf, and the U.S. Security and Exchange Commission's failure to heed warnings about Bernard Madoff's investment practices, represent disasters that were allowed to develop because small failures were ignored. Likewise, terrorist attacks can almost always be traced back to pieces of intelligence that have either been ignored or not communicated to appropriate agencies. Even less far reaching but still dramatic failures, such as the fatal drug error that killed a *Boston Globe* correspondent at Boston's Dana Farber Hospital, occur after mistakes were missed, problems ignored, and warnings dismissed.[3] Most large failures have multiple causes, and some of these causes are deeply embedded in organizations. These are rarely simple to correct. But the fact is, small failures are early warning signs that are vital to avoiding catastrophic failure in the future.[4]

What Failure Means

The word *failure* encompasses a broad spectrum of phenomena. Similarly, failures in organizations can take vastly different forms. Any conversation about how to better avoid and learn from failure must include a definition of the term. Simply put, a failure is a deviation from a desired outcome. This includes both avoidable mishaps and unavoidable outcomes of experiments or other risky actions. To build intuition about the social psychology of failure management, it's important to understand two facts about the term. To begin with, the word failure carries both psychological weight and organizational stigma, so it should be used carefully. Second, the word failure is terribly imprecise, covering events that range from small problems to major accidents.

An intelligent process of organizational learning from failure, whether in the hospital operating room or the executive boardroom, requires proactively identifying and learning from small failures. Small failures are often overlooked. Why? Because when they occur they appear to be minor mistakes or isolated anomalies hardly worth the time to contemplate. Small failures arise not only in the course of purposeful experimentation, but also when daily work is complex and interdependent. When problems inevitably arise during the course of business in these situations, workers have two choices: they can compensate for problems, which would likely make the small failure go unnoticed. But compensating for problems can be counterproductive if doing so isolates information and obscures the opportunity to learn. The other choice is they can seek to resolve the underlying cause of the small failure by notifying those who can help correct the problem. This, however, would expose poor performance. Due to a natural desire to protect their image or status, very few people would voluntarily choose to publicize their own mistakes. But to capture the value of small failures, individuals and groups must learn to acknowledge their performance gaps.

Although seemingly insignificant, small failures can offer opportunities for substantial organizational learning. Take radiologists' mammogram readings. When Dr. Kim Adcock became chief of radiology at Kaiser Permanente in Colorado, there was an expected 10–15 percent error rate due to inherent difficulties in reading mammograms. Standard practice dictated that a failure to detect one, or even several tumors, did not reflect negatively on a radiologist's ability. These missed tumors were considered small failures, and were therefore easily ignored. Adcock, however, sought a way to learn from these small failures. By analyzing the large data sets that accumulate after multiple mammogram readings, he found meaningful patterns and produced detailed feedback, including bar charts and graphs, for each individual radiologist that helped to proactively identify and avoid failure.[5] For the first time, the doctors could learn whether they were falling near or outside of the acceptable range of errors, allowing them to improve their accuracy rates.

Organizations that make timely use of the seemingly small, but important, learning opportunities contained in failure are more able to improve, innovate, and prevent catastrophes than those who ignore or hide failures. If small failures are not widely identified, discussed, and analyzed, it's very difficult for larger failures to be prevented.[6] But knowing this fact doesn't make it any easier to embrace and learn from failure. Regardless of intention or incentives, it's still difficult to overcome the psychological, cognitive, and social barriers to admitting and analyzing failure.

Why It's Difficult to Learn from Failure

Most of us have been primed to aim for success. We've been schooled from an early age to focus on good grades, regular promotions, performance awards. As a result, most of us see failure as unacceptable.[7] We would just as soon avoid it altogether, even if we know that failure is inevitable and creates important learning opportunities. It's hard to be the nurse who administers the wrong medication or the marketing executive who squanders a window of opportunity to launch a new product. And so, people at work often remain silent about the potentially informative mistakes, problems, or disappointments they've experienced, which means that companies miss the learning that could be gained from failures. This barrier to learning from failure is rooted in the strong psychological and social reactions that most people have to failing.[8] Self-serving biases that bolster self-confidence and protect one's public image make these barriers even stronger. And natural biases and their corresponding emotions are exacerbated by most organizations' inclination to punish failure, as well as by the strong connection between the concepts of failure and fault.

Self-Esteem and Positive Illusions

Being held in high regard by other people, especially by one's managers and peers at work, is a strong fundamental human desire.[9]

Most people believe that revealing failure will jeopardize this esteem. Even though people may intellectually appreciate the idea of learning from failure and are sympathetic to others' disclosures of failure, they have a natural aversion to disclosing or even publicly acknowledging their own failures. People have an instinctive tendency to deny, distort, or ignore their own failures. The fundamental human desire to maintain high self-esteem is accompanied by a desire to believe that we have a reasonable amount of control over important personal and teaming outcomes. Psychologists argue that these desires give rise to "positive illusions," which are unrealistically positive views of the self, accompanied by illusions of control that contribute to helping people be energetic and happy. Some even argue that positive illusions are a hallmark of mental health.[10] However, the same positive illusions that boost our self-esteem and sense of control are at odds with an honest acknowledgment of failure.

The challenge isn't just emotional. Human cognition introduces perceptual biases that reduce the accuracy of our causal attributions. Even without meaning to, all of us favor evidence that supports our existing beliefs rather than alternative explanations. Similarly, the psychological trap known as the fundamental attribution error—the tendency to ascribe personal rather than situational explanations for others' shortcomings (discussed in Chapter Two) makes us less aware of our own responsibility for failures and very willing to blame others for the failures we observe. People tend to be more comfortable considering evidence that supports what they believe, denying responsibility for failures, and attributing problems to others. Understandably, these individual-level emotional and cognitive barriers have a dramatic affect on our ability to discuss failure effectively.

Failure Is Tough to Talk About

Even when failures are identified, social factors inhibit constructive discussion and analysis. Most managers lack the skills for handling the strong emotions that often surface in discussions that focus on mistakes and failure. This means that conversations attempting to unlock the potential learning from failure can easily degenerate into opportunities for scolding or finger-pointing. People experience negative emotions when examining their own failures, and this can chip away at self-confidence. Most people prefer to put past mistakes behind them rather than revisit them for greater understanding. In addition, most managers admire and are rewarded for efficiency and action, not for deep reflection and painstaking analysis.

But effective teaming requires its members to be comfortable in some uncomfortable situations like not being right, asking for help, or admitting mistakes. Analyzing and discussing failure requires openness, patience, and a tolerance for ambiguity. These behaviors must be embedded in the company culture. Consider the following example from Toyota Motor Company: James Wiseman was already a successful businessman by the time he joined Toyota in Georgetown, Kentucky, to manage its statewide public affairs program. Fujio Cho, later Chairman of Toyota worldwide, was then the head of the Georgetown factory. Wiseman recalled an important lesson about success and failure:

> I started going in there and reporting some of my little successes. One Friday, I gave a report of an activity we'd be doing . . . and I spoke very positively about it. I bragged a little. After two or three minutes, I sat down. And Mr. Cho kind of looked at me. I could see he was puzzled. He said, "Jim-san. We all know you are a good manager, otherwise we would not have hired you. But please talk to us about your problems so we can work on them together."[11]

Wiseman said that it was "like a lightning bolt. . . . Even with a project that had been a general success, we would always ask,

'What didn't go well, so we can make it better?'" Jim Wiseman later became Toyota's Vice President of corporate affairs for manufacturing and engineering in North America, and Fujio Cho became the chairman of Toyota worldwide. At least part of their success had to do with their ability to ask and discuss that critical question: What didn't go well so we can make it better? They were able to consistently reframe failure so that it was seen as a learning opportunity, rather than as an embarrassing event. More generally, they understood the need to create productive policies and norms for dealing with failure that helped overcome the organizational tendency to punish failure.

Organizations Punish Failure

You might think that those highest in organizational hierarchies would be confident enough to disclose failures. Surely an occasional slip-up is understandable given their overall track record, right? Wrong. Managers have an added incentive to disassociate themselves from failure because most organizations reward success and penalize failure. This means that holding an executive or leadership position in an organization doesn't imply an ability to acknowledge one's own failures. Dartmouth business professor Sydney Finkelstein's in-depth investigation of major failures at over 50 companies suggested that the opposite might be the case: The more senior the manager, the greater the social and psychological penalty for being fallible.[12] In his study, Finkelstein wrote:

> Ironically enough the higher people are in the management hierarchy, the more they tend to supplement their perfectionism with blanket excuses, with CEOs usually being the worst of all. For example, in one organization we studied, the CEO spent the entire forty-five-minute interview explaining all the reasons why others were to blame for the calamity that hit his company. Regulators, customers, the government, and

even other executives within the firm—all were responsible. No mention was made, however, of personal culpability.[13]

Organizational structures, policies and procedures, and senior management behavior can discourage people from analyzing failures and embracing experimentation.[14] A natural consequence of punishing failures is that employees learn to avoid identifying them, let alone analyzing them or experimenting if the outcome is uncertain. Even in more tolerant organizations, most managers fail to reward these behaviors through raises or promotions, and instead rely on punitive actions that often reflect a misunderstanding of the relationship between failure and fault.

The Blame Game

Failure and fault are inseparable in most cultures. Every child learns at some point that admitting failure means taking the blame for a disappointment or breakdown. And yet, the more complex the situation in which we find ourselves, the less likely we will be to understand the relationship between failure and fault. Executives I've interviewed in organizations as different as hospitals and investment banks admit to being perplexed about how to respond constructively to failure. If people aren't blamed for failures, their reasoning goes, what will ensure that they do their best? This concern is based on a false dichotomy. In actuality, a climate for admitting failure can coexist with high standards for performance.

To understand why this dichotomy exists and how leaders often misperceive the relationship between failure and fault, consider Figure 5.1. Listing nine possible reasons for failure, the figure represents the range and diversity of causes identified in research on organizational failure.

Which of these nine causes involve blameworthy actions? People may disagree at the margins, but most will draw the line

<table>
</table>

Blameworthy	**Deviance** An individual chooses to violate a prescribed process or practice. **Inattention** An individual inadvertently deviates from specifications. **Lack of Ability** An individual doesn't have the skills, conditions, or training to execute a job. **Process Inadequacy** A competent individual adheres to a prescribed but faulty or incomplete process. **Task Challenge** An individual faces a task too difficult to be executed reliably every time. **Process Complexity** A process composed of many elements breaks down when it encounters novel interactions. **Uncertainty** A lack of clarity about future events causes people to take seemingly reasonable actions that produce undesired results.
Praiseworthy	**Hypothesis Testing** An experiment conducted to prove that an idea or a design will succeed fails. **Exploratory Testing** An experiment conducted to expand knowledge and investigate a possibility leads to an undesired result.

Figure 5.1. A Spectrum of Reasons for Failure

Source: Edmondson, A. C. "Strategies for Learning from Failure," *Harvard Business Review* 89, no. 4 (2011). Reprinted with permissions from *Harvard Business Review*.

either before or after cause number two. In other words, most people agree that deliberate deviance—intentionally violating a rule or a procedure—warrants blame. But inattention, next on the list, may or may not deserve condemnation. If created by a lack of employee effort, then perhaps inattention is blameworthy. If created instead by a physiological limitation due to an overlong shift, inattention can be blamed on the manager who assigned the shift, not on the employee whose attention wandered. As we go down the list, it becomes more and more difficult to find blameworthy acts. In fact, failures that occur as a result of thought-ful experimentation can even be recognized as praiseworthy acts that generate valuable information. Accordingly, the list presents a spectrum that goes from obvious blame to obvious praise.

When I ask executives to consider this kind of causal spectrum and then estimate what percentage of the failures in their organiza-tions are caused by blameworthy events, the answers usually come back between 2 and 5 percent. But when I then ask what percent-age of failures are treated as if caused by blameworthy events, after a pause or laugh, their responses often yield a much higher number in the 70–90 percent range.[15]

The difference between failures that are truly blameworthy and those that are simply treated as blameworthy reveals a gap between logic and practice. Logically, we can see that many of the things that go wrong in organizations couldn't have been prevented, or may come from thoughtful exploration of a new area. But emotion-ally, failure is unpleasant regardless of the reason or circumstance. This unpleasantness helps explain the punitive connection between fault and failure even when the failure is fault-free. The unfortunate consequence of this gap between logic and practice is that many failures go unreported or misdiagnosed and their lessons are lost. As the next section explains, the importance, costs, and ramifications of these failures differs greatly across the Process Knowledge Spectrum.

Failure Across the Process Knowledge Spectrum

The role failure plays in a teaming effort or within a learning organization varies in important ways across the Process Knowl-edge Spectrum. Although a 90 percent failure rate might be expected in a biology research lab, if 90 percent of the food Taco Bell served was wrongly prepared or used spoiled ingredients, obvi-ously that would be unacceptable. Likewise, if 70 percent of com-mercial airline flights never made it to their destination or 50 percent of new automobiles broke down as they were driven off the dealer's lot, consumers would be incensed. If even a 1 percent failure rate occurred in any of these three settings, the offending companies would soon be out of business. Clearly, the frequency and the meaning of failure shifts as we move across the Process Knowledge Spectrum. The following sections outline critical distinctions between how failure should be viewed in routine, complex, and innovation operations.

Failure in Routine Operations

Even in routine tasks, small mistakes and failures happen because people are fallible. These failures are usually caused by small process deviations and generally involve reasons one through three (deviance, inattention, and inability) in the previous list of nine possible causes of failure. Most of these mistakes can be quickly corrected and the work goes on. But some small failures in routine processes provide valuable information about improvement opportunities for enhancing quality or efficiency. The key for learning from failure in routine operations, such as assembly plants, call centers, and fast-food restaurants, is to establish and maintain an organizational system that enables people to find, report, and correct errors.

The quintessential routine process is the automotive assembly line, and no system for managing a routine process surpasses the Toyota Production System (TPS) in learning from failures. TPS builds continuous learning from tiny failures and small process deviations into its systematic approach to improvement. When team members on the assembly line at Toyota spot a problem on any vehicle, or even a potential problem, they are encouraged to pull a rope called the Andon Cord to initiate a rapid diagnostic and problem-solving process. Production continues unimpeded if the problem is solved in less than a minute. Otherwise, production is halted despite the substantial loss of revenues until the failure is understood and resolved.

Failure in Complex Operations

Failures in complex operations, which require the work to be tailored to a specific customer or patient and in which multiple interacting processes create uncertainty, are particularly challenging because the stakes tend to be high. Such failures are usually due to faulty processes or system breakdowns. This means that most failures occur due to reasons in the middle of the previous causal spectrum (process inadequacy, task challenge, and process complexity). Not surprisingly, analysis usually reveals an organization's process, rather than a human, to be at fault when disaster strikes.

Important failures in complex operations are usually the result of an unfortunate combination of many small failures. James Reason, an error expert, uses Swiss cheese as a metaphor to explain how failures occur in these settings. Failures occur when multiple events accidentally line up, like holes in Swiss cheese, forming an unexpected tunnel that allows a number of separate failures to pass through without correction. Therefore, the risks inherent in complex systems call for extraordinary vigilance to help organizations detect and respond to the inevitable small failures, in order to avoid the large, consequential ones.

Because many complex organizations, such as nuclear power plants, air traffic control facilities, and aircraft carriers, present extremely high levels of risk, it would be wrong to say that failures are encouraged or rewarded. But, as previously mentioned, failures are inevitable. Recognizing this fundamental tension, some scholars have studied how high-risk organizations are able to operate safely in a remarkably consistent way and earn the designation High Reliability Organizations (HROs).[16] These organizations are resilient, able to adjust on the fly, and bounce back under challenging conditions.[17] Rather than trying to prevent all errors, HROs devise ways to contain and cope with errors as they occur, minimizing their effects before they escalate. Termed "heedful interrelating" by University of Michigan professor Karl Weick, this unusual level of vigilance includes the ability to detect and recover from small failures before real harm occurs.[18] Facing the potential for larger failure when smaller failures interact, leaders in complex organizations must promote resiliency by acknowledging that failure is inevitable, making it psychologically safe to report and discuss problems, and promoting habits of vigilance that support rapid detection and responsiveness.

Failure in Innovation Operations

Where knowledge is less well developed, it stands to reason that failures are more likely. Indeed, as we move to the right on the Process Knowledge Spectrum, failure is not only expected, it is essential to progress. To innovate, people must test ideas without knowing in advance what will work. Therefore, failures in innovation operations are usually due to reasons seven through nine on the causal spectrum presented in Figure 5.1 (uncertainty, hypothesis testing, and exploratory testing).

Researchers in basic science, tireless laboratory experimenters who have discovered such advances as human genome sequencing or the latest insights into galactic dust, know that the experiments they conduct, often for decades, will have a high failure rate, alongside the occasional spectacular success. Scientists in some fields confront failure rates that are 70 percent or higher. All pharmaceutical companies have had to learn from failure to succeed. The daunting reality is that over 90 percent of newly developed drugs fail in the experimental stage and never make it to market.

In innovation operations, the keys to success are thinking big, taking risks, and experimenting, while remaining fully aware that failure and dead ends are inevitable on the road to innovation. Award-winning design firm IDEO employs the slogan: "Fail often in order to succeed sooner."[19] This simple motto reveals an attitude that has given rise to products that appear in ISDA and *Business-Week* magazine's IDEA awards and regularly ranks them in the Fast Company 50, a list of the world's most innovative companies.

Teams at IDEO truly believe that success comes more quickly when they fail early and often, so long as they learn the lessons each failure has to offer.

Sometimes learning from failure in innovation operations means further investigation and analysis to ascertain if a failed product or design may prove to have a viable alternate use. Pfizer's lucrative Viagra was originally designed to be a treatment for angina, a painful heart condition. Eli Lilly discovered that a failed contraceptive drug could treat osteoporosis and consequently developed the billion-dollar-a-year drug Evista.[20] Strattera, a failed antidepressant, was discovered to be an effective treatment for attention deficit/hyperactivity disorder. Clearly, a one-size-fits-all-failures approach is too rigid for today's complex organizations and markets. This means an important aspect of developing a learning approach to failure includes understanding how to match failure to both its cause and context.

Matching Failure Cause and Context

I have found that managers rarely understand or appreciate the need for context-specific approaches to failure. As a result, it's common for them to apply an approach to failure that's appropriate for one context (for example, routine operations where failures should be prevented) to another context where it's inappropriate (for example, innovation operations where failures are valuable sources of new information). Take, for example, statistical process control (SPC), which uses statistical analysis of data to assess unwarranted variance from specified processes. SPC works well for identifying deviations from otherwise routine and visible patterns, but falters when used to catch and correct an invisible glitch like a poor clinical decision in the emergency room. As obvious as this example may seem, organizations make such errors all the time.

One well-meaning executive seeking to increase research productivity at Wyeth implemented financial incentives to reward scientists for steering more new compounds into the pipeline. Sure enough, more compounds went in. But, much to everyone's disappointment, more viable drug candidates didn't come out the other end. His strategy was a mismatch between the uncertainty of scientific research and the counting mindset that works well in ensuring process control in routine operations. A better approach would be to build a culture that rewards experimentation and early detection of failure.

Determining the correct strategy for learning from a failure depends on the failure's causes and context, which often go hand in hand. The word *failure* is terribly imprecise. This imprecision and ambiguity contributes to misdiagnosis of many failures. Although there are an infinite number of potential things that can go wrong in organizations, failures can be grouped into the three broad categories summarized in Exhibit 5.1.

Not surprisingly, these three types of failures generally correspond with the three different Process Knowledge Spectrum categories: preventable failures with routine operations, complex failures with complex operations, and intelligent failures with innovation operations. As organizations have become more complex in today's knowledge-based economy, however, this is not always true. Many times the boundaries between processes and problems become blurred. Take, for example, a software glitch that

---

Exhibit 5.1: Three Types of Failures

- **Preventable failures:** process deviations in well-understood domains, usually caused by behavior, skill, or support deficits.

- **Complex failures:** process or system breakdowns that arise due to inherent uncertainty and may or may not be identified in time to prevent consequential accidents.

- **Intelligent failures:** the unsuccessful trials that occur as part of thoughtful experiments and provide valuable new information or data.

Table 5.1: Organizational Failure Types

	Preventable	Complex	Intelligent
Common Causes	Behavior, skill, and attention deficiencies	Complexity, variability, and novel interactions	Uncertainty, experimentation, and risk taking
Descriptive Term	Process deviation	System breakdown	Unsuccessful trial
Sample contexts	Production line, manufacturing Fast-food services Basic utilities and services	Hospital care NASA Shuttle program New technology launch Aircraft carrier Nuclear power plant	Drug development New product design
Key Resources	TQM Stop order/ Andon cord SPC Training in root cause Problem solving	Vigilance Teaming skills Cross-functional analysis Training for difficult conversations	Scientific method Technical expertise Willingness to take risks Willingness to declare failure

negatively affects a manufacturing production line. The manufacturing process may be a routine operation, but the software issue is most like a system breakdown that represents a complex failure. The overview presented in Table 5.1 reveals that each of the three types of failure has its own causes, context, and solutions.

Preventable Failures

Behavior, skill, or support deficits in predictable operations constitute preventable failures. Most failures in this category can be considered "bad." In high-volume, routine operations, well-specified processes, with proper training and support, can and should be followed consistently. When there are failures, gaps in skill, motivation, or supervision are likely the reason. These causes can be readily identified and solutions developed. In these instances, leaders should diagnose why their predictable operations are not performing well and design ways to motivate employees to get the job done correctly every time, or fix faulty processes.

Complex Failures

A large and growing number of organizational failures are the result of system complexity. When novel combinations of events and actions are to be expected, some necessarily give rise to failures. Such failures are not preventable in a conventional sense. Instead, they arise due to the inherent uncertainty of work in complex systems, where a particular combination of needs, people, and problems may have never previously occurred. Sample contexts include managing a global supply chain, responding to enemy actions on the battlefield, or running a fast-growing start-up. Though serious failures may be avoided by following safety and risk-management best practices, small process failures will occur. To consider these inevitable small failures "bad" not only indicates a lack of understanding of how complex systems work; it's also counterproductive. Doing so blocks the rapid identification through which small failures are corrected and major failures are avoided.

Intelligent Failures

These types of failures generally occur in frontier or cutting-edge endeavors where experimentation is required to learn and succeed. Failures in this category shouldn't be called "bad." In truth, these types of failures can rightly be considered "good" because they provide valuable data that can help an organization leap ahead of the competition. Intelligent failures are essential in developing new knowledge. In innovation operations, the right kind of experimentation strategy helps to ensure the future growth of the company. Managers who operate on the assumption that change is constant and novelty is everywhere are more likely to get the most out of the failures that invariably will occur. In addition, they're more apt to avoid the unintelligent failure of conducting experiments at a larger scale than is necessary. Plainly, when mistakes are inevitable and innovation is crucial, developing an environment that encourages learning from failure is an organizational imperative. Even with the best of intentions, however, such learning is hard to do.

Developing a Learning Approach to Failure

Because psychological and organizational factors inhibit both failure identification and analysis, a fundamental reorientation is needed to successfully learn from failure. Individuals and groups must be motivated to embrace the difficult and often emotionally challenging lessons that failures reveal. Doing so requires a spirit of curiosity and openness, as well as exceptional patience and a tolerance for ambiguity. These traits and behaviors are best characterized by what, in the management literature, has been termed an *inquiry orientation*. This type of orientation is presented as a contrast to an *advocacy orientation*. Both terms describe contrasting communication behaviors and distinct approaches to group decision making.

Advocacy and Inquiry Orientations

As discussed earlier in the chapter, organizational structures and processes can hinder the ability of a group to learn from failure. In groups characterized by an advocacy orientation, these structures and processes support a top-down management approach and the organizational status quo. Therefore, when trying to incorporate the unique knowledge of different members, the unintentional results often include antagonism, a lack of listening and learning, and limited psychological safety for challenging authority. Recall the story of the *Columbia* space shuttle disaster at the beginning of Chapter Four. Thoughtful inquiry could have generated new insights about the threat posed by the foam strike that ultimately lead to the death of seven astronauts. Instead, NASA's rigid hierarchy, strict rules, and reliance on quantitative analysis discouraged novel lines of inquiry that may have helped prevent the disaster.

In contrast, an inquiry orientation is characterized by the perception among group members that multiple alternatives exist and that frequent dissent is necessary. These perceptions result in a deeper understanding of issues, the development of new possibilities, and an awareness of others' reasoning. This orientation can counteract common group tensions and process failures. Learning about the perspectives, ideas, and experiences of others when facing uncertainty and high-stakes decisions is critical to making appropriate choices and finding solutions to novel problems. But how can leaders promote an inquiry orientation to facilitate learning? The terms *exploratory response* and *confirmatory response* have recently been used to describe distinct ways that leaders can orient individuals and groups to respond to potential failures.[21]

Confirmatory and Exploratory Responses

Leaders play an important role in determining a group's orientation to a perceived failure. Facing small or ambiguous problems, leaders can respond in one of two basic ways: confirmatory or exploratory responses. A confirmatory response by leaders reinforces accepted assumptions, naturally triggering an advocacy orientation. When individuals seek information in this mode, they look for data that confirms existing beliefs, which is a natural human response. Leaders encourage or reinforce a confirmatory response, when they act in ways consistent with established frames and beliefs. This often means they're passive or reactionary rather than active and forward-looking.

In uncertain, risky, or novel situations, an exploratory response is more appropriate. Rather than supporting existing assumptions, an exploratory response requires a deliberate shift in the mindset of a leader. This alters the way a leader interprets and diagnoses the situation at hand. This shift involves challenging and testing existing assumptions and experimenting with new behaviors and possibilities. When leaders adopt an exploratory approach, they embrace ambiguity and openly acknowledge gaps in knowledge. They recognize that their current understanding may require revision, and so they actively search for evidence in support of alternative hypotheses. Rather than seeking to prove what they already believe, exploratory leadership encourages inquiry and experimentation. This deliberate response helps to accelerate learning through proactive information gathering and simple, rapid experimentation.

It would be nice if transforming an organization into a learning enterprise was just a matter of altering the orientation and perspective of a single leader. But of course it's not that simple. A productive approach to failure requires leadership, exercised by many individuals, to cultivate diagnostic acumen. In this way, an organizational culture of curiosity and analysis can be developed and nurtured. This helps people to develop a clearheaded understanding of what happened, rather than just "who did it" when something goes wrong. Doing this well means insisting on consistent reporting of failures, encouraging deep and systematic analysis, and promoting the proactive search for opportunities to experiment.

Strategies for Learning from Failures

Failure tolerance is a smart strategy for any organization wishing to gain new knowledge. Because organizations are more and more likely to encompass complex work and face unpredictable environments, a growing number of failures are of the complex type, and it's crucial to anticipate and respond to them quickly. Moreover, great strategic advantage can be gained from intelligent failures. But neither type of failure can be put to good use without a rational approach to diagnosis and discussion. Given that failure is inherently emotionally charged, responding to it requires specific, purposeful strategies. Three activities—detection, analysis, and experimentation—are critical to learning from failures. As Table 5.2 shows, these three activities apply to all types of failures, although how they're carried out varies in important ways.

Failure Detection: Support Systems for Identifying Failure

The first crucial strategy to master is the proactive and timely identification of failure. This is especially true of the type of small and seemingly inconsequential failures that lead to large, often catastrophic, failures. Any organization can detect big, expensive failures. It's the little ones that often go unnoticed. In many organizations, any failure that can be hidden is hidden, so long as it's unlikely to cause immediate or obvious harm. Even more common is the tendency to withhold bad news related to pending failures as long as humanly possible.

Recognizing this, Allan Mulally, soon after being hired as CEO of Ford Motors, created a new system for identifying failures. Understanding how difficult it is for early-stage failures to make it up the corporate hierarchy, he asked his managers to color code their reports: green for good, yellow for caution, red for problems. Mulally was frustrated when, during the first couple of meetings, managers coded most of their operations green. He reminded managers how much money the company had recently lost and asked pointedly whether everything was indeed going along well. It took this prodding for someone speak up, tentatively offering a first yellow report. After a moment of shocked silence in the group Mulally clapped, and the tension was broken. After that, yellow and red reports came in regularly.[22]

Ford's is not an isolated story. In companies around the world, even the most senior executives can be reluctant to convey bad news to bosses and colleagues. Shooting the messenger remains an enduring and problematic phenomenon, so it's essential for leaders

Table 5.2: Strategies for Learning from Failure

	(1) Detect Failure	(2) Analyze Failure	(3) Promote failure
Strategies for Learning from Preventable Failures	Make it safe for employees to check with managers and peers when unsure what to do. Reward problem detection. Reward "false alarms" (potential failures that turn out fine) for their value in learning and practicing.	Develop and employ classic techniques for process improvement.	Encourage small tests to ensure process viability, especially in the face of gradual changes in technology or customer preferences.
Strategies for Learning from Complex Failures	Make it safe to report errors and problems. Reward finding system vulnerabilities. Reward rapid reporting of small and large failures.	Convene cross-functional groups to identify what happened from multiple perspectives.	Encourage off-line tests to identify new failure modes so as to add new fail-safe mechanisms into processes.
Strategies for Learning from Intelligent Failures	Make it safe to experiment. Reward early detection of failed experiments. Reward early declaration of failed projects.	Employ scientific method to analyze data systematically. Avoid superficial assessment of trends or patterns. Include multiple perspectives.	Experiment more often, with more variety. Conduct pilots as experiments to identify failure modes rather than as demonstrations of success.

to proactively create conditions in which messages of failure travel up and across an organizational hierarchy. To do this, leaders need to engage in three essential activities: embrace the messenger, gather data and solicit feedback, and reward failure detection.

Embrace the messenger. Savvy managers understand the risks of unbridled toughness. An overly punitive response to an employee mistake may be more effective in stifling information about problems than in making your organization better. This is obviously not a good result. Managers' ability to quickly diagnose and resolve problems depends upon their ability to learn about them. Organizations with a habit of punishing mistakes or errors will discourage this process. This means that psychological safety, as explained in Chapter Four, is the bedrock of any genuine failure identification and analysis effort.

Gather data and solicit feedback. My research has found that a lack of access to data on failures is the most important barrier to managers learning from them. This is especially true for preventable and complex failures. In these circumstances, people often believe that no failures are acceptable, so hiding them can seem the only feasible approach. That inaccessibility can be due as much to human resistance to identifying failure as to technical difficulties in understanding small mistakes. To overcome this barrier, organizational leaders must develop systems, procedures, and cultures that proactively identify failure.

Soliciting feedback is an effective way of gathering data and surfacing many types of failures. Feedback from customers, employees, and other sources can expose failures such as communication breakdowns, the inability to meet goals, or a lack of customer satisfaction. Proactively seeking feedback from customers often helps manufacturers and service providers identify and address failures in a timely manner. If you believe identifying customer dissatisfaction is a luxury, bear in mind that only 5–10 percent of dissatisfied customers choose to complain following a service failure. Instead, most simply switch providers.[23] This means that if service companies fail to learn from their failures, they're guaranteed to lose customers.

Reward failure detection. Failures must be exposed as early as possible to allow learning in an efficient and cost-effective way. This requires a proactive effort on the part of managers to surface available data on failures and use it in a way that promotes learning. The detection challenge for intelligent failures lies in knowing when to declare defeat in an experimental course of action. The human tendency to hope for the best impedes early failure identification and is often exacerbated by strict organizational hierarchies. As a result, fruitless research projects are frequently kept going much longer than is scientifically rational or economically prudent. We throw good money after bad, hoping to pull a rabbit out of a hat. In innovation operations, this happens more often than most managers realize. Engineers' or scientists' intuition can be telling them for weeks that a project has fatal flaws, but making the formal decision to call it a failure may be delayed for months. Considerable resources are saved when such projects are stopped in a timely way and people are freed up to explore the next potential innovation.

Failure Analysis: Support Systems for Analyzing and Discussing Failure

Once organizations detect problems, they must use discipline and sophisticated analytic techniques to delve deeper than the obvious, superficial causes of failure, to go beyond quick fixes, and to learn the right lessons and implement the best remedies. After detection, failure analysis is one of the most overlooked activities in organizations today. This is true even though discussing failures has many important organizational benefits. By discussing failures, the valuable learning that might result from analyzing simple mistakes won't be overlooked. Discussion also provides an opportunity for other group members or employees who may not have been directly involved in the failure to learn from it, too. These employees can then bring new perspectives and insights that deepen the analysis and help to counteract self-serving biases that may color the perceptions of those most directly involved in the failure. The U.S. Army conducts After Action Reviews that enable participants to analyze, discuss, and learn from both the successes and failures of a variety of military initiatives.[24] Similarly, hospitals use Morbidity and Mortality (M&M) conferences in which physicians convene in brutally candid sessions to discuss significant mistakes or unexpected deaths.

The primary danger in failure analysis is that people tend to leap prematurely to conclusions, unless the analysis emphasizes a careful consideration of all possible causes and effects. For example, a retail bank that was losing customers conducted a failure analysis to figure out why customers were switching to other banks. The data showed that most customers who closed their accounts picked "interest rates" as the reason for switching banks. However, once the bank actually compared their interest rates to others in the area they found no significant differences. Might the customers' real reasons for leaving be something different from what they actually said? Careful interviews with the dissatisfied customers revealed a less obvious reason for customer defections: they were irritated by being aggressively solicited for a bank-provided credit card, and then subsequently turned down for the card. The deeper failure analysis concluded that the problem lay in the bank's marketing department. Consequently, changes were made so the marketing department could do a better job of screening candidates for bank-provided credit cards.[25]

This type of rigorous analysis, however, requires that people put aside their resistance to exploring unpleasant truths and instead take personal responsibility. Analysis can only be effective if people speak up openly about what they know and if other members of the organization listen. To develop an environment that overcomes organizational and social barriers to failure analysis, leaders should take actions such as implementing systems for total quality management (especially in routine operations), convene interdisciplinary groups to look for potential vulnerabilities (especially in complex operations), and take a systematic approach to experimenting and analyzing data (especially in innovation operations).

Develop and employ systems for total quality management. Preventable failure analysis is best accomplished through the classic techniques of process improvement such as total quality management (TQM), with its discipline of root-cause problem solving. The major management challenge lies in motivating people to keep going beyond first-order observations (procedures weren't followed) to second- and third-order diagnoses about why the failure occurred and what underlying conditions contributed to the problem. Process improvement techniques like TQM work best in routine operations, because high-volume activities allow large amounts of data on process and performance to be collected and analyzed with statistical methods. These analyses reveal process deviations (problems) that might otherwise go undetected, and thereby point to improvement opportunities. In the absence of the repetitive processes characteristic of routine operations, TQM and statistical analyses are less useful in learning from failure, and so alternative techniques for systematic analysis are presented.

Convene interdisciplinary groups. Formal processes or forums for discussing, analyzing, and applying the lessons of failure are needed to ensure that effective learning occurs. Learning from complex failures requires the use of interdisciplinary teams with the diverse skills and perspectives necessary for both anticipating and analyzing complex incidents. Multidisciplinary groups are able to combine their areas of expertise to identify potential vulnerabilities in complex systems. They can discuss how processes work from different perspectives and recognize the potential for things to go wrong. They also can work together to figure out the causes of failures that do occur. Such groups are most effective when people have technical skills, expertise in analyzing data, and diverse perspectives, allowing them to explore different interpretations of a failure's causes and consequences. Diverse perspectives are essential because most failures have multiple contributing factors related to different departments or requiring different areas of expertise to understand them. Because this process usually has the potential for creating conflict, expert facilitators skilled in interpersonal or group process can help keep the process productive.

Analyze data systematically. The intellectual challenge of analysis intensifies as we move from preventable to complex to intelligent failures. As noted, statistical data analysis is a useful tool for analyzing large amounts of qualitative data—for example, the weight or dimensions of batteries in a production run—to assess consistency. Statistical analysis prevents mistaking what's called normal variation for problematic variation. It helps separate signal from noise. Complex and intelligent failures instead require deep qualitative analysis, to identify what happened and why, and to brainstorm the implications of these conclusions. Complex and intelligent failures are often unique, unprecedented events. Complex failures occur when multiple factors come together in new ways and give rise to a system breakdown. Analysis thus involves figuring out all the possible contributors to the failure—a creative task that benefits immensely from the involvement of a motivated team. Intelligent failures also must be analyzed systematically, so as to avoid drawing the wrong conclusions from the failure. For example, when a new experimental chemotherapy drug developed at Eli Lilly failed in clinical trials, the doctor conducting the trials analyzed the failure systematically—rather than assuming the drug simply didn't work—and discovered something important. Patients who didn't do well with the drug had a folic acid deficiency. Sure enough, further study showed that giving patients folic acid along with the drug solved the problem, thereby rescuing a drug that the organization had been ready to discard.[26]

Failure Production: Establish and Support Systems for Deliberate Experimentation

The third critical, and possibly most provocative, action a leader can take in establishing a culture conducive to learning from failure is to strategically produce failures for the express purpose of learning and innovating. For scientists and researchers, failure is not optional; it's part of being at the forefront of scientific discovery. They know that each failure conveys valuable information, which they're eager to obtain more quickly than the competition. Exceptional organizations, therefore, go beyond detecting and analyzing problems by intentionally generating intelligent failures that increase knowledge and suggest alternative courses of action.

It's not that managers in these organizations enjoy failure. They don't. But they recognize that failure is a necessary by-product of experimentation. Thus, these organizations devote some portion of their energy to experimentation in order to find out what works and what doesn't. Despite the increased rate of failure that accompanies deliberate experimentation, organizations that experiment effectively are likely to be more innovative, productive, and successful than those that don't take such risks.[27] Devoting resources to experimentation doesn't have to mean dramatic experiments with large budgets. In one study, for example, I found that hospital care improvement teams devised solutions to improving such mundane activities as clinician hand-washing behavior by experimenting with different persuasion techniques.[28]

On a larger scale, Google institutionalized 20 Percent Time, which is a portion of paid employee time allotted to independent projects. Although the projects must be officially approved by a supervisor, employees have come to expect that most proposals will be given the go-ahead. Although the real or immediate work takes precedence, employees are encouraged to devote one day a week to these exploratory projects, in the hopes that they lead to the next big innovation. Although 20 Percent Time is universally lauded for the invention of such lucrative breakthroughs as Gmail and Adsense, what's not usually mentioned is how many of these independent projects fail. Companies like Google that are known for innovation understand that for one successful new product or service, there are usually countless well-intentioned failures.

Leaders can sanction and even institutionalize deliberate experimentation. Unfortunately, this is both technically and socially challenging to implement intelligently. Purposefully setting out to experiment and generate both failures and successes is particularly difficult when failures are stigmatized. Conducting experiments requires acknowledging that the status quo is imperfect and could benefit from change. One of the advantages of most forms of experimentation is that failures can often take place off-line in simulations and pilots. However, even in these situations, the fear of stigma or embarrassment can still make people reluctant to take risks. Therefore, strong leadership is needed to encourage people to engage wholeheartedly in experimentation. This type of leadership includes rewarding both experimentation and failure, understanding the power of words, and designing intelligent experiments that increase knowledge and ensure learning.

Reward experimentation and its inevitable failures. Experimentation is difficult when organizations emphasize and reward only success. Research in social psychology has demonstrated that espoused goals of increasing innovation through experimentation are not as effective when rewards penalize failures as when rewards are aligned with the goal of promoting experimentation.[29] In addition, explicit messages that both recognize the inevitability and value of failures can counteract the corporate stigma otherwise associated with failure. To help reduce this stigma and encourage timely declaration of failure, the chief scientific officer at Eli Lilly introduced "failure parties" to honor intelligent, high-quality scientific experiments that failed to achieve the desired results. Redeploying valuable resources, particularly scientists' time, to new projects earlier rather than later can save hundreds of thousands of dollars. Rewarding failure is tricky. Many managers worry about creating a permissive, anything-goes atmosphere, imagining that people will start to believe failure is just as good as success. In reality, however, most people are highly motivated to succeed, based on the natural desire to do well and to be recognized for their competence. They are less motivated, however, for the reasons discussed in this chapter, to reveal and analyze failure, and so it takes leadership encouragement to make it happen. It is not a matter of formal metrics and cash rewards, but rather informal acknowledgment and celebration of the lessons learned from failure.

Words matter. One way to counteract failure's stigma and promote increased experimentation is through the use of more precise terminology. This simple truth is recognized in the notion of trial and error, a discovery strategy for finding out what works when little is known. Strictly speaking, the phrase *trial and error* is a misnomer. Instead, "trial and failure" is more appropriate. Error implies that you could have done it right, and not doing so constitutes a mistake. But a trial is needed when results are not knowable in advance.

Why does it matter if managers treat a trial's unfavorable outcomes as errors rather than as failures? Errors are preventable deviations from known processes. Failures include both the preventable (errors) and the unpreventable. Just as many hospitals have learned to call certain adverse medical events "system breakdowns" rather than clinician errors, leaders can call experiments that fail "unsuccessful trials." The difference both cognitively and emotionally between these terms is palpable. Such small changes in language can have a major impact on organizational culture and counterbalance the well-established psychological barriers to learning from failure.

Design intelligent failures for learning. When learning from failure is taken seriously, experiments, simulations, and pilot programs are planned and executed in a way that stretches current knowledge and capacities. Designing these types of experiments for learning means testing limits and pushing the boundaries of what works. Therefore, successful experiments are often those that are designed to fail.

In my research, however, I've found that far too many experiments are designed to endorse or confirm the likelihood of success. Consider the way in which many pilot programs—a common example of experimentation in business—are devised and implemented. In their hunger for success, many managers in charge of piloting a new product or service typically do whatever they can to make sure it's perfect right from the beginning. Paradoxically, this tendency to make sure a pilot is wildly successful can inhibit the more important success of the subsequent full-scale launch. Pilots should instead be used as tools to learn as much as possible about how a new service performs well before allowing shortcomings to be revealed by a full-scale launch. However, when managers of pilots work to make sure they succeed, they tend to create optimal conditions rather than representative or typical ones. Exhibit 5.2 offers six useful questions to help leaders design pilots that increase the probability of producing intelligent failures that generate valuable information.

As the questions demonstrate, managers hoping to successfully launch a new, innovative product or service shouldn't try to produce success the first time around. Instead, they should attempt to engage in the most informative trial-and-failure process possible. A truly successful pilot is designed to discover everything that could go wrong, rather than proving that under ideal conditions everything can go right. This strategy for learning from pilot-size failures is a way to help ensure that full-scale, online services succeed. And, as a result, it is also the very essence of how organizations master the art of learning from failure.

Exhibit 5.2: Designing Successful Failures

Managers of successful pilots must be able to answer "yes" to the following questions:

- Is the pilot program being tested under typical circumstances instead of optimal conditions?

- Are the employees, customers, and resources representative of the firm's real operating environment?

- Is the goal of the pilot to learn as much as possible, rather than to demonstrate to senior managers the value of the new system?

- Is the goal of learning as much as possible understood by everyone involved, including employees and managers?

- Is it clear that compensation and performance ratings are not based on a successful outcome of the pilot?

- Were explicit changes made as a result of the pilot program?

Source: Edmondson, A. C. "Strategies for Learning from Failure," *Harvard Business Review* 89, no. 4 (2011). Reprinted with permissions from *Harvard Business Review.*

Leadership Summary

Teaming brings the occasional failure. This creates an imperative for organizations to master the ability to learn from failure. Yet few organizations have a well-developed capacity to dig deeply enough to understand and capture the potential lessons that failures offer. Research demonstrates that this gap can't be explained by a lack of commitment to learning. Instead, the processes and incentives necessary to identify and analyze failure are lacking in most organizations. Add the human desire to avoid the unpleasantness and loss of confidence associated with acknowledging failure, and it's easy to understand why so few organizations have made the shift from a culture of blame to a culture in which the rewards of learning from failure can be fully realized.

This is regrettable for a number of reasons. Many failures provide valuable information about improvement opportunities for enhancing quality or efficiency. In addition, organizations that pay more attention to small problems are more likely to avert large or catastrophic failures. Most important, however, organizations that embrace failure are likely to learn and innovate faster than their competition. An environment that supports failure identification and analysis encourages the type of purposeful experimentation essential to progress. These types of experiments, and the intelligent failures they produce, increase knowledge and help to ensure that new products and services succeed.

Creating an environment in which people have an incentive to reveal and discuss failure is the job of leadership. This means executives and managers must resolve not to indulge in the natural tendency to express strong disapproval of what may at first appear to be incompetence. Instead, by providing appropriate rewards and using language that helps destigmatize failure, leaders can create a culture conducive to inquiry, discovery, reflection, and experimentation. To understand what went wrong and how to prevent it in the future, learning from failure often requires working with people from different groups, specialties, or even regions. The next chapter will examine the specific challenges of teaming across these types of boundaries and how to manage cultural and occupational differences.

LESSONS AND ACTIONS

- When bringing together people with different perspectives and skills, failure is inevitable because of both technical and interpersonal challenges.

- Failures provide valuable information that allows organizations to be more productive, innovative, and successful. But due to strong psychological and social reactions to failing, most of us see failure as unacceptable.

- Logically, we can see that many failures in organizations cannot be prevented, but emotionally, it's hard to separate failure from blame. This leads to the types of punitive reactions that cause many failures to go unreported or misdiagnosed.

- The causes of failure vary across the Process Knowledge Spectrum. In routine operations, failures are usually caused by small process deviations. Failures in complex operations are usually due to faulty processes or system breakdowns. In innovation operations, failures are usually due to uncertainty and experimentation.

- Although there are an infinite number of things that can potentially go wrong in organizations, failures can be grouped into three broad categories: preventable failures, complex failures, and intelligent failures.

- Leaders looking to develop a learning approach to failure should adopt an inquiry orientation that reflects curiosity, patience, and a tolerance for ambiguity. Doing so makes it safe to talk about failures and reinforces norms of openness.

- Failure detection, failure analysis, and purposeful experimentation are critical to learning from failures.

- To encourage failure detection, leaders need to embrace the messenger, gather data and solicit feedback, and reward failure detection.

- To support failure analysis, leaders should convene interdisciplinary groups and take a systematic approach to analyzing data.

- To promote purposeful experimentation, leaders must reward both experimentation and failure, use terminology that counteracts psychological barriers to learning from failure, and design intelligent experiments that generate more smart failures.

chapter six

teaming across boundaries

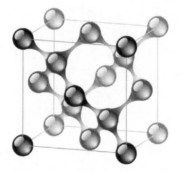

On August 5, 2010, more than half a million tons of rock suddenly caved in, completely blocking the entrance to the San Jose copper mine in Chile.[1] Mining accidents are unfortunately common. But this one was unprecedented for several reasons: the distance of the miners from the Earth's surface, the sheer number of miners trapped, and the hardness of the rock, to name a few. Thirty-three men were buried alive 2,000 feet under rock harder than granite. By way of comparison, an earlier rescue at the Quecreek Mine in Pennsylvania, with nine miners trapped 240 feet below ground, had been considered a remarkable feat.[2] In Chile, initial estimates of the possibility of finding anyone alive were put at 10 percent—odds that diminished sharply two days later when rescue workers narrowly escaped a secondary collapse and forever shut down the option of extracting miners through the ventilation shaft.[3]

Most readers will already know that within 70 days all 33 miners would be rescued. What happened during those 70 days was an extraordinary teaming effort involving hundreds of individuals spanning physical (those 2,000 feet of rock), organizational, cultural, geographic, and professional boundaries.

Teaming took place in three main arenas. First, and most painful to consider, were the miners facing the challenge of physical and psychological survival. In the second arena, engineers and geologists came together from multiple organizations and nations to work on the technical problem of locating, reaching, and extracting the trapped miners. The political and managerial sphere comprised the third arena, where senior leaders in the Chilean government and elsewhere made decisions and provided resources to support the actions of those above and below ground at the San Jose site. At the outset, these three arenas contained independent teaming activities; by the end, their successes brought them together in a dramatic, magnificently choreographed rescue.

———————

Below ground, amid shock and fear, leadership and teaming took shape after a tumultuous beginning. Immediately after the collapse, the miners scrambled to safety in the mine's small "refuge."[4] Luis Urzúa, who had formal leadership over the group as the shift supervisor, started by checking provisions in the refuge. Calmly and quickly, he began to focus on crucial survival needs, especially in terms of the limited food available (roughly the amount of food two miners would eat over two days). Calm did not prevail, however. Mario Sepulveda, a charismatic 39-year-old, outraged at the state of the mine and the company's long-standing lack of attention to safety, reacted angrily to the collapse. His energy attracted followers; factions and conflict soon emerged. Some wanted to take action of any kind to reach the outside rather than sitting helplessly to await rescue. Others wanted to follow Urzúa's guidance. By the end of their first twenty-four hours, the miners were exhausted by failed attempts to communicate with the outside world and disoriented by the lack of natural light. With scant attention to sanitation or order and subdued by hunger and fatigue, they attempted to sleep.

On the second day, miner Jose Henriquez stepped in to urge the group to start each day with a collective prayer. Soon this became a sustaining routine and helped unite the group around a shared goal of survival. With no blueprint for how to survive in these conditions, conversation and experimentation were essential to discovering a way forward. In the days that followed, facing darkness, hunger, depression, filth, and illness, the miners cooperated intensely to maintain order, health, sanitation, and sanity. They used the lighting system to simulate day and night, each lasting twelve hours. Sepulveda, determined now to pull people together, assigned specific tasks to people based on skills, experience, and mental stability. No responsibilities were imposed on miners who were hallucinating or were otherwise incapable of focused action. When some miners began to develop skin mold and canker sores from the heat and humidity, miner Yonni Barrios, well read on various illnesses, volunteered as a medic. A grim but functional routine took hold, dampening the cycles of despair and hope. Seventeen days later, when rescuers finally bored a narrow hole into the chamber, the miners received additional food and supplies and the lifeline of communication by special telephone.

Above ground, the Chilean Carabineros Special Operations Group—an elite police unit for rescue operations—arrived a few hours after the first collapse. Their initial attempt at rescue led to the ventilation shaft collapse that was the rescue effort's dismal first failure. As news of a mine cave-in spread, family members, emergency response teams, rescue workers, and reporters also flooded to the site. Meanwhile, others in the Chilean mining community dispatched experts, drilling machines, and bulldozers. Codelco, the state-owned company overseeing the San Jose mine, sent Andre Sougarret, an engineer and manager with over twenty years of experience in mining who was known for his calm, composure, and ease with people, to lead the operation.

Working with numerous other technical experts, Sougarret formed three teams to oversee different aspects of the operation. One searched for the men, poking drill holes deep into the earth in the hopes of hearing sounds to indicate that the men were alive. Another worked on how to keep them alive if found, and a third worked on how to extract them safely from the refuge. The teams originally came up with four possible rescue strategies: the first, through the ventilation shaft, was quickly rendered impossible, as noted earlier. The second, drilling a new mine ramp, also proved impossible once the rock's instability was discovered. The third, tunneling from an adjacent mine a mile away, would have taken eight months and was also excluded. The only hope was to drill a series of holes at various angles in an attempt to locate the men.

But the extreme depth and small size of the refuge made the problem of location staggeringly difficult. With the drills' limited precision, the odds of hitting the refuge with each painstaking drill attempt were about one in eighty.[5] Even that was optimistic, because the location of the refuge was not precisely known. Available maps of the tunnels were inaccurate, having not been updated in years. Worse, the drillers couldn't take the most direct route, mounting equipment in such a way as to drill straight down on top of the mine because it would increase the danger of collapse. Instead, they would have to set up off to the side and drill at an angle, further complicating the accuracy problem.

To maximize the chances of success, teams worked separately at first to come up with different strategies for drilling the holes. Several early attempts failed to reach the miners, but at least revealed crucial features of the mine and the rock. Unfortunately, much of this learning brought bad news. For instance, the drillers and geologists discovered that fallen rock trapped water and sedimentary rocks, increasing drill deviations and further reducing the chances of reaching the refuge in time. They also learned that drilling at an inclined angle shifted the drill to the right, while the weight of the drill bars pushed the drill upright, giving rise to an overall drift downward and to the right. This was the kind of technical detail that engineers had to quickly incorporate into their plans, which were changing rapidly and radically with each passing day.

One dramatic change to procedure was the discovery and use of frequent, short action-assessment cycles. In normal drilling operations, precision was measured after a hole was completely drilled. Here, in contrast, drillers realized that to hit the refuge, they would have to make measurements every few hours and promptly discard holes that deviated too much, starting again—discouraging as that might be. As they learned more about the search challenge, the odds of success diminished further, with one driller putting it at less than 1 percent.

Fortunately, the different teams came up with remarkably complementary pieces of an ultimately viable solution. For example, in one piece of good luck, a Chilean geologist named Felipe Matthews, who had developed a unique technology for measuring drilling trajectories with high precision, showed up at the site with his innovation. He discovered quickly that his measurements were inconsistent with those of other on-site groups. Based on a rapidly improvised series of tests, Matthews's equipment was found to be most accurate, and he was put in charge of measuring the accuracy of all drilling in progress.

The various subgroup leaders met for a half hour every morning and also called for quick meetings on an as-needed basis. They developed a protocol for transitioning between day and night drill shifts and for routine maintenance of machinery. "We structured, structured, structured all aspects of execution"[6] As drill attempts continued to fail, one after another, Sougarret communicated gracefully with the families. Despite these failures, Sougarret and his new colleagues persevered.

Meanwhile, in Santiago, the newly elected Chilean president, Sebastian Piñera, had met with Mining Minister Laurence Golborne on the morning of August 6, 2010. The president sent Golborne to the mine with clear instructions: Get the miners back alive and spare no expense. Further, this intention was to be made entirely public. This was a critical decision by a man with prior experience in business rather than government; someone with political savvy might have avoided staking his reputation on a promise so unlikely to be realized. Golborne and Piñera quickly reached out to their network, which comprised colleagues around the world. As the president put it, "We were humble enough to ask for help."[7] Michael Duncan, a deputy chief medical officer with the U.S. National Aeronautics and Space Administration (NASA) who was contacted by the government, concurred, reporting that the Chilean officials basically said, "Let's try to identify who the experts are in the field—let's get some consultants in here that can give us the best information possible."[8] Duncan, for example, brought experience with long space flights to bear on the question of the miners' physical and psychological survival in small quarters. NASA engineers played a crucial role in the design of the escape capsule, leading us to the final teaming endeavor in the technical realm, thousands of miles from the site.

Clint Cragg, a top NASA engineer, went to Chile in late August with a few NASA health care experts to volunteer to help.[9] Cragg later teamed with engineers in the Chilean navy to design the rescue capsule, after first going back to the United States to pull together a group of 20 NASA engineers. For inspiration, the NASA team looked to a precedent dubbed the "Dahlbusch Bomb," built in 1955 to rescue three men trapped in the Dahlbusch coal mine in western Germany. The engineers developed a twelve-page list of requirements, used by the Chilean navy in the final design for the capsule, which was called the Fenix. The Fenix interior, just barely large enough to hold a person, was equipped with a microphone, oxygen, and spring-loaded retractable wheels to roll smoothly against the rock walls. The engineers designed three nearly identical capsules. The first was used during tests—experiments and dry runs—and the second was used during the rescue operation. The third, presumably, was a backup. On October 13, the Fenix started its life-saving runs to bring miners one by one through the fifteen-minute journey to the surface of the Earth. Over the next two days, miners were hauled up one by one in the twenty-eight-inch-wide escape capsule painted with the red, white, and blue of the Chilean flag. After a few minutes to hug relatives, each was taken for medical evaluation.

Teaming Despite Boundaries

Reflecting on the Chilean rescue, it is clear that a top-down, command-and-control approach would have failed utterly. No one person, or even one leadership team, could have figured out how to solve this problem. It's also clear that simply encouraging everyone to try anything they wanted would have produced only chaos and harm. Family members, miners, and others with good intentions had to be held back numerous times from rushing headlong at the rock with pickaxes. Instead, what was required, facing the unprecedented scale of the disaster, was coordinated teaming—multiple temporary groups of people working separately on different types of problems, and coordinating across groups, as needed. It also required progressive experimentation. This section considers key factors to the operation's success, and what we can learn from the case about teaming across boundaries more generally.

First, the most senior leadership committed publicly to a successful outcome, risking both resources and reputation on an unlikely outcome. In his decision to do this, President Piñera resembles other leaders facing nearly impossible challenges who have been willing to declare an early and total commitment to success. Take, for example, the explosion that occurred in an oxygen tank during the *Apollo 13* mission on its journey to the moon. Despite limited resources, unclear options and a high probability of failure, NASA flight director Gene Krantz insisted, "Failure is not an option." He authorized problem-solving efforts in previously trained teams that tirelessly worked out scenarios for recovery using only materials available to the astronauts.[10] Ultimately, Kranz and his teams safely returned the crew to Earth. Piñera and Golborne were also willing to ask for help and to seek out expertise in any organization or nation willing to provide it.

Second, the teaming utilized rapid-cycle learning. Technical experts worked collaboratively to design, test, modify, and abandon options, over and over again, until they got it right. They organized quickly to design and try out various solutions, and just as quickly admitted when these had failed. They willingly changed course based on feedback—some obvious (the collapse of the ventilation shaft), some subtle (being told that their measurements were inaccurate by an engineer intruding mid-process with a new technology). Perhaps most important, the engineers did not take repeated failure as evidence that a successful rescue was impossible. Similarly, the miners successfully teamed to solve the most pressing problems of survival, despite the desperate odds.

Third, the structure of the teaming is interesting to consider. The separate efforts—managerial, technical, and survival—were intensely focused. In each arena, problem solving was intelligent and persistent, and the combined efforts equaled more than the sum of the parts. The intermittent coordination between the arenas was as important as the intense improvisation and learning within them.

As this example demonstrates, when teaming across boundaries works, the results can be awe-inspiring. Managing a complex rescue operation, launching a space shuttle, producing a big-budget movie, or delivering a large engineering and construction project are all examples of complex uncertain work that requires multiple areas of expertise, and even multiple organizations, for its completion. The problem is that all too often teaming is thwarted by communication failures that take place at the boundaries between professions, organizations, and other groups. People think they're communicating, they participate in endless meetings, and they work hard, only to have their projects fail. Why? As individuals bring diverse expertise, skills, perspectives, and goals together in unique team configurations to accomplish challenging goals, they must overcome the hidden challenge of communicating across multiple types of boundaries. Some boundaries are obvious—2,000 feet of rock, or being in different countries with different time zones. Others are subtle, such as when two engineers working for the same company in different facilities unknowingly bring different taken-for-granted assumptions about how to carry out a particular technical procedure to a collaboration.

This chapter describes the boundaries that team members frequently must cross while working together on complex problems. After examining why boundaries matter, I describe three types of boundaries that confront teaming in today's global organizations. I then provide guidelines for successfully teaming across boundaries to create possibilities for organizational learning.

Visible and Invisible Boundaries

Boundaries refer to the divisions between identity groups. An identity group exists around any meaningful category in which a person belongs, such as gender, occupation, or nationality. Some identity groups, and their corresponding boundaries, are more visible than others. Gender, for example, is visible. Occupation is less visible—except where clothing gives it away. What is invisible, however, are the taken-for-granted assumptions and mindsets that people hold in different groups. For teaming to be successful, managers and team members must be aware that they come together with different perspectives, often taking for granted the "rightness" of their own beliefs and values. This means it's not enough to simply say, let's band together, and it will all work out. No matter how much goodwill may be involved, boundaries limit collaboration in ways that are often invisible but nonetheless powerful.

Taken-for-Granted Assumptions

Processes of education, licensing, hiring, and socializing contribute to beliefs that lead people to favor their own group or location, and to unconsciously view the knowledge of their own group as especially important. It's as if there's a wall that separates engineers from marketers; nurses from doctors; and designers in Beijing from designers in Boston. Most people take knowledge that lies on their side of a boundary for granted, making it hard to communicate with those on the other side. Paraphrasing an observation once made by communications theorist Marshall McLuhan, we don't know who discovered water, but it wasn't the fish. In other words, the context in which we work, day in and day out, is often invisible to us. Presumably, fish don't think much about water; they take it for granted. Research on cross-functional new product development teams conducted by Professor Deborah Dougherty of Rutgers found that team members from different areas of expertise occupied different "thought worlds"—taken-for-granted assumptions that each expert was unaware of holding.[11] Similarly, each of us takes for granted many of the values and norms of identity groups (profession, organization, country, and so on) of which we're members. At its core, teaming is about reaching across or spanning these kinds of boundaries. To do this, we must first be keenly aware of what they are. Many boundaries were created and strengthened by the very people—experts, department heads, authorities—who now must play a role in helping to break them down.

Communication with anyone from a different group, whether the difference is demographic or organizational, is fraught with small hurdles. Teams within organizations often must coordinate objectives, schedules, or resources with other teams, departments, or locations. This requires discovering and revealing taken-for-granted assumptions to avoid misunderstanding and error. But by their very nature, taken-for-granted assumptions are notoriously hard to recognize, so it helps to be aware that they exist and to be on the lookout for them. Consider the real-life example of two aeronautical organizations that joined forces to collaborate on a new aircraft. At the first planning meeting, everyone agreed on ambitious goals and a rigorous schedule. However, the conversation kept getting mired in misunderstanding and miscommunication. Finally, it was discovered that the two groups meant something different when they used the simple phrase "the plane has been delivered." One organization understood it to mean the plane has been physically delivered to a control station. But the other organization understood the exact same phrase to mean the plane has been delivered to the physical site and the machinery has passed all technical inspection. In addition to the head-scratching in the room, this semantic difference was crucial to the project because it affected how data was to be collected and categorized. This subtle difference in semantic use between two aeronautical groups is just a single example of the kind of misunderstanding that can be multiplied many times over when teaming spans boundaries.

To further add to the challenge, research by Miami University professor Gerald Stasser and his colleagues shows that unique information held by any one team member, as opposed to information shared by most team members, is often ignored in team decisions, much to the detriment of team performance.[12] It is natural for people from different groups to come together and spend precious time discussing the subset of knowledge with which everyone is already familiar. Unique information rarely surfaces, even when that information is critical to making the decision. Groups don't mean to do this. In fact, people in groups often believe they are leveraging group member expertise to make an informed decision. These well-documented findings describe groups that are left to their own devices, without leadership or tools to guide their process. Fortunately, as we will see later in this chapter, it is possible to avoid these traps.

Specialization and Globalization

Two related trends have increased the need for teaming across boundaries. First, knowledge and expertise evolve ever more rapidly. In most fields, the rate of new knowledge development requires people to invest considerable time just to stay current in their own area of expertise. Especially in technical fields, the explosion of new knowledge leads inexorably to greater specialization. Fields spawn new subfields, and new subfields spawn even more specialized subfields. For example, electrical engineering, once a subfield of physics, became its own discipline by 1900, and today splits into the several distinct subfields of power systems, signal processing, and computer architecture. More generally, technical knowledge and specialized jargon proliferate, making it difficult to keep up with other, even closely related, fields of inquiry. Highly specialized professionals thus find themselves needing to collaborate to carry out the important work of the organization, whether developing a new cell phone or caring for a cancer patient.

Second, global competition has led to ever more compressed time frames: product life cycles are shrinking; lead times for getting new products to market are shorter; and scientific researchers face more threats of being scooped in their work by a lab halfway around the world. Time pressures mean that a structured approach, in which managers plan each aspect of a large development project with specialized tasks to be accomplished separately in carefully structured phases, are unrealistic. This planning becomes even less realistic when completed tasks are "thrown over the wall" to other functions or disciplines. Instead, the walls between disciplines have come down, and simultaneous work on related tasks must be coordinated and negotiated in a dynamic teaming journey.

Individuals or departments cannot accomplish meaningful results in isolation. The chances of individual components, developed separately, coming together into meaningful, functional wholes—new product, feature film, or rescue operation—without intense communication across the boundaries are exceedingly low. Considering these two factors—increasing specialization and global competition—there are numerous benefits to learning how to transcend boundaries that exist between people, departments, or specialties. Understanding how to break down these walls includes developing a deeper understanding of the varieties of diversity and how they relate to the boundaries that exist both within and between work groups.

Three Types of Boundaries

Diversity is an important topic in research on teams and teaming, yet researchers lack consensus on a single clear definition of diversity. Katherine Klein and Dave Harrison, professors at Wharton and Penn State, respectively, defined diversity as "the distribution of differences among the members of a unit with respect to a common attribute X."[13] Common attributes include gender, ethnicity, professional status, and educational degree. A team is considered diverse if its members differ in respect to at least one attribute. Conceptually, Klein and Harrison grouped diversity into three basic groups, *separation, disparity*, and *variety*, which provides a helpful starting point. Exhibit 6.1 uses these distinctions to suggest three common boundaries that often confront teaming in complex organizations.

The following sections look at examples of each of these types of boundaries and consider their impact on collaboration. Of course, sometimes people must cross multiple boundaries at once, such as when two team members have differences in terms of

---

Exhibit 6.1: Three Types of Boundaries

- **Physical distance:** *Separation diversity* includes differences in location—different time zones or the building down the street.

- **Status:** *Disparity diversity* ranks people according to the social value of a particular attribute. Teaming often confronts differences in status between people who need to work together to get a job done.

- **Knowledge:** *Variety diversity* describes differences in experience, knowledge, expertise, or education. When teaming, the major boundaries confronted in this category are differences in knowledge based on organizational membership or expertise.

---

nationality, profession, gender, and time zone. Fortunately, leadership that helps establish process discipline and good communication can help overcome the challenges described in this section.

Physical Distance

An increasingly common teaming challenge is created by the need to span geographic distance. In many global companies, work teams in geographically dispersed locations all over the world, so-called *virtual teams*, are relied on to integrate expertise. A virtual team is a group of individuals who work across physical and organizational boundaries through the use of technology. (Later in this chapter, I describe one such project in a global company.) Geographic regions in some organizations present nearly impermeable boundaries, even within the same country. At the Internal Revenue Service, for example, before Commissioner Charles Rossotti led the agency in an ambitious organizational transformation during his five-year tenure under President Bill Clinton, regional centers had acted like fiefdoms for decades, sharing neither information nor resources, despite the need to do both. Service representatives were unable to respond to the volume and variety of complex tax questions that would come into the regional center. The result was poor service and frustrated customers. Rossotti took down the regional barriers by combining all service representatives into one centralized national call center. Employees did not physically move. They still lived and worked in the old geographic locations, but they became part of one large virtual service team that was able to spread the workload in sensible and equitable ways.[14] This organizational change allowed taxpayers' technical queries to be routed to those individuals with expertise in a particular aspect of the tax code—no matter where they were located.

Status Boundaries

Disparity diversity may be the most challenging boundary to cross in teaming. When those at the top have the most power and those at the bottom have the least, lower-power individuals usually find it hard to speak up. Perhaps the most common power differences within work teams are professional status and ethnicity. Professional status can significantly affect beliefs about taking interpersonal risks and speaking up. In health care, for example, physicians have more status and power than nurses, who in turn have more status than technicians. Yet members of these professions often must team to take care of patients. Even people from the same profession can have status differences. Consider resident-level and senior ("attending") physicians working together to care for patients. Fears about taking interpersonal risk can prohibit candid discussion and hinder collaboration. Yale professor Ingrid Nembhard and I conducted a study of intensive care units (ICUs) in which we found that the status differences that exist between physicians, nurses, and respiratory therapists led to significant differences in psychological safety across these groups, which affected their willingness to speak up, ask questions, and participate in improvement efforts.[15] When we looked at the data more closely, we discovered that some unusual ICUs didn't show any status-based difference in psychological safety. Instead, these units were workplaces where everyone, no matter what role, felt equally engaged and able to participate in the collaborative work of caring for patients. These units also showed significantly more clinical improvement in outcomes over the two years of the study.[16]

My recent research with Professor James Detert of Cornell (described in Chapter Two) uncovered taken-for-granted beliefs about speaking up in hierarchies that pose a real challenge to cross-status teaming. Each of us, without consciously realizing it, has well-learned taken-for-granted rules for when to openly share our ideas, concerns, or questions with people above us in an organizational hierarchy. For example, many tacitly assume that ideas for change will be seen by senior managers as a criticism (whether or not that's accurate). And most people are naturally reluctant to avoid criticizing people in positions of power.[17]

Note that demographic differences (differences based on gender, race, religion, and other social categories), which may readily be seen as variety diversity, sometimes also enforce a power hierarchy due to the nature of social power in various cultures and countries. For example, power and status differences in organizations have been documented for both gender and race.[18] In addition, individuals aware of negative stereotypes associated with cultural identity may become hindered by self-fulfilling prophecies or a perceived need to overcome negative stereotypes.[19] Similarly, unconscious negative stereotypes significantly hinder group performance because individuals tend to skirt or avoid the issue, allowing negative stereotypes to arise in other, more subtle ways.[20]

Knowledge Boundaries

Work teams often confront differences in expertise. In product and process development teams, for example, it is increasingly common to bring together people from different organizational functions for a limited period of intense teaming. The value of teaming is that different experts bring different knowledge and skills to the collaborative task. In product development, engineering offers insight into design and technology; manufacturing into feasible production processes, accurate cost estimates, pilot and full-scale production; and marketing into customer receptivity, customer segments, product positioning, and product plans. Teaming is the process of integrating these diverse skill sets and perspectives, as well as coordinating timelines and transferring resources across groups, when appropriate. However, diverse groups often have difficulty accessing and managing disparate knowledge, for two reasons. Misunderstandings arise due to different meanings embedded in different disciplines, and mistrust arises between groups.

Teaming Across Common Boundaries

Sharing knowledge across boundaries may not be natural in large organizations, but it's certainly worth the effort. Successfully overcoming the obstacles of teaming across boundaries offers valuable learning for individuals and provides a vital competitive advantage for organizations. Working across the three types of boundaries described in the previous section requires attention to their unique challenges and to techniques for overcoming them. For reference, Table 6.1 summarizes these common boundaries and their accompanying tactics.

As shown in Table 6.1, physical and status differences arise from distance and hierarchy, respectively, whereas knowledge boundaries arise from two distinct origins—membership in different organizations and membership in different occupations. The following sections explore the implications of teaming across each boundary and present strategies for successful teaming and learning within diverse groups.

Teaming Across Distance Boundaries

"Sharing is not a natural thing," said Benedikt Benenati, the organizational development director at the multinational food company, Groupe Danone.[21] With subsidiaries in 120 countries, Groupe Danone is a multinational corporation that sought to promote teaming across the geographical boundaries of its many divisions.

Table 6.1: Common Boundaries That Impede Teaming and Organizational Learning

Boundary Type	Physical Distance	Status	Knowledge-Based	
Arises due to:	Dispersed geographic locations	Hierarchy	Different organizations collaborating	Different experts collaborating
Composition of team:	Geographically dispersed team members	Different levels of power or status	From different companies or different sites within a company	Diverse skills and expertise from education or function
Team challenges:	Misunderstandings, miscommunication, and coordination difficulty	Social norms of deference to authority	Competing taken-for-granted assumptions derived from organizational goals or values Competing incentives	Team member allegiance to expertise-based subgroups
Collaboration enabled by:	Periodic visits to other sites Focus on shared goal Knowledge repositories and exchanges	Leadership inclusiveness to minimize experienced status gaps	Explicitly sharing individual perspectives Emphasizing value brought by each organization Focus on shared goal	Proactive sharing of expertise-based knowledge Use of boundary objects like drawings, models, and prototypes

In addition to sharing common problems, such as getting retailers to stock the right amounts of Danone products at the right time, managers in different countries were focused on their own regions, and rarely considered the opportunity to seek ideas from their counterparts in other regions. As Benenati pointed out, the company's senior managers may be part of the problem: "Managers may be reluctant to let their teams discuss among themselves. If members of their team find solutions, then perhaps managers are of no further use."[22] Such reactions and fears are very human, of course, but they also leave opportunities for small process improvements around the globe to go untapped.

Benenati put the need for knowledge sharing in blunt, practical terms: "In a company with 90,000 employees, solutions to the problems of one team are likely to exist elsewhere."[23] To facilitate knowledge sharing and immediate collaborations among people in different locations, but with similar responsibilities, Benenati and his colleague, Franck Mougin, executive vice president of human resources, created what they called Knowledge Marketplaces. These marketplaces were like small improvisational performances punctuating the usual business routine. Nested within regular company conferences, Knowledge Marketplaces took place when managers from across the globe were gathered in one location. Participants in the marketplace wore costumes to mask hierarchical levels and encourage sharing of business and operations ideas. Interacting with a senior vice president in a Yoda mask was less intimidating than approaching that same executive dressed in a suit and tie. Likewise, a new associate dressed as Darth Vader might feel empowered to speak up in ways she might not feel in regular office attire. The atmosphere was clearly playful, and many remarked that the costumes made it easy to trade ideas and practices.

Although spontaneous exchanges of ideas and practical suggestions abounded in the Danone Knowledge Marketplaces, some knowledge exchanges were orchestrated in advance. For these, selected managers were instructed to prepare books with stories of best practices that facilitated successful knowledge sharing. One such book described how the marketing team at Danone Brazil helped the marketing team in Danone France launch a new fat-free dessert. By adapting an existing product from Brazil, Danone France was able to bring a new product to the French market in less than three months. Not only was time saved, but a €20-million business was created with sales superior to the closest competitor. This occurred, however, as a result of Danone's leadership designing a kind of social engineering to overcome the natural tendencies for practical knowledge not to flow across geographic boundaries. When teams or groups do not have the ability to physically meet and exchange ideas, they must rely on technology to span distances, and communicating through information technology brings its own problems.

The information technology that allows us to shrink global distances by sending e-mails hurtling through cyberspace and to fax documents to machines across continents gives us a false sense of security, lulling us into believing that teamwork among geographically dispersed employees requires nothing more than a fast Internet connection or new videoconferencing equipment. In fact, there are substantial barriers to sharing and integrating knowledge that virtual teams must overcome. In some organizations, however, it's the different mindsets across geographic regions, rather than the actual physical distance between them, that present nearly impermeable boundaries. In addition to the obvious challenges brought on by language and time zone differences, some types of knowledge just do not travel well. This is because certain, often very valuable, information is taken for granted by those who are closest to it. This tacit knowledge can be situated in ways that make it invisible to distant team members.

Collaboration across distance boundaries is greatly enabled by coming together physically, if possible, for a rare but valuable face-to-face meeting. This helps build trust and awareness of differences that might have to be taken into consideration during collaborative work. The Knowledge Marketplaces at Danone were an example of this technique. It's also helpful to emphasize a shared goal, to motivate the effort of communicating across distances. A shared goal clearly helped motivate teaming across distance boundaries in the Chilean rescue, for example. And, despite the various challenges of using IT systems effectively, computer-based knowledge management (KM) systems in large companies remain a crucial tool for helping people team across distance boundaries. Recent research shows that globally dispersed software project teams that used knowledge repositories more frequently than their counterparts performed better in both quality and efficiency.[24] The use of stored knowledge, developed by engineers around the world, provided these complex temporary teams with valuable information and techniques that accelerated and improved their collaborative work.

Teaming Across Status Boundaries

Most organizations contain vestiges of hierarchical boundaries. Although a command-and-control model of authority may have been productive in the past, the knowledge economy increasingly requires interactive communication and collaboration. The many problems that hierarchy creates for collaboration have been mentioned in previous chapters. I have also offered practical solutions to the corrosive and stifling effect of hierarchy. (See especially Chapter Four, Making It Safe to Team.) The principal strategy for developing the necessary level of collaboration, however, is leadership inclusiveness, in which higher-status individuals in a group actively invite and express appreciation for the views of others.[25]

Consider the case of Patti Bondurant, senior clinical director at the Regional Center for Newborn Intensive Care at Cincinnati Children's Hospital. Bondurant felt that having the respiratory therapists, rather than the physician-director of the unit, lead an improvement project was a key driver to their improvement. She described this new relationship as follows:

> The turning point for us was when our respiratory therapy clinical managers in all three of the units said, "With all due respect, doctor, this is our expertise and you need to let us do our job." It was a really defining moment for this group. The doctor sat back and said, "I believe you're right. I don't need to hang onto control when there are people willing to do the work." . . . Those doctors were open to say, "Yes, you're the experts and we're going to let you do your job." The dynamic shifted from doctor sitting at the head of the table, to all of us becoming common denominators at the table.[26]

This is a "textbook moment" of teaming across hierarchical boundaries. The respiratory therapy clinical managers, lowest on the ladder, felt valued enough to speak clearly and directly to their institutional superiors with both expertise and a point of view. The doctors, at the top of the ladder, were able to sit back, listen, agree, and learn, thereby relinquishing control over every aspect of the project. Most important, spanning this boundary allowed a renegotiation of responsibilities, which in turn allowed improved care for the newborn patients.

Teaming Across Knowledge Boundaries

Organization and occupation are two important sources of knowledge boundaries. The former exists anytime people from different companies—or even sites within companies as we saw at the IRS—have to work together. The latter is driven by differences in areas of expertise, within and between organizations.

Organization-based. Organizational membership brings with it taken-for-granted, or "tacit," knowledge shared by other members of the same organization. People working together acquire shared experiences and practices that begin to seem (to them) like the obvious right way to do things. This tacit knowledge might consist of expectations about a particular supplier's reliability, the performance of a particular piece of equipment, or even awareness of who knows what in a given facility. Some things you just have to be on site to know. And because this kind of knowledge is taken for granted, people often don't realize that what they know is important to share. It is also the case that these kinds of knowledge boundaries often coexist with distance boundaries, which further raises the communication hurdle.

Consider the example of a new product development team in a large highly technical business charged with carrying out a project to develop a polymer for a new customer in a strategic market sector. With seven people dispersed across five sites on three continents, teleconferencing allowed the team extensive brainstorming and discussion, yet one ingredient for the new polymer proved unexpectedly difficult to source. One member of the team, an engineer in the United Kingdom whom I'll call David Thompson, turned to his local, on-site colleagues for help. As Thompson tells it, he was "just talking" when a colleague at his site happened to mention that he was making the difficult-to-source ingredient and could reserve a barrel for Thompson's team. It's the "just talking" around the proverbial watercooler that is situational, often crucial, and easily misunderstood by distant colleagues.[27]

Perhaps it's no surprise that tacit knowledge still figures prominently in the twenty-first century, despite vast technical advances. One of the greatest challenges of teaming is finding ways to augment high-tech mediated collaboration by actively seeking out tacit knowledge to use in other locations. The trick for accomplishing this is for each team member to enroll his or her local colleagues by keeping them in the loop with basic project updates. That way, they can offer relevant knowledge, both technical and organizational, when needed. This scouting activity often involves lateral and downward searches through the organization to understand who has relevant knowledge and expertise.[28] Periodic visits are also wonderful ways to uncover tacit knowledge! Research on virtual teams has shown that visiting each other's sites is a powerful way to foster trust, understanding, and collaboration.[29] When teams are able to discover and leverage site-specific tacit knowledge, they are better able to take advantage of their diverse knowledge. Emphasizing the value brought by each organization helps this happen.

Occupation-based. Training for any one profession is often a long process of mastering a specialized body of knowledge, terminology, and above all, a mindset or way of knowing. Business students learn about marketing, management, and how to interpret company problems. Medical students learn about ligaments, blood vessels, and how to recognize disease. Writers learn about how to use language. Each profession is trained to make particular assumptions and epistemological assertions, which often become taken for granted. Jargon, acquired in specialized education and practice, often means that occupations speak different languages. This makes sharing across the "thought worlds" of occupational communities highly vulnerable to misunderstanding. In many cases, meaning is lost, errors are made, and synergy fails to materialize.

Expertise diversity is a key source of innovation. Individuals from different groups weave their ideas and knowledge into new, integrated forms. This type of synthesis is tricky even in mature industries, but particularly when confronting new or novel problems, as occurred in the Autodesk building project (discussed later). Colocation, along with a lot of communication, and excitement about the innovative building they were trying to build, were essential to the team's ability to build trust across occupational boundaries that had long been antagonistic in the industry. Working across occupational boundaries is replete with technical and interpersonal challenges. It also comes with the territory of *cross-functional teams.*

Teams with occupational and expertise differences aligned with organizational departments or functions are termed *cross-functional teams*. Such teams are on the rise in organizations, especially for innovation projects. The goal of cross-functional teaming is to bring together experts of various kinds who can combine knowledge gleaned from their distinct training to produce results that can't be achieved by any single discipline. Cross-functional teams are useful in organizations because they serve as a mechanism for combining different sets of highly specialized skills into one cohesive group. The obvious benefit of this form of collaboration is the qualified, high-level information that can be provided by each team member.

For example, cross-functional teaming allowed Dr. Fred Ryckman, a transplant surgeon at Cincinnati Children's Hospital and Medical Center, to overcome seemingly insurmountable capacity constraints in operating room scheduling. The hospital needed at least one more operating room (OR) to accommodate the increased surgical volume. Because of this limitation, patients had to wait longer for care and surgeons had to work longer hours than might be safe. But a new operating room costs upwards of $2.5 million; money that would be difficult and time-consuming to raise. Unfortunately, tackling the capacity problem with the other surgeons failed to produce any viable solutions. Everyone understood the need to share available resources, but no one could figure out how to stretch the hours in a day to meet the rising demand.

Instead, by teaming with a computer scientist and a statistician, Ryckman was able to explore different, innovative possibilities. The statistician abstracted the problem into one of numbers: arrival times, procedure times, and dates. The computer scientist reorganized the data and ran complex analyses. In very little time, a team of experts with varied backgrounds was working to figure out ways to redesign the existing system for operating room allocations. Only when Ryckman began teaming cross-functionally did a solution begin to seem possible. Professionals outside the operating room asked questions that Ryckman had never considered. The resulting changes reoriented what were previously thought of as natural assumptions about OR capacity and scheduling. Together, Ryckman and his team created a model that dramatically altered and improved how operating rooms were used. They discovered that how patients flowed through the hospital system made a huge difference in how well operating rooms were used. The details, in Ryckman's own words, illuminate how this works:

> By smoothing our OR flow and dedicating different ORs for scheduled surgeries versus unscheduled emergency surgeries, we were able to increase throughput by five percent. This doesn't seem like a big deal, but we run 20 operating rooms, so a five percent increase equals one additional OR being available. It costs $2.5 to $3 million to build a standard OR that can do typical procedures. A neurosurgery room with an integrated MR [magnetic resonance] suite can cost almost $10 million. If you can go in and manage it better, you won't have to build a new room.[30]

Research has shown that the challenge of occupational boundary spanning can be mitigated through the use of what are called *boundary objects* around which diverse groups can coalesce. Boundary objects like drawings, prototypes, and components are tangible representations of knowledge. Professor Paul Carlile of Boston University studied knowledge barriers in new product development teams in the automotive industry. He found that boundary objects facilitated spanning occupation and expertise boundaries. By pointing to and discussing elements in a model or schematic, the obfuscating qualities of jargon can be overcome.[31] Similarly, University of California, Davis professor Beth Bechky has found that while working face to face in a production facility engineers, technicians, and assemblers can cocreate meaning, reaching across the boundaries between practices to do so.[32] This process, which generates fuller understanding of the products and problems they face, involves more than just discussion, but also shared action; for example, convening around a common machine or drawing to articulate different perspectives and develop a shared understanding. It also facilitates sharing expertise-based knowledge.

Occupation and organization combined. When knowledge boundaries based on expertise or profession are confounded with knowledge boundaries that exist between companies, the challenge intensifies. A complex building project, for example, brings together multiple areas of expertise as well as multiple companies to produce a customized product with unique constraints and goals. Participants in this process—owners, architects, engineers, and builders—have traditionally managed the manifold risks they face through legal contracts rather than through teaming, leaving the industry with a history of deep mistrust between professions.[33] The next section includes discussion of a strategy for overcoming the mistrust and misunderstandings that these organizational boundaries have created.

Some recent innovative building projects have attempted to change the counterproductive dynamics in the construction industry by teaming across boundaries from the beginning of a project until the very end. The goal is to avoid the small failures that are nearly inevitable in complex, unique projects, and of course to avoid large failures, too. My colleague Faaiza Rashid and I studied a project that employed such an approach, called Integrated Project Delivery (IPD). Individuals from the multiple companies and professions in a large building project agreed to work together closely from project start to completion. Locating together in one workplace near the building site, everyone signed a single legal contract. Despite aggressive targets in budget, deadline, aesthetics, and environmental sustainability that made the project especially challenging, the teaming worked, trust grew, and the result was an award-winning building for the Boston area headquarters of software company Autodesk.[34]

Teaming across boundaries of all kinds has the potential to help participants increase their knowledge of other fields. Working in diverse teams can expand participants' networks of colleagues from other areas of the organization and improve their boundary-spanning skills. This last point is particularly important because most teams must work across more than one diversity type or organizational boundary to solve today's most complex problems. In the next section, I offer suggestions to help leaders facilitate cross-boundary communication.

Leading Communication Across Boundaries

There are three actions leaders can take to facilitate communication across boundaries. First: frame a shared goal that unites people and motivates willingness to overcome communication barriers. Second: display curiosity to legitimize sharing information and asking questions. Third: provide process guidelines to help structure collaboration. Let's look at each of these actions to see how they can make teaming across boundaries smoother in spite of the obstacles we've discussed.

Establish a Shared Superordinate Goal

In a complex teaming effort, individuals and subgroups have many small goals to achieve along the way (drill a hole without collapsing more rock, complete an aesthetically pleasing building design), but sharing an overarching or "superordinate" goal (rescue the miners, complete an ambitious building project on time and under budget), helps motivate people to communicate thoroughly and carefully. Emphasizing a shared goal (as discussed in Chapter Four) should be recognized as one of the core leadership framing tasks. A goal can be framed as something important and inspiring (helping patients recover faster) or as just another job (implementing a new technology). When the path forward to its completion is unclear, a superordinate goal should be framed as a learning opportunity. Framing a shared goal as a learning opportunity helps level the playing field and facilitates speaking up. This also helps to build a psychologically safe environment. Team members must feel safe asking what could be considered a "dumb question" in an effort to better understand each other's "thought worlds." They must be able to share their perspectives without embarrassment.

One extraordinarily successful cross-boundary teaming project was the design and construction of the Water Cube, the aquatics center built for the Beijing Olympics. The goal was clear and exciting: build a memorable, iconic building for swimming and diving that would reflect Chinese culture, integrate with the site, and minimize energy consumption. Because the design would compete in an international competition, everyone wanted it to be novel, exciting, and unique. And, of course, it had to be finished before the Olympic Games began. Moving from concept to completion in record time, the Water Cube utilized cross-disciplinary, cross-continent, and cross-organizational teaming. Led by Tristram Carfrae, principal and senior structural engineer at Arup in Sydney, Australia, the teaming involved more than 80 individuals from four organizations (Arup, PTW Architects, China State Construction and Engineering Company, and China Construction Design International), spread across twenty disciplines and offices in four countries.

Be Curious

To help people cross boundaries, leaders must display and encourage genuine curiosity about what others think, worry about, and aspire to achieve. By cultivating one's own curiosity about what makes others tick, each of us can contribute to creating an environment where it's acceptable to express interest in others' thoughts and feelings. MIT professor Edgar Schein, a preeminent researcher on corporate culture, uses the term "temporary cultural island" in his description of a process for sharing crucial professional and personal information in a multicultural work group. The process involves talking about concrete experiences and feelings, and is fueled by thoughtful questions on the part of a leader, acting as a facilitator. Schein explains that cultural assumptions related to authority and intimacy are crucial issues in culturally diverse teams. When someone violates an authority rule that is taken for granted in one culture—for example, by speaking in an overly familiar manner to a high-status person—someone from another culture may experience it as jarring. By sharing stories in which these issues are exposed, boundaries begin to dissolve.[35] Note that the term *culture* applies to nations, companies, professions, and other identity groups.

The Water Cube team similarly fostered curiosity by bringing people together at several points to talk about design ideas, brainstorm possibilities, and dig into how cultural meanings of design elements differed across nations. Interacting across different cultures was a significant challenge for the team. One technique that worked well was exchanging specialists who had familiarity with both cultures, asking them to go work *in* the other firm for a period. These literal boundary-spanners helped project members to get interested in each other's language, norms, practices, and expectations.

Provide Process Guidelines

In any complex teaming effort, it is important to establish process guidelines that everyone agrees to follow. A strategy for boundary management is essential. Guidelines are needed for specifying points at which separate teaming activities must come together to coordinate resources and decisions. Carfrae and his team thus adopted a strategy for "interface management" that divided the project into "volumes" based on physical and temporal boundaries. Each volume was owned by a subteam. An interface existed when anything touched or crossed a boundary. Regular interface coordination meetings were held to manage physical, functional, contractual, and operational boundaries. Through extensive documentation, the team eliminated mistakes that might otherwise occur at these boundaries—saving materials, funds, and headaches.[36]

Leadership Summary

The complex, interdependent tasks of learning and innovation can no longer be accomplished by a single individual or even by a set of individuals working sequentially (in a hands-off scenario). Whether developing new products, delivering health care, or collecting and processing a nation's taxes, multiple disciplines and locations increasingly need to work together to get the job done. Teams that succeed today don't just work around a shared conference table—they collaborate across boundaries of several kinds. But the barriers to teaming across boundaries are often underestimated. In some workplaces, daily face-to-face interactions allow people to talk to each other and share ideas easily. In others, thousands of miles separate those with shared responsibilities, and communicating is more difficult. And borders aren't the only boundaries that must be crossed when teaming. Occupational, hierarchical, and cultural divisions also exist. Effective teaming, therefore, starts with identifying and acknowledging boundaries.

Diversity gives rise to novel possibilities by combining knowledge across intellectual, functional, and other boundaries. Research has clearly shown that groups and individuals both can learn more when they span boundaries between disciplines and locations. But it's not easy to do it well. Team leaders and team members must learn to span the boundaries within and between organizations that stifle the flow of information and inhibit collaboration.

Fortunately, such ordinary behaviors as asking for help, offering help, expressing curiosity, and voicing interpretations all can work magic in lowering the obstacles to collaboration.

Leaders play an essential role in breaking down the boundaries that impede knowledge sharing and collaboration. Through leadership inclusiveness, the creation of knowledge exchanges, and the use of boundary objects, leaders can increase best practice sharing and innovation. It's essential to remember that fear in teams where status differences are prominent can hinder communication and sharing. Research finds that psychological safety makes it easier to communicate and experiment across boundaries.[37] When organizations create an inclusive environment and master the ability to trade and employ knowledge across organizational boundaries, they can begin implementing a new way of operating called execution-as-learning. Explored in depth in the next part of this book, execution-as-learning is an iterative process that combines continuous learning and improvement with productivity.

LESSONS AND ACTIONS

- People teaming in today's workplaces are unlikely to be homogenous in beliefs, attitudes, or opinions. When not managed consciously and carefully, these differences can inhibit collaboration.

- The term *boundaries* refers to both visible and invisible divisions between people, including gender, occupation, or nationality. Boundaries exist based on the taken-for-granted assumptions and diverse mindsets that people hold in different groups.

- Boundary spanning involves deliberate attempts to reach across the barriers that exist within and between groups of all kinds. Rapid developments in technology and the greater emphasis on globalization have greatly increased the significance of boundary spanning in today's work environment.

- The three most common boundaries confronted in teaming are: physical distance (differences in location), knowledge-based (differences in organization or expertise), and status (differences in hierarchical or professional status).

- Establishing a superordinate goal, fostering curiosity, and providing process guidelines are important leadership actions for promoting good communication across boundaries.

- To overcome geographic boundaries, group members should make periodic visits to other sites, pay close attention to unique local knowledge, and contribute to knowledge repositories and exchanges.

- To overcome knowledge boundaries created by organizational diversity, group members should share individual perspectives, emphasize the value brought by each organization, and establish a collective identity.

- To overcome knowledge boundaries created by occupational diversity, groups should share expertise-based knowledge, establish a collective identity, and use boundary objects, such as drawings, models, and prototypes.

- To overcome hierarchical boundaries and minimizing experienced status gaps, leaders should be inclusive and proactively engage group members in conversation.

part three

execution-as-learning

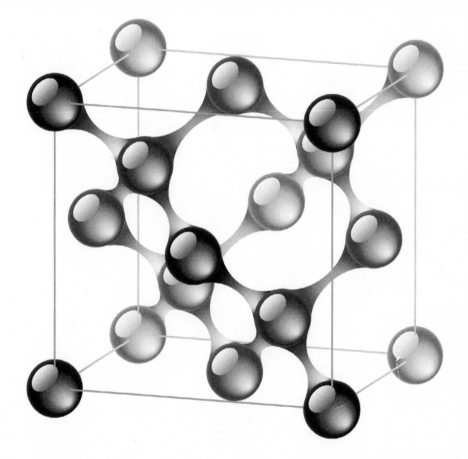

chapter seven

putting teaming and learning to work

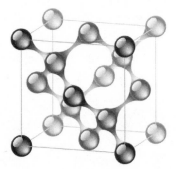

This chapter explores execution-as-learning as a way of operating that contrasts with a more traditional managerial approach that separated learning from execution. Rare in practice, execution-as-learning provides a competitive advantage at any organizational level: product development teams, hospital emergency rooms, and automotive assembly plants alike. Put simply, execution-as-learning is how a learning organization works. Every aspect of execution is conducted with a learning mindset and the liberal use of learning behaviors.

Learning is an imperative for any organization to stay competitive over time. As we saw in Chapter Six, some of this learning takes place among people working across disciplines, nationalities, and even continents. Figuring out new and better ways to do things in an organization, or even finding ways to improve current processes, is more often accomplished by working in flexible, team-based arrangements than by individuals working alone. Research over the last twenty or so years, including my own, has found that teams are a fundamental source of learning and organizational effectiveness.[1] It's little wonder, then, that the workplace of the twenty-first century places a premium on team-based learning.

This chapter takes a closer look at execution-as-learning: how to do it, how to get started, and what it looks like in organizations across the Process Knowledge Spectrum. I offer a diagnostic framework for tailoring execution-as-learning according to where your organization sits on the Process Knowledge Spectrum. A detailed case study shows what happens when this tailoring doesn't occur. I describe the elements of execution-as-learning, explain how it differs from execution-as-efficiency, and provide four essential steps to practicing it.

Execution-as-Learning

Execution-as-learning means operating in a way that allows organizations to learn as they go. It means that work groups, departments, or entire companies can adjust, improvise, or innovate while at the same time successfully delivering products or services to customers. It is a way of operating that is deliberately and consciously iterative, where action and reflection go hand in hand. Figure 7.1 depicts execution-as-learning as comprised of four steps—diagnose, design, act, reflect—supported by a foundation of teaming and organizing to learn.

Execution-as-learning takes place in small groups or teams. Some groups are relatively stable, such as might be found in a factory production line. Others are temporary, including those who care for patients in a hospital, or design new products in cross-

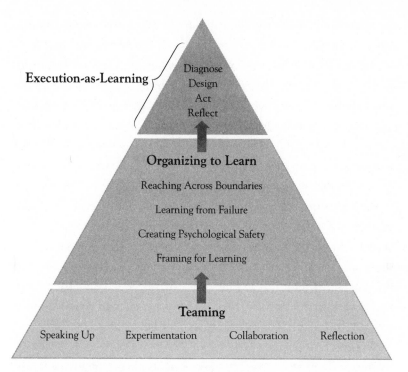

Execution-as-Learning

Diagnose
Design
Act
Reflect

Organizing to Learn

Reaching Across Boundaries

Learning from Failure

Creating Psychological Safety

Framing for Learning

Teaming

Speaking Up   Experimentation   Collaboration   Reflection

Figure 7.1. Foundations of Execution-as-Learning

functional teams. But execution-as-learning is collaborative either way, because varied skill sets and perspectives are needed to suggest possibilities for action and to make sense of results. Working collaboratively means that you always have a sounding board to test out new ideas.

Team-Based, Work-Focused Learning

The use of teams is important for execution-as-learning even when the work itself does not seem to require intensive back-and-forth teaming. For example, each assembly line in a Toyota production facility works as a team—not because the nature of automotive assembly work requires teaming, but rather because continuous improvement activities require it. When undertaking continuous improvement in a Toyota assembly plant, people work together to diagnose and identify problems, to brainstorm possible fixes, and to experiment with solutions. In this setting, the problem-solving cycle is lightning fast—often requiring less than a minute to go from problem identification to solution, as detailed later in this chapter. Toyota worked for decades to build learning into execution, steadily accumulating economic value and quality awards. Later in this chapter, I discuss what happened at Toyota when execution-as-learning faltered in recent years.

Execution-as-learning is also baked into day-to-day operations in the very different setting of Intermountain Healthcare, in Utah and Idaho, widely considered one of the best health care delivery systems in the world. As described in more detail later in this section, an interconnected set of teams identify best practices in the medical literature, modify them if needed, build them into computer-supported protocols, and invite all caregivers to routinely give feedback to help make them better and better.

Southwest Airlines is another good example of team-based learning. Employees execute super-fast airport gate turnarounds; the airline consistently outperforms its competitors in operational measures of all kinds, without sacrificing customer satisfaction.[2]

Swimming Upstream

The good news is that execution-as-learning is a winning formula in almost any context. Toyota, Intermountain, and Southwest are each top performers in their respective industries. The bad news is that it's rare because it doesn't happen naturally. Working in this way requires people to fight against the desire for instructions that specify process steps and guarantee results. It requires swimming upstream. Embracing execution-as-learning as a way of operating means accepting that every process is necessarily inadequate and can always be improved, even if only a little.

Execution-as-learning requires relentless discipline to keep people aware of the imperfection of today's answers and eager to work together to discover new and better ways to do things. It's not that the goal of learning is placed above the goal of meeting today's performance standards; rather it's about doing work in such a way that learning is a valued by-product of action. Execution-as-learning is challenging because most people enjoy the certainty of having a process that works and knowing that they won't be blamed as long as they adhere to that process. Most of us would prefer to have reliable solutions to the problems we face, and we certainly like to feel that we are good at what we do. But execution-as-learning requires us to accept our individual and collective fallibility. Moreover, it requires us to understand that "nothing fails like success." Complacency and arrogance are natural by-products of repeated successes and tend to block awareness of the ways in which yesterday's formula for success slowly, but surely, loses its power.

Execution-as-Learning Versus Execution-as-Efficiency

Execution-as-learning can best be understood in contrast to execution-as-efficiency, a stylized description of classic management approaches to managing work in organizations. In execution-as-efficiency, leaders provide answers. It's assumed that those at the top know more about how to get results than those who do the work at the front lines of production or customer service. Those at the top, along with the smart, technical people they employ, invest considerable effort into figuring out and installing optimal work processes. This investment makes process change unattractive (and rare), because everyone knows that implementing change is a huge undertaking. Feedback is usually a one-way street: bosses tell subordinates whether or not they did what they were supposed to do, and subordinates are not expected to offer solutions or judgments. Finally, execution-as-efficiency tends to use fear as a tool to keep people in line. Indeed, when tasks require little judgment or ingenuity, when they are done by independent individuals, and when quality can be easily observed, then fear can motivate effort without appreciably harming results. Fear may make working conditions unpleasant, but it is unlikely to lower production quality or efficiency for individualistic, routine work. In contrast, when teaming and learning are part of the work, fear is crippling.

For execution-as-learning, leaders are not providing answers, but rather setting direction. Setting direction means describing the priorities that matter most to the organization. Depending on the circumstances, this may mean transforming customer service, improving production quality, or discovering cures for disease. The leader does not, and cannot, specify how to get it done. And so, the "answers" have to be jointly discovered or improved along the way. To a manager seeking to "get the job done," this process might at first seem laborious and slow. But when the effort to engage people as active thinkers and learners gathers momentum, employees' attention and interest can lead to independent initiatives at the front lines. And lowering fear, as already noted, is critical to making that happen. Table 7.1 summarizes this distinction.

Table 7.1: Differences Between Execution-as-Efficiency and Execution-as-Learning

Execution-as-Efficiency	Execution-as-Learning
Leaders have the answers.	Leaders set direction.
Stable work processes are put in place.	Deliberately tentative work processes are put in place as a starting point.
Implementing change is seen as a huge undertaking.	Constant small changes are a way of life.
Feedback is one-way.	Feedback is two-way.
Employee judgment is discouraged.	Employee judgment is essential.
Fear of the boss is normal.	Fear inhibits experimentation, analysis, and problem solving.
Goal: Capture profits today.	Goal: Create long-term value.

Best Practice Is a Moving Target

In execution-as-learning, tentative work processes are provided as a starting point—a way of inspiring improvement as more is learned about what works and what doesn't. One of the exemplars of this approach is Intermountain Healthcare (IHC), the integrated network of hospitals and clinics that has been praised for the quality of its care and for the efficiency of its processes. At Intermountain, teams of senior clinicians who are experts in different areas of medicine use their experience and medical research to develop a protocol, which is essentially a list of steps that clinical staff in the hospital should follow when treating patients with particular diseases. These protocols are then built into the hospital's computer support systems to help guide clinical decisions shaping patient care in the hospital. Actual clinical actions are recorded. This learning system is the brainchild of Dr. Brent James, a physician, statistician, and chief quality officer at IHC. If you're thinking that doctors might not be willing to be told what to do by a computer, you understand the challenge well. So how did Dr. James pull this off?

The secret sauce for encouraging compliance is this: All clinicians are invited to use the protocol as a starting point, not as the law. Anytime a physician's clinical judgment suggests a different action than what is in the protocol, she should rely on her judgment—not on the protocol. The only requirement? Physicians are asked to record what they *actually* did for the patient, feeding this information back to IHC by way of its clinical support information technology (IT) system. This feedback allows the expert teams to learn from physicians' on-the-job experience. Periodically, these teams study the process data to discover what changes may be needed. Through this execution-as-learning system, patients are given care that is rooted in knowledge of the latest medical literature, and, at the same time, the system allows the state of the art to continue to develop through an ongoing learning loop, as depicted in Figure 7.2.

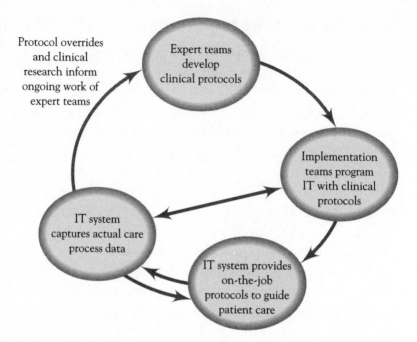

Figure 7.2. A Team-Based Learning System at Intermountain Healthcare

As the expert teams accumulate feedback, two types of improvement are enabled. The first is that practicing physicians discover errors or weaknesses in the protocols, and these are corrected in revised protocols. The second is that the protocols become more fine-grained, that is, more customized for different subgroups of patients. For instance, instead of a one-size-fits-all diabetes protocol, groups of patients based on age, gender, weight, and so forth, are provided with protocols that have been refined to work for their specific situations.

Rather than believing there is one best way to get the work done that can be put to uniform and stable use, many managers, across a variety of industries, recognize that "best practice" is a moving target. Therefore, they seek to inspire people to help current practices get better and better. Through small experiments and by proposing improvements, people working in an execution-as-learning system participate in helping that system evolve. Clearly, employee judgment is essential, and feedback flows both from managers to subordinates and from subordinates to managers.

Using the Process Knowledge Spectrum

Implementing execution-as-learning starts with understanding crucial features of the operating context. It is especially critical to assess the extent to which there is knowledge currently available to produce desired results—that is, where the operation sits on the Process Knowledge Spectrum. Knowing where one's work sits on this spectrum helps frame the learning challenge as one of improvement, problem solving and risk reduction, or innovation.

Knowing Where You Are on the Process Knowledge Spectrum

Although most organizations encompass multiple work contexts in their operations—routine work, complex systems, and innovation—one usually dominates the organizational culture and managerial approach. This is why thoughtful diagnosis of the work ahead, which seems an obvious first step, is often not done. Most managers take their dominant context for granted. For instance, the heart and soul of the automotive industry is high-volume production; the identity of an academic medical center lies in providing complex customized services for unique patients; and basic science is all about discovery.

Because it's easy to take for granted that one's work is routine, or customized, or creative, it's important to pause for thoughtful diagnosis. A manager might ask herself, for example: even though I am working in a century-old car company, does the situation I am managing call for a well-understood process, or are we trying to do something complex or innovative? A manager in a research setting might stop to think: even though this is a scientific laboratory, perhaps a particular aspect of the operation, such as managing payroll or supplies, calls for a more streamlined routine. Because most managers don't consciously think about where their work typically sits on the process knowledge spectrum, they often fail to recognize when a shift in the environment calls for a different approach.

Some work takes the form of well-specified processes that give rise to repeating routines within a defined group or department (for example, assembly lines, call centers), whereas other work presents unfamiliar situations that involve improvisation and active coordination across groups (for example, medical care for a patient with multiple diseases). In other situations, how to accomplish a goal—say, a cure for diabetes or an economically viable source of renewable energy—is still unknown. Only through discovery and innovation will it be achievable. Clearly, the learning challenge in each case is different. As shown in Table 7.2, the managerial focus, the level of uncertainty, the nature of planning, the role of failure, and the nature of success differ across the three types of operations in the Process Knowledge Spectrum.

Diagnosing Uncertainty and Interdependence

Managers face all kinds of uncertainty, depending on the extent and quality of available knowledge—from practically complete to totally inadequate. High uncertainty means that figuring out the best way to achieve the desired results will involve trial and failure. In contrast, when uncertainty is low, achieving desired results does not call for experimentation, but rather presents an opportunity for small refinements to streamline or speed up an existing process. Great scientists intuitively adhere to product design company IDEO's slogan, "Fail often in order to succeed sooner," but this would be a poor system for ensuring success in a manufacturing plant, where learning is characteristically about steady but small improvements. To illustrate, a few years ago, an MBA student at Harvard Business School recalled the instructions given to him as

Table 7.2: How Operating Contexts Differ Along the Process Knowledge Spectrum

	Routine Operations	Complex Operations	Innovation Operations
Work design	Well-established processes	Mix of established, tentative, and novel processes	Consistent process guidelines, unique process details
Uncertainty	Low: results are predictable	Medium: inputs and results are both somewhat unpredictable	High: results are unpredictable
Managerial Focus	Control and measurement	Building a culture of openness and vigilance	Inspiring and supporting focused exploration
Planning	Interdependencies are managed in advance	Many interdependencies must be managed real-time through back-and-forth communication	Understanding of interdependencies has to be developed along the way

(Continued)

Table 7.2 (Continued)

	Routine Operations	Complex Operations	Innovation Operations
Failure Frequency (Dominant Type)	Avoidable and infrequent (Process Deviation)	Expected—vigilance essential (System Breakdown)	Frequent and even desirable (Unsuccessful Trial)
Organizational-Learning Goal	Continuous improvement	Problem solving	Innovation
Critical Learning Tools	Total Quality Management (TQM); Statistical Process Control (SPC); Andon Cord	A psychologically safe culture; Vigilant interpersonal communication	Structured innovation processes; Cross disciplinary teams
Measure of Success	Efficiency/Reliability	Safety/Quality	Innovation/Discovery
Exemplar	Automotive Assembly Plant	Tertiary Care Hospital	Product Design Consultancy

a newly hired engineer at Toyota: stand in that small square (drawn on the floor of the assembly plant) and look around until you can find something to improve. Although the factory was renowned as one of the best in the world, its leaders believed deeply that a smart young person, new to the system, could help make it better. The experience also conveyed to the new hire that the company was serious about learning.

Another important diagnostic dimension is the level of interdependence the work requires. Some tasks can be done by a single individual working alone; others require people with different skill sets or access to different information to engage in coordination or collaborative problem solving. When interdependence and uncertainty are both high, getting it right the first time is unlikely, and those doing the work have to play an active role in the design for action. A detailed example of this, in which IDEO pioneers a new type of consulting service, is provided in Chapter Eight. Recognizing its lack of knowledge about how to proceed, the firm experimented at a small scale in an effort to learn quickly. Designs to build in continuous learning differ according to the levels of predictability and complexity in specific contexts.

Achieving Congruence

Achieving congruence between the management approach and the business context doesn't happen automatically. To begin with, the force of habit is powerful. All of us are vulnerable to wielding a hammer and treating everything as a nail. Many managers have a signature style or approach that they will bring to any situation. In addition, managers often fail to notice that technological or market shifts have changed the game in important ways. They are slow to realize that the situation may call for a different response from the one that worked so well in the past.

Consider the following example from one of the earliest large-scale industries. Founded soon after the telephone was invented, the telecommunications industry experienced steady growth for more than a century as populations and economies grew. In recent years, of course, telecommunications transformed from the immense regulated national monopolies of the past to the dynamic, competitive, high-technology information businesses of the present. In the midst of that transformation, a major telecommunications company I studied, which I will call Telco, was poised uneasily between the routine business of the past and the innovative and uncertain businesses ahead. As you will see, in a successful routine operations business, uncertainty does not always announce itself.

Facing a Shifting Context at Telco

Bruce Madison, senior vice president of business development at Telco paced his carpeted office, contemplating the decision.[3] In his long and satisfying career at Telco, he'd made plenty of tough decisions that helped make the telephone company one of the most successful and well run in the industry. But new technologies were bringing changes, known and unknown, that would affect Telco's future. With only two months left in the twentieth century, change was in the air. The question Madison faced was: How, and how quickly, should Telco take advantage of digital subscriber line (DSL) technology as a way to offer customers high-speed Internet access? Madison wanted his company to be positioned at the forefront of new technology. He certainly wanted to gain a first-mover advantage in a competitive marketplace. But he did not want to implement something too soon and too complex, especially if it would end up frustrating customers and tarnishing Telco's excellent reputation.

Put simply, Madison didn't want to fail.

Installing the new technology would require new steps at the interface between Telco and its customers. For instance, technicians would have to ensure a separation between voice and data streams on each customer's premises, and they would have to install a modem to connect each customer's unique computer to the data stream. Old wires would need to be replaced. Thousands of access lines would have to be inspected and approved for DSL use. All of these small and large tasks were vulnerable to missteps and failures, especially when performed for the first time. And customer frustration would harm the brand the company had worked so hard to build. Telco's reputation rested upon the reliability of thousands of repeating transactions that produce phone service that works every time.

A History of Successful Execution

Madison wanted to expand Telco's service offerings while maintaining the company's long-standing record of successful execution. Customer access problems would bring phone calls and complaints, and should be avoided. Telco's high-quality customer service had long been key to the company's success. A strong culture, impeccable attention to detail, extensive training (customer service reps received three months of training when they joined the company), and endless measurement combined to give the company a great reputation. Managers did not take success for granted. New service representatives were given a script detailing what to say to customers who called with complaints, billing inquiries, or requests for new telephone service. On the job, employees were routinely monitored, and a customer satisfaction index (CSI) tracked the mood of customers. Management objectives were set with care, and performance was constantly evaluated against them. Customer surveys evaluated customer satisfaction with all aspects of service, including resolution of problems, placing orders, and so on. Telco's discipline was truly remarkable.

It should be easy to recognize Telco's approach as *organizing to execute*. Its well-developed systems and measurements allowed the company to predict, with enormous precision, the level of demand for and satisfaction with its services. Even predicting the duration of an average service call was feasible. To ensure management interest and compliance, Telco tied managers' bonuses to CSI performance. And the system worked! For years.

Yet the very methods that had made Telco's customer service a success proved to be its downfall when implementing DSL.

Surprised by Failure

Despite the risks, Madison and his team made the decision to go full speed ahead with a full-scale DSL rollout. The strategic opportunity was irresistible. And Telco was expert at high-volume operations. The outcome, unfortunately, was a dismal failure—one that persisted longer than any of them would have thought tolerable. The CSI, normally in the high 80s, dove down to the teens for the DSL operation, which missed 75 percent of its commitments and accumulated 12,000 late orders. As many as 500 customers a day were waiting to hear back about some aspect of service. Twenty percent of complaints were taking 30 or more days to resolve. Morale suffered throughout the company, not just in the DSL group, and Madison feared employee burnout. In short, recalled Madison: "We had so many more problems than we anticipated, and we didn't have the resources to fix everything instantly."

Bruce Madison was a smart and effective executive with the best intentions for his company, employees, and customers. The disaster that Telco inadvertently spawned had to do with how much Madison and his colleagues managed according to principles designed for routine operations. The problem was that DSL, which would become routine soon enough, was new at the time. Its implementation was thus not the kind of routine, well-understood process conducive to precise measurements and definitive targets. Despite executives' near certainty about customer *demand* for high-speed Internet service, the process knowledge for how to *deliver* that service reliably across diverse customer situations was still woefully immature. Not consciously considering this mismatch, Telco was in a position of managing an initiative that should have been treated as a complex new operation, as a routine operation.

Until variability could be diagnosed and numerous new processes developed and codified to cover the wide and uncertain terrain, there could be no metrics, no precision, no guaranteed results. No one knew exactly how long it would take to repair thousands of miles of customer access lines, much less provide actual DSL service. Telco would have to work across department and company boundaries to integrate systems of multiple vendors. They would have to learn, and learn as teams, as they went along. That meant that service representatives could not simply follow scripts carefully compiled from a comprehensive database of troubleshooting events. Nor could they be extensively trained in procedures. A script can only be written if you already know what needs to happen to get the job done—and you expect the process to remain fixed for a while.

Organizing to Learn

Instead, on-the-job learning was needed to discover and use new answers simultaneously. Without a script, employees would have to improvise. This meant they would make mistakes. Managers would have to act in ways that made it clear they understood that excellent performance did not mean *not making mistakes*. Instead, it meant learning quickly from mistakes and sharing the lessons widely—the very essence of organizing to learn. Table 7.3 summarizes the difference between organizing to execute and organizing to learn, in the context of Telco's new initiative.

Many technology companies serve early adopters first. These are the pioneers, eager to be on the leading edge of technology, technically savvy, and tolerant of early hiccups in a new product or service. Those who need more hand-holding can wait until the kinks are worked out. At Telco, marketing rhetoric (which reflected an organizing-to-execute mindset) over-promised the miracle of high-speed Internet access. Customers trusted Telco and expected the new offering to work seamlessly and effortlessly, just like a home phone works effortlessly every single time you pick up the

Table 7.3: Contrasting Approaches for Routine Versus Complex Operations

Routine Telephone Service	Brand-New DSL Service
Follow a script	Improvise
Learning before doing	Learning on the job
Adherence to procedures	Deliberate experimentation
Mistakes are rare	Mistakes are frequent, learned from, and shared
Organizing to execute	*Organizing to learn*

receiver. These expectations, fueled by the company's own decisions about how to introduce the new service, were too often profoundly disappointed.

The crucial question that no one had asked before the launch was this: How do we organize to learn? The company's organizing-to-execute mindset made it difficult for managers to think differently, especially in the middle of a crisis. Recognizing the imperative of getting things done—on time and under budget—managers at Telco had long focused on making sure employees were provided with answers, were trained to execute them, and understood the consequences of not following through. As discussed in Chapter One, this mindset works well when the work is well understood. But even the most detailed plans and disciplined execution cannot guarantee success when knowledge about how to do something is still in flux.

In reality, reliability (of the *it-works-every-time* sort) was still some months, maybe over a year, away. Of course it was achievable. By organizing to learn, the systems needed to produce reliable, routine performance in the future would soon be discovered. Rather than a top-down, execution machine, Telco had to use a new approach, allowing a small part of its organization to forge a path into the new terrain. Organizing to learn for a new initiative is often a temporary state. After a while, when done well, new systems are developed, standardized, and ready for high-volume efficient execution.

More generally, facing novelty and uncertainty, managers must stimulate and guide a collective learning process. This process involves trading in the traditional role of monitoring, measuring, and rewarding people for adherence to procedure. The new role— one that can aptly be described as "chief scientist" or "principal investigator"—involves helping to design and motivate the small experiments through which a new procedure can be jointly discovered.

Don't Roll Out, Cycle Out!

Rather than a full-scale, widely advertised "rollout" of the new service, Telco might have engaged a few pioneering customers who would happily tolerate blips and flops along the way to success. Motivated by their role as coinvestigators, these pioneers might even relish the blips and flops. Similar to Amazon.com customers who voluntarily review books and post their thoughts on the website, Telco's customer coinvestigators would voluntarily report not just problems encountered, but also solutions devised. Together, company and customer would learn as they go. Eschewing a mass-market push, Telco would seek out early adopters carefully—the computer cognoscenti and the merely curious with slack time— customers who were willing to try and fail together. It would not be long before the problems all would be solved, the kinks discovered and worked out, in an inevitable march toward reliable easy-to-use DSL service, which today's customers take for granted. A *rollout*, as one might roll out a carpet, implies that something is ready to go, all set, just needs a bit of momentum to propel it forward. Cycling out involves iteration and learning.

The trick, therefore, for Telco or any company undertaking an uncertain new endeavor is to learn from early experiences (preferably at a small scale) as quickly as possible so as to later provide a high-quality product or service to a mass market. With this mindset, each customer encounter is implicitly conceptualized as an experiment, rather than as a mere service transaction. Instead of a rollout, this is a "cycle out"—each step, each experiment, is different from the one before. Its design has benefited from the knowledge gained in the prior cycle. Sure, the process rolls out, but bumpily. For example, Netflix introduced its Watch Instantly offering in successive waves of 250,000 customers at a time, taking six months to cycle out its instant downloading technology. During this time the company constantly checked in with customers via follow-up e-mails that inquired about the quality of specific movies watched. It also set up and actively monitored a Netflix Blog to explain operations, step-by-step, and to respond to frequent customer posts about problems, requests, and suggestions. This is the kind of practice that companies use when organizing to learn.

Above all, the goal for a new or complicated service delivery is to *fully exploit employee capabilities and experiences to help the firm learn*. This approach is both obvious and counterintuitive at the same time. Although it makes sense to experiment and learn as you go when all the kinks aren't worked out, too often managers accustomed to managing for efficiency—to meet the numbers— might miss the opportunity to change their approach.

The Telco case shows what happens when there is a mismatch between the managerial approach (organizing to execute) and the situation (launching a complex new service). Eventually, the DSL problems were all solved and the service became routine. Happily, efficient execution again became the norm. But execution-as-learning could have dramatically lowered the costs of this transition. The four steps of execution-as-learning are described in the next section.

Learning That Never Ends

Execution-as-learning builds on classic models of individual learning, in which conceptual and practical knowledge grows through iterative cycles of action and reflection.[4] In execution-as-learning, people must communicate with each other; this is the only way the learning can be collective in nature.[5] Individuals can learn when they think, decide, act, and reflect privately, but collective learning requires spoken or written conversation. A growing literature on team learning has investigated how teams learn new tasks, as well as how teams engage in continuous improvement, problem solving, and innovation.[6] Across the board, learning occurs in cycles. Learning cycles in teams may take months or minutes depending on the nature of the work.

As depicted in Figure 7.3, execution-as-learning involves four essential steps:

- **Diagnosing** the situation, challenge, or problem facing the organization, including how much is currently known about how to execute in such a situation.

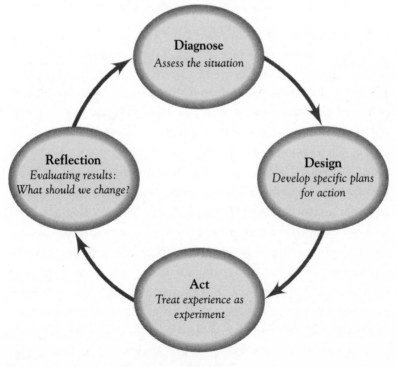

Figure 7.3. Practicing Execution-as-Learning

- **Designing** an appropriate action plan for execution-as-learning.

- **Acting** on the new plan, while viewing it as an experiment from which to learn.

- **Reflecting** on the process and the outcomes, to begin a new cycle.

Let's take a look at each step, using examples and specific suggestions for implementation, where appropriate. However, keep in mind while reading this section that the steps are neither as separate, nor as a linear, as they are presented. Diagnosis, for example, is a form of action. And action at its best is a form of diagnosis. One of the biggest mistakes managers make is conducting extensive diagnostic phases, ostensibly before acting, which can serve both to postpone the kind of critical learning that occurs from trying things out, and to obscure the fact that the diagnosis is itself an intervention.

Diagnosis

The first activity in execution-as-learning is diagnosis. Simply put, diagnosis is sizing up the situation and the challenge that might lie ahead. This means identifying performance shortcomings, process problems, or opportunities for innovation. Diagnosis may take the form of extended analysis, or it may be a quick exchange of one or two ideas to consider. Diagnosis may also involve initial experiments or interventions to find out how the system will respond.

Leaders of both small groups and large enterprises should cultivate a habit of diagnosis. To do this, they have to be actively and constantly seeking to answer the question they are most afraid to ask. The CEO of a major U.S. pharmaceutical company recently described this practice as the core element of his success. Knowing in advance that an anticipated breakthrough drug under development may be late, or worse, may not work at all, is better than finding out later, when investor, customer, and board scrutiny is at its highest level. Knowing bad news early provides more time to develop a new approach. When this does not happen, the results can be tragic. For instance, recall the *Columbia* shuttle mission in 2003 described in Chapter Four. Mission Manager Linda Ham did not draw effectively on the insights of NASA engineers like Rodney Rocha, whose expertise turned out to be critical in diagnosing the threat posed by foam that struck the shuttle during its launch. Diagnosis takes slightly different forms across the Process Knowledge Spectrum, as shown in Table 7.4.

Routine operations. In routine operations, diagnosis usually means assessing performance in a known dimension, using known

Table 7.4: Execution-as-Learning in Three Contexts

	Routine Operations	Complex Operations	Innovation Operations
Diagnose	How are we performing against target measures?	What risks do we face?	What opportunities might we explore?
Design	Select a performance dimension and an approach for improving it.	Identify a problem to solve and brainstorm alternatives.	Decide on one possibility for experimentation and design the first step.
Act	Follow a structured or scripted approach to improvement.	Test an alternative—off-line if in a high-risk operation.	Experiment with prototypes.
Reflect	Did the targeted performance improve?	Did the alternative work to solve the problem or lower the risk?	What do we learn from the failures that occur?

measures. For example, in a call center, a manager might examine customer service ratings, or call duration, to see how the center is performing against targets. Or in a fast-food restaurant chain, it might mean customer satisfaction scores, or simply restaurant cleanliness. When David Novak became CEO of YUM! Brands, the company that runs fast-food restaurant chains including Taco Bell, Pizza Hut, and KFC, he examined customer satisfaction as one crucial measure of the company's performance, and found room for improvement. Diagnosis was followed quickly by improvement efforts, as described later in this section.

In routine operations, diagnosis often involves benchmarking. For example, a public water utility seeking to improve its efficiency can start by visiting a high-performing water utility, thereby identifying both an aspiration level and a set of transferable process solutions at the same time.

Complex operations. In complex operations, diagnosis is usually related to assessing the risks—obvious and latent—faced by the operation. Clinical areas within hospitals that use execution-as-learning frequently stop to consider what risks they may have overlooked or not previously considered. Risks in health care delivery can include the possibility of overt harm to a patient, or simply the possibility of failing to do something to streamline a process or improve a patient's comfort. Similarly, a global supply chain manager might be scanning the news for information about impending hurricanes or supplier problems. Especially in complex operations, diagnosis benefits from asking questions such as: What do we know about this situation? What do we not know (and wish we knew)? What might we be missing altogether in our portrayal of the situation? Psychological safety is critical for diagnosis in this context. Without it, people may not be speaking up about the problems and errors they know exist.

As in routine operations, diagnosis in complex operations also means assessing performance, but safety and quality performance are usually more important than efficiency performance. The most important diagnostic task relates to considering interactions among elements of a system, rather than assessing the performance of separate elements. Thus, as we saw in Chapter Two, participants in the execution of a CT scan may individually be performing perfectly, but the interactions between the separate tasks can create a major malfunction.

Innovation operations. Finally, in innovation contexts, diagnosis is about identifying areas of opportunity. This is part market and technical analysis and part vision. In this setting, it's crucial both to consider unmet customer needs and to daydream about brand-new areas worthy of exploration. At Intuit, the financial software company, for example, engineers sometimes observe customers interacting with the software directly so as to diagnose how easy or difficult it is for them to use the various features built into the product. This diagnostic step allows engineers to observe unmet user needs firsthand, needs that the customers themselves lack either the experience or the vocabulary to voice. Part of diagnosis in innovation is assessing what's feasible, given the current state of technology or the costs of inputs. Opportunities may be wide, but they are not infinite.

Design

The next step, design, shifts from sizing up the situation to considering and selecting possibilities for action. This often involves brainstorming and then narrowing options to a single possibility for action. The design step thus ends with a preliminary commitment to action; this may take the form of a formal decision or plan, or it may be a more gradual shift into agreement about something to try next. A design is simply a statement of what a team will do—or, more precisely, what it will try—to achieve a goal. In general, a design's purpose is to guide action. It sounds simple, but design fosters learning by making action more deliberate and conscious. Figuring out how to accomplish a goal often starts with seeking out existing best practices from experts, publications, or even competitors. These can provide inspiration or even models to copy. But the key to design for execution-as-learning is the recognition that an initial design is just a best guess, a starting point. It may be a very educated guess (when process knowledge is well developed), or just a stab in the dark, a trial that will surely fail to achieve hoped-for results but will provide valuable information. It depends, of course, on the context, as depicted in Table 7.4.

Routine operations. In a routine context, design involves targeting a dimension of performance to improve, which can benefit from structured approaches to improvement. Because process knowledge is so well developed in a routine context, designs for action are limited in scope. The managerial goal is usually to continue what we are doing—but do it better, sometimes much better. In routine operations, a core principle for producing excellence is commitment to continuous improvement, or *kaizen* in Japanese. Designs for action typically rely on structured tools and techniques for improvement, such as are found in the discipline of total quality management (TQM). When Novak decided to target cleanliness at YUM!, he included the reduction of trash in restaurant parking lots. It was then up to local restaurant managers and employees to design ways to make that happen, as well as how to track progress.[7] For example, they might consider the visibility of trash bins, or reduce the sources of trash by considering the amount of packaging used in the food.

Complex operations. In complex operations, the design step works best when it draws on the insights of a diverse group to help identify as many alternatives for action as possible. This diversity was a crucial resource in the successful rescue of the Chilean miners, for example, as described in Chapter Six. Hospitals routinely use teams to design strategies for improving care processes, eliminating errors, or improving patient compliance with instructions, as shown in Chapter Eight. The designs that such teams develop are necessarily imperfect, but they are a starting point, to be modified as more is learned about the challenge.

Innovation operations. In innovation, designing the next experiment thoughtfully can save time and expense later. Recall how the RAZR team (in Chapter Two) brainstormed shapes and features for their telephone, and then tried out mock-ups made of clay before getting too far down the path with real materials. Note that as we move to the right in the Process Knowledge Spectrum, we are less able to predict what will happen as a result of any given design. So, the design—a plan for action—is often just a starting point. It may comprise only a single step forward, one that we expect to revise as soon as we learn more. Thus, for innovation, a focus group might be used to react to an experimental new service or product idea before figuring out all of the details of execution.

Action

The shift from talking to doing, from considering to trying, also happens in teams. A key to effective action in execution-as-learning is making sure to track what actually happens, as well as the results that these actions produce. Traditional management controls emphasize outcome data, which capture results. Execution-as-learning pays just as much attention to process data that describe how work unfolds.

Routine operations. In a routine context like restaurant operations at YUM!, after managers and employees worked together to figure out ways to reduce trash, action took the form of placing trash bins in visible places, with well-marked slots for trash and recycling. Their participation led employees to feel ownership of the goal of reducing trash, and the goal's measurability made it easy to see progress.

Action to improve operational processes is best accomplished by teams. If teams don't yet exist in a routine setting, a crucial action step is forming and training them. For example, at the Washington Suburban Sanitation Commission (WSSC), a water utility in Maryland, General Manager John Griffith instituted self-managed teams throughout the company. Building the new teams was a critical action step on the road to achieving improved operational efficiencies of more than 30 percent in the first couple of years.[8]

Complex operations. In complex operations, action involves the conscious use of new (or existing) designs, to assess their effectiveness, as well as experiments with small changes to assess their impact. At Intermountain, action unfolds when clinicians start to use the protocols designed by the expert teams. As described earlier in this chapter, process data are routinely collected, which allows Intermountain to assess both whether protocols were being used, as well as whether they produced the best outcomes for patients.

In settings where the stakes are too high, making experimentation too risky, simulation is a valuable option for assessing new actions. Simulation is a realistic situation that imitates a real context, either in a virtual (computer) scenario, or in an off-line practice field, either way allowing practice with a new action without the risk of actual harm. Recent research by Rotman School of Management professor Marlys Christianson, who also happens to be trained as a physician, finds that participating in simulated medical event scenarios helps clinicians improve teaming coordination and performance with real patients back on the job.[9] The Water Cube, described in Chapter Six, included 22,000 steel beams, with unimaginably complex shapes and sizes to comprise its iconic soap-bubble design. As Tristram Carfrae explained, "Changing the size of one element would affect the sizes of the other 21,999."[10] Clearly, real-world experiments with changing beam lengths would have been both dangerous and expensive. But it could be done with computer simulation. So the building was designed, tested, and optimized in the virtual world of computer modeling first. In fact, the calculations to do this required computing power that just a year earlier had not been readily available at the cost and speed the project required.

Innovation operations. Rapid, unconstrained action is at the heart of innovation. It's called experimentation. Scientists, of course, routinely experiment, hoping to be first to make an important new discovery in the process. Experiments range from those for which outcomes are all but unknown in advance to those in which strong hypotheses are being tested. In basic research, a scientist with a 70 percent failure rate in the experiments she runs might be in the process of earning a Nobel Prize. The RAZR team tried out several configurations before hitting on the idea of putting the battery next to the circuit board (prior phones had them stacked) to reduce thickness. Teams at IDEO routinely build quick prototypes to see what ideas for new products might look like in three dimensions. The point is simply to try things to see what happens. It's easy to stay in the conceptual plane—to talk about ideas and possibilities forever. A key to successful innovation is making frequent, small forays into action.

Reflection

The goal of collecting process data as part of the action step is to understand what worked and what didn't, and to prevent any detected failures from recurring. Frequent evaluation is essential to execution-as-learning. Reflection is an analytic task. Some reflection is formal and thorough—after-action reviews, or rigorous studies, for instance—but other times evaluation is informal and quick. Through periodic reflection, execution-as-learning enables both small and large improvements to current practices, which are then integrated into the diagnosis and design of the next iteration. At the Cleveland Clinic, for example, teams of physicians study process data and identify areas for improvement throughout the organization's many sites. When I studied it in 2006, the clinic had seven such teams, including heart failure, stroke, diabetes, and orthopedic surgery. Each included doctors from hospitals throughout the system.

As we move to the right in the Process Knowledge Spectrum, evaluation relies less on large, systematic data sets and becomes more qualitative in nature.

Routine operations. Routine operations often require statistical analysis of quantitative data to assess the impact of an action. Detailed information on techniques for data analysis is beyond the scope of this book, but its essential features are the disciplined systematic use of data to detect process failures and to assess the impact of new actions. At Toyota, relentless reflection, or *hansei*, is an essential element of continuous improvement.[11] The literal meaning of *hansei* is to acknowledge your mistake and commit to improvement, which adds to the notion of reflection the idea of taking personal responsibility for improvement. At Toyota, reflection occurs in the moment when a small process problem is detected, addressed, and resolved, real-time as the assembly line moves along.[12] Reflection also occurs periodically, off-line, through the analysis of accumulated data from operations, customers, and so on.

Complex operations. Teams in complex operations reflect on simulated or real changes to assess their impact on risk and quality. Sometimes they reflect on unique events, such as a specific event of medical error, to understand what happened. In my study of 16 cardiac surgery teams discussed in Chapter Three, reflection in the surgical teams that learned the fastest took the form of steady reflection-in-action, rather than infrequent extensive reviews of patient outcomes. The teams that most successfully learned the new procedure engaged in a steady banter about what they were doing, what was happening, and what it was teaching them about how to improve the process. In some contexts, more data are needed for useful reflection. As noted in Chapter Five, Kaiser Permanente needed to accumulate large numbers of mammogram readings to have enough data to detect meaningful patterns from which to learn about different radiologists' performance. Similarly, the expert teams at Intermountain require data from large numbers of patients before they can find ways to improve a clinical protocol.

Innovation operations. Innovation teams consider what can be learned from unique trials and the frequent failures these produce, so as to conduct new trials. Reflecting on failure is rarely fun, but it's essential to figuring out the true causes of a failure, in order to help determine what gets tried next. It's important not to short-change reflection in the desire to move quickly to the next experiment, because high-quality reflection can help avoid predictable failures in subsequent actions. Ed Catmull, founder and president of Pixar, lamented that Pixar employees would just as soon avoid post-project reflection altogether, preferring to relish the success of a film than to stop and identify what could have gone better. To get more out of this critical step he instituted the following: ask participants to list the five things they would do again, and then to discuss five things they wouldn't do. According to Catmull, the positive-negative balance created a safe environment conducive to discussing every aspect of a project thoughtfully.[13]

In any context, in addition to the analysis of data, reflection may involve formal or informal feedback given by team members to each other. The work itself, along with periodic customer comments, may also provide plenty of feedback. Teams should put aside time, periodically, to carefully evaluate what they're learning from the work they're doing and the results they're getting.

It's not easy for a hospital, or any other organization facing cost constraints, to do this. Disciplined evaluation can take productive resources off-line, and conventional management wisdom views this as lost productivity. Nonetheless, the only way to achieve and sustain excellence is for leaders to insist that their organizations invest in the slack time and resources that support the evaluation of process data that is integral to execution-as-learning. As the next section notes, this learning cycle never ends.

Keeping Learning Alive

Great companies and organizations never say, "We're done. We're as good as we can get." Successfully implementing execution-as-learning is about continuously innovating and building toward the future. As companies like IDEO, Intermountain, Microsoft, and Apple demonstrate, what's good today may only be adequate next year. Because of this, successful organizations are constantly looking for new ideas and different approaches. An implicit belief captured by the saying "If it ain't broke, don't fix it" is common. If recent history has taught us anything, however, it's that in today's environment good is never good enough, fast is never fast enough, and new is never new enough. Learning is not a one-time event or a periodic luxury. Great leaders in great companies recognize that the ability to constantly learn, innovate, and improve is vital to their success. Successful companies—like Microsoft and Apple, Southwest and Intermountain, Toyota and YUM!—constantly work to make their processes and products better. They're not waiting for the market to do it. So, don't set aside a day a week, or a day a month, to ask: What can we learn? What can we do better? Ask yourself that every day.

Recent events at Toyota provide an object lesson for what happens when execution-as-learning breaks down. Problems with floor mats and sudden acceleration in Toyota vehicles several years ago led to extensive federal investigation. The report, released in May 2011, found no evidence of an electrical problem, as some had predicted. The culprit? Hubris. As Nick Bunkley of the *New York Times* wrote, "Toyota had been slow to discover the pedal and floor mat issues because it viewed complaints made to the company or to federal regulators about sudden acceleration skeptically and defensively." The report concluded that "Toyota had failed to apply the principles of its manufacturing process, known as 'the Toyota Way' and built around the concept of detecting and responding to problems quickly, to evaluate the criticism from external sources."[14] In short, as Toyota settled into its new position as the world's dominant automaker, it began to feel invincible. Feedback was no longer enthusiastically embraced. Reflection was for mortals. Humility in the form of *hansei* and *kaizen* had eroded. (Let's hope not for long.)

The key to developing an execution-as-learning mindset is creating a cyclical operating process. The ultimate goal is to create a learning enterprise that will always learn, improve, and excel in order to compete in a crowded marketplace. The four steps to execution-as-learning presented earlier fit together to create an ongoing, regenerative cycle of learning, improvement, and innovation.

Implementing execution-as-learning takes leadership, because the relationship between learning and performance is complex. To begin with, the costs of learning often are more visible than the benefits. To illustrate, if an organization invests money in a program to build leadership skills, the costs are measurable and immediate. The benefits are difficult to quantify: they accrue over time, and accrue through second- and third-order effects. Leaders influence the actions of others, producing results at some distance from the original investment in learning.

The time delays between learning and results also bring what Peter Senge calls the better-before-worse problem.[15] This happens when a complex organization starts a learning journey, and "bad news" about problems, mistakes, and other failures starts to surface first. In hospitals, for example, undertaking a learning effort to improve patient safety may increase the number of *reported* safety problems in the short term. Or, police in a community undertaking an effort to radically lower crime, may see crimes appearing to increase in the short term. If citizens believe the police are serious about change, they may become willing to report more incidents. In reality, such upswings in bad news are (and should be treated as) "good news." An organization and its leaders are better off when they have a more realistic assessment of what's happening.

The costs, uncertainty, and delays of learning must be embraced when seeking to implement execution-as-learning. Leaders must anticipate and explain the hurdles ahead, so that people are not surprised and disappointed when progress is not smooth. They must motivate immediate action, while also displaying patience about results. The primary leadership tool for doing this is framing, as discussed in Chapter Three. Framing involves an organizing-to-learn mindset that recognizes the need for psychological safety (Chapter Four), anticipates failure along the way (Chapter Five), and helps people build bridges across organizational divides (Chapter Six). The right framing helps to shift a culture to a psychologically safe environment where execution-as-learning can thrive.

Leadership Summary

Organizing to learn and organizing to execute represent starkly different managerial mindsets, with different goals, actions, and outcomes. As the Telco case illustrated, the most basic tenets of organizing to execute—ensuring control, eliminating variance, rewarding conformance—inhibit rapid organizational learning in new domains. The result, as we saw, is that successful executers can fail when they confront complex or dynamic new contexts. Adopting the mindset and practices of organizing-to-learn is a strategy for avoiding these kinds of predictable failures. In some organizations, the organizing-to-execute mindset is a powerful habit that does not easily relax its grip. However, by experimenting with the four leadership best practices discussed in Part Two of this book, leaders can build learning into the fabric of how work gets done.

It's not that execution-as-efficiency should be abandoned altogether. Obviously, there are certain workplaces (airport gates, assembly plants) in which doing things faster and more efficiently than the competition is critical. But even in such organizations, people must learn to succeed over the longer term.

In work environments characterized by fear, the four steps described above become difficult, if not impossible, to follow. Fostering an atmosphere in which trust and respect thrive, and flexibility and innovation flourish, pays off in most settings, even the most deadline-driven. Healthy teaming environments, in which managers empower, rather than control; ask the right questions, rather than provide the right answers; and focus on flexibility, rather than insist on adherence, allow organizations to move to a higher form of execution. And when people know their ideas are welcome, they will offer innovative ways to lower costs and improve quality, thus laying a more solid foundation for their organization's success. While execution-as-learning environments are rare, it *is* possible, following steps that counteract some of our most basic behaviors, to make it happen. Teaming can be, and often is, an important piece of the puzzle. Chapter Eight shows how, in routine, complex, and innovation environments, managers correctly identified the contexts in which they operated and made critical changes to create and support execution-as-learning environments.

LESSONS AND ACTIONS

- Execution-as-learning is a way of operating that builds learning into ongoing operations.

- Execution-as-learning is defined in contrast to execution-as-efficiency, which values control over flexibility and adherence over experimentation, and often relies on fear to promote control and adherence.

- Execution-as-learning starts with diagnosing the situation to consider where it sits on the Process Knowledge Spectrum.

- It's easy to take for granted that one's work is routine, or customized, or creative, and so it's important to pause for thoughtful diagnosis.

- When a novel situation is misdiagnosed, the routine use of execution-as-efficiency can produce dramatic service failures.

- Execution-as-learning is comprised of four essential steps—Diagnose, Design, Act, and Reflect—which vary in form based on the Process Knowledge Spectrum

- It requires leadership to keep execution-as-learning alive.

chapter eight

leadership
makes it happen

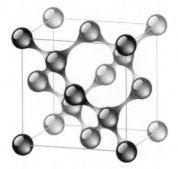

Τhis chapter presents three case studies that illustrate how
leadership, teaming, and execution-as-learning vary across
contexts. The Process Knowledge Spectrum, outlined in Chapter
One, differentiates between routine, complex, and innovation
contexts (see Figure 1.2 and, in Chapter Seven, Table 7.2). In this
chapter, we look at real-life situations to see how leaders assess
uncertainty, mobilize people, and meet their goals in each of these
three contexts. To be effective, learning and teaming must be
tailored to the context, taking into consideration the level of
process knowledge available.

The first case looks at a company in a setting that is undeniably
routine—the manufacture, sales, and distribution of mattresses to
retailers across the United States. Unfortunately, the company's
performance had been deteriorating for a number of years, and a

new CEO was brought in to reverse this trend. The second case tells the story of the chief operating officer in a complex operation, a Midwestern children's hospital, who wanted to dramatically improve patient safety. Her challenge was to engage people in an organizational learning journey through which safer, better ways of operating could be discovered and implemented at the same time. The third case takes place in the renowned product design consultancy, IDEO, which epitomizes an innovation operation. Here company leaders and project team members routinely experiment with both small and large changes. Unafraid to fail, they do fail! But they learn fast, try again, and ultimately succeed in transforming parts of the operation to generate new lines of business while successfully providing innovative product designs to corporate clients of all kinds.

In each of these situations, ask yourself: What is the context? What is the goal? How is teaming used? What makes it safe for people to team? What does execution-as-learning look like in this setting? And finally, ask yourself at the start and finish of each case: Does the leadership style match the context?

Leading Teaming in Routine Production at Simmons

In routine operations, leadership is especially critical when a company has lost its way. It is a common story: an organization with a history of success fails to keep up with new technologies, shifting customer preferences, or heightened competition, and performance suffers. In this situation, teaming is a useful strategy for turning the company around. Leaders play a vital role in identifying a viable path forward as well as in inspiring teams throughout the company to help implement and improve the basic formula for serving customers. Examples we've seen in prior chapters in this book include CEO David Novak, who steered YUM! Brands through a period of remarkable growth and performance improvement, and Commissioner Charles Rossotti, who led a dramatic turnaround of the U.S. Internal Revenue Service to improve efficiency and customer service. This section looks in depth at a turnaround in the mattress industry, to show how leading teaming in a routine operation works.

The Context

When Charlie Eitel arrived at Simmons Bedding Company, the venerable 130-year-old mattress manufacturer that had once sponsored Eleanor Roosevelt's radio show was struggling. Financial performance was anemic, morale was poor, and product and service quality were uninspiring. Eitel had a warm and easy-going manner and a solid track record as a turnaround leader of mid-sized manufacturing companies. He had been recruited by the firm's new private-equity owners to join the company as its CEO. Eitel brought a simple vision to Simmons employees: "I want us, together, to create the kind of company where all of us want to get up and come to work in the morning."[1] He continued, "And the kind of company that others want to do business with."

When he arrived at Simmons, it was pretty clear that few employees were eager to get up and come to work in the morning. Morale in some plants and divisions was abysmal. People worked hard when the boss was watching. Teaming was virtually nonexistent. Not only were relations poor within the eighteen manufacturing plants, but between them it was even worse. Plant employees tended to view each other as competitors rather than collaborators, and sharing best practices was virtually unheard of. In addition to suffering along with the rest of the U.S. economy from the fallout of the September 11, 2001, terrorist attacks, Simmons lost three of its biggest customers to bankruptcy three months later. Making matters worse, one of the company's suppliers had shipped foam used for bed cushioning that was starting to give off a terrible smell.

Eitel recognized a lack of disciplined execution when he saw it. He saw low-hanging fruit everywhere. Processes could certainly be made more efficient. The workforce morale problem was an open invitation to make a difference. Eitel believed that his success depended on communicating a compelling direction to get people's attention and, better yet, to inspire them to believe in themselves and in the firm. He was confident that the employees had what it took to do the work effectively and efficiently and he could see that they had not previously been supported in doing so. Eitel also believed in the power of a soft skills approach to make it happen. He decided to engage front-line employees throughout the company, site by site, in a program designed to build team skills and establish a culture of worker empowerment.

The Goal

Obviously, neither team building, nor even a vastly improved culture, will alone turn around a business. Eitel's focus on personal growth and culture change had to be combined with clearly speci-fied goals and skills, in order to channel employees' new enthusi-asm and teaming behaviors into performance results. In any turnaround, there are numerous problems and opportunities for improvement, but picking one reasonably clear target area to direct participants' motivation into something measurable is key. For routine operations like mattress manufacturing (unlike DSL in its early days), this kind of specificity is realistic.

Eitel chose Zero Waste as the goal to rally and focus the teaming energy. Zero Waste had the right elements for this focus, for two reasons. First, everyone can relate to waste. No matter what your job, you can find opportunities to reduce waste, whether in materi-als, time, steps, or energy, and work teams can help brainstorm ways to do so. Second, many dimensions of waste are relatively easy to measure—allowing the demonstration of small wins and steady progress, if successful. Simmons's focus on Zero Waste was intended to channel enthusiasm created by the team-building program into something measurable.

Much of Eitel's confidence in the program came from a successful pilot he authorized in one of the firm's eighteen manufacturing plants. The Charlotte, North Carolina, plant was one of the two worst-performing in the company. With eleven languages spoken by workers—whose duties included sewing, panel and border repair, flat panel cutting, creating new sewing methods, or machine maintenance and repair—perhaps this was inevitable. Plant managers relied on a dictatorial micromanaging style. Coordination between groups, such as panel cutters and panel sewers, was problematic—lacking precision and colored by finger-pointing. To test the premise that the program could help improve the company's performance, Eitel proposed starting with Charlotte. A good test is a tough test.

In retrospect, it's not difficult to see how the team program had a profound impact on almost everyone in the Charlotte workforce. When Eitel decided to try it, however, his decision was met with resistance by his own team as well as by the company's owners. For one, money was tight and spending a sizable amount on training didn't seem to some executives to be a wise move. Two, some people felt the command-and-control culture in most of the plants was too entrenched to change. But Eitel's hunch—that bringing the program to the Charlotte plant was "the right thing to do," as he put it—turned out to be right. The plant manager perhaps made the most dramatic change of all, from a highly dictatorial approach to an engaging and inclusive style. In his own words, "I thought I *had* to act that [dictatorial] way. It's how I had always seen [plant management] done. But I didn't like it." Two people who worked for him had been planning to leave Simmons, but, as a result of his changed behavior, decided to stay. The plant saw performance improvement quickly, and within the next year was awarded "Plant of the Year," followed, as improvements continued, by an OSHA safety award. Charlotte's success emboldened Eitel's team to spread the program across the company's other plants. In this case, a roll-out mindset was appropriate, and was used, with minor improvements in logistics.

Building a Teaming Infrastructure

Facing a turnaround situation such as this one, many new CEOs might have sought to restructure, cut jobs and costs, or close plants. Instead, Eitel invested a substantial sum in a team-building program with outdoor "ropes course" activities followed by classroom learning, to engage people in personal growth and teamwork, and to focus their attention on the company's goals.[2] This certainly didn't seem like a quick fix. Spending seven million dollars over three years to send plant managers and employees to off-site team-building sessions for two or three days each? But Eitel believed that turning around the business hinged on changing the Simmons culture. By putting people in challenging physical teaming experiences, where they experienced firsthand what it was like to depend on, and be supported by, their colleagues, Eitel hoped to reframe and transform poor work relationships to improve the company's sluggish performance. Once people's eyes were open, he hoped they would see the possibilities of being a part of a collaborative, learning-oriented culture, and become motivated to deliver the operational excellence that would restore Simmons's profits.

Some managers opposed the plan and opted out by leaving the company, incidentally not harming the bottom line. Most, however, went along and found the program a highly positive experience. The program helped them reframe the situation, inviting them to view and participate at Simmons in a very different way. One plant employee called it among the five most important experiences of her life, "right up there with marriage and childbirth." Many managers waxed enthusiastic about how time spent with colleagues during the physical challenges of the ropes course taught them to trust one another's support, tap new strengths, and work collaboratively toward a common goal.

The team-building program built on foundational psychological principles by providing team experiences that require trust and cooperation, to give people who work together an experience of a new way of working. In this way, the guy who is afraid of heights and must climb a telephone pole is able to find the courage to do so because of the group's support.

Execution-as-Learning

Teaming focused on improvement, whether in manufacturing or fast food, starts with the recognition that the basic process knowledge for achieving the products or services customers want is well developed. It's codified—that is, there's a kind of recipe for action that can be (and usually is) documented. Collective learning in this setting is thus usually focused on improvement—making the existing process better, more efficient, less expensive, difficult, or time-consuming. Execution-as-learning, then, is about driving continuous improvement for greater efficiency and reliability. This was the essential nature of the journey that Simmons faced.

Eitel and his team went to great lengths to ensure that the emotional impact of the team program would translate into the daily work of people in the company. Zero Waste became the rallying cry to help channel employee energy toward specific operational goals. Appropriately, for a routine operations setting, the Zero Waste initiative stemmed from lean production principles. It drew inspiration from the Toyota Production System, which includes the drive to reduce waste (*muda*) as a core principle. The goal of teaming on the manufacturing floor was to constantly modify, refine, fail, and learn toward this end.

Perhaps this seems too reminiscent of Taylor's time and motion studies, intended to break up tasks into the most efficient—that is, the least wasteful—steps. Henry Ford, nearly obsessed with waste's drain on efficiency, criticized the waste he saw in farming, noting, "The average farmer puts to a really useful purpose only about five percent of the energy he spends. . . . A farmer doing his chores will walk up and down a rickety ladder a dozen times. He will carry water for years instead of putting in a few lengths of pipe. His whole idea, when there is extra work to do, is to hire extra men. He thinks of putting money into improvements as an expense. . . . It is waste motion—waste effort—that makes farm prices high and profits low."[3]

There's one big difference, however. Zero Waste invited those doing the work to figure out how to make the tasks more efficient. For Ford and Taylor, that was the job of managers and engineers.

At Simmons, the drive toward Zero Waste, fueled by team training, produced $21 million in measurable cost reductions in the first year alone, while sales and revenue grew. Supplemented by follow-up training in teaming and problem-solving skills, people had begun to embrace a new culture of learning in the company, emphasizing the idea that Simmons's employees' fates were linked together.[4] A new incentive program tied 25 percent of workers' weekly compensation to a plant's overall quality and productivity, encouraging cooperative effort. Final product quality, percentage of a product scheduled to ship that did ship, and productivity were tracked daily. Perhaps because of interconnected destinies, Simmons employees very often helped one another on the job.

Teaming skills development followed the team-building exercises for several months, supported by systematic assessment. This helped employees develop technical and interpersonal skills, collaboratively. Five stages of teamwork were outlined for each part of the operation. For example, the five stages for Teaming for Production were:

- Level 1: Employees could understand daily production goals, production zones, and learn manufacturing concepts.

- Level 2: Teams could monitor their work in progress, meet existing goals, clear zones, and understand lean principles.

- Level 3: Teams could set, measure, post, and report team production goals.

- Level 4: Teams could consistently meet goals and initiate production improvements.

- Level 5: A team could reevaluate goals and continuously improve, as well as coordinate production between teams and shifts.

Similar five-level trajectories were outlined for Safety, Quality, Service, Cost, Cross-Training, and Visual Management. When a team's members thought they were ready to advance from one stage to the next, they made a formal presentation to the leadership team at the plant. This systematic approach tied on-the-job skills learning, personal growth, incentives, and results together in ways that were motivating and easy to understand.

Update

Simmons implemented a curriculum that raised awareness, built skills, and rewarded people for learning and teaming. Employees were helped in moving up the cognitive ladder from, for example, meeting preset production goals to independently setting viable production goals, estimating time, materials, and labor. This was a classic routine operations turnaround—accomplished through motivating and supporting teaming for continuous improvement. The company's performance showed dramatic and robust improvements for the next six years, until the financial and housing crises of 2009 sharply lowered demand for mattresses.

Leading Teaming in Complex Operations at Children's Hospital

In complex operations, leaders confront the challenge of ever-present risk. Whether global supply chain or tertiary care hospital, a Complex Operation faces the possibility of failure around every corner. In this situation, teaming is a strategy for identifying vulnerabilities, brainstorming designs to prevent failures, and analyzing those failures that do occur. Leaders play a vital role in inspiring and supporting teaming in this context. Examples of complex operations in prior chapters include NASA's space shuttle program and Intermountain Health Care. This section looks in depth at a leadership initiative that transformed a large hospital to show how teaming in a complex operation can help identify and reduce risks in patient care.

The Context

Children's Hospital and Clinics in Minneapolis, Minnesota, is a major tertiary care hospital for children, with six facilities located throughout the Minneapolis–St. Paul area. When Julie Morath took the job of chief operating officer at Children's, she understood the complexity of patient care operations and clearly recognized the challenge ahead as one with neither a manual nor a successful predecessor to emulate.

All complex organizations face unknowns (Will the supply chain face disruptions? Will the aircraft carrier successfully land its aircraft in a stormy sea?), but hospitals confront more than their fair share. The timing and type of patients who come through the door of the emergency room or show up in a hospital bed, and the services they will need, can be difficult to predict. Moreover, treatment protocols and medications are constantly changing as a result of advances in science, technology, and clinical research. Chronic diseases such as cystic fibrosis or advanced diabetes require ongoing customized care, and new diseases, such as the H1N1 virus, periodically show up, demanding intense discovery and problem solving. Problems—small and catastrophic, unique and recurring—are the norm. The kind of teaming that is needed to find and solve problems involves keen observation from multiple perspectives, timely and open communication, and quick decision making. The stakes are high—particularly in the ICU or an operating room. Errors can have dire consequences. Yet, counter to expectations of achieving Six-Sigma quality in a manufacturing plant, hospital processes are seen by many experts as too complex to perfect.

To better understand the potential for safety failures, consider this episode in one young patient's hospital stay. Nurse Ginny Swenson[5] wheeled ten-year-old Matthew from the intensive care unit to Children's surgical floor, despite needing medications usually reserved for the ICU, because of capacity constraints. Swenson described Matthew's condition to Patrick O'Reilly, a newly graduated nurse, and instructed him to program the electronic infusion pump for the morphine dosage prescribed by the physician.

Matthew's care was dependent, at the very least, on accurate communication between a physician and two nurses. O'Reilly, unfamiliar with the particular morphine pump, asked another nurse, Molly Chen, for help. Unfortunately neither she nor any of the other nurses in the unit had much previous experience using pumps for continuous pain control. Chen, an experienced nurse, felt rushed. She was taking time from her many other duties to help O'Reilly. A conscientious, capable professional, she peered at the unfamiliar machine's dials.

To program the pump, one needed to enter both the morphine concentration and the appropriate rate of infusion. Neither Chen nor O'Reilly saw a concentration listed on the medication label (it turns out the label had been printed in a way that folded critical information inside the cassette where it could not be seen), but Chen used the information visible on the label to calculate and program the machine with what she believed was the correct concentration. She entered the rate of infusion as Swenson had instructed. Following hospital procedure, O'Reilly verified Chen's calculations and settings. Then Chen left to care for other patients.

Within minutes, Matthew's face turned blue. He was having trouble breathing. O'Reilly sprang into action, turned off the infusion machine, called for the doctor, and began ventilating the child with a breathing bag. The doctor arrived within a very few minutes and confirmed O'Reilly's suspicion that Matthew had been given a morphine overdose—several times more than was appropriate. The doctor administered a different drug to reverse the effect, and within seconds, Matthew's breathing returned to normal.

The Goal

In contrast to Eitel at Simmons, Morath's challenge was not to inspire employees to follow her down a well-worn path of improvement in a routine operation, but rather to create a self-organizing learning system that would pioneer new terrain. Morath had a single-minded goal—to avoid harming hospitalized children. She aspired to achieve 100 percent patient safety at Children's at a time when medication errors were rarely discussed among caregivers, let alone by senior management, and were widely considered inevitable by industry insiders. Thus, knowledge of how to improve safety dramatically was not only limited, but it was likely to differ in various parts of the organization based on the nature of the procedures. Counterbalancing this challenge of venturing into new territory, however, was the fact that this was indeed a goal that everyone could buy into. No one wants to harm a hospitalized child.

When Morath interviewed for the COO job, she was already talking about patient safety. She had twenty-five years' experience in patient care administration and had previously been a registered nurse. With her calm demeanor and ready smile, she exuded an unflappable, can-do attitude that was both reassuring and inspiring. After joining Children's, she continued her "carefully constructed conversations around the topic of safety with people who would have to be on board with the initiative."[6] In the beginning, this was not easy. As Morath noted, it was "difficult to broach the topic of safety because most people get defensive. Talking about safety implies that we are doing things, 'wrong.'"[7] For example, recall the teaming failure that led to Matthew's overdose. Fortunately, an episode of successful teaming was quickly triggered, and Matthew made a full recovery. This is not the kind of story that makes newspaper headlines or even one that would have necessarily been reported a decade ago in a busy urban hospital. It was, however, clear to Morath that avoiding these kinds of failures was of the utmost importance for the goal of 100 percent patient safety. To prevent this kind of failure in the future, it was important to understand who or what was to blame.

Looking at the string of events, this is not an easy question to answer. Did the problem lie with Chen, who programmed the machine? O'Reilly, who verified her settings? The administrator who placed the postsurgical patient in a unit where nurses were unfamiliar with using a pain pump? The pharmacist who delivered a morphine cassette with an ambiguous concentration? The computer programmer who made the medication labels too large to fit on the cassette, obscuring some text? Or perhaps Swensen, who left Matthew in the care of a novice nurse? In a word, yes. All of them contributed to the failure. We cannot single out anyone as the culprit; the events succumb to a multicausal analysis, which ultimately points to a system breakdown. A novel situation combined with a number of small deviations from optimal practice to produce a potentially fatal failure. Unfortunately, because of the complexity of the activities and the idiosyncratic nature of individual patients' situations, incidents like this happen over and over again in hospitals around the world.

The power of teaming in complex operations is the ability— with the right leadership, interpersonal awareness, and discipline —to anticipate, problem solve, diagnose, and reduce system risks, so as to avoid consequential failures. How do leaders create this kind of learning organization? The answer is not exactly the same as what Eitel did to lead change at Simmons—communicate a compelling goal, make it safe to team, and support teaming for improvement throughout the company—but it's not completely different, either.

Leading in a complex operation starts with communicating a compelling goal to motivate people to take action without easy answers. The need to tie that goal to a meaningful shared purpose that contributes to making a better world is far greater in complex operations than in routine operations. This is because people have to cope with greater uncertainty. They have to take greater interpersonal risks—such as admitting mistakes and pointing out flawed systems to bosses and others. The opportunity to make a positive difference in the world supports and promotes the greater willingness to sacrifice that these interpersonal risks require. Tying the work the organization does to the larger purpose of creating a better world is itself a reframing. Leaders in complex operations must pay even more attention to creating an environment of psychological safety, where people can tolerate the risks of learning, than in routine operations. The interpersonal risks in complex operations are that much greater.

When leaders inspire and support teaming in this setting, they are seeking coinvestigators: people willing to work together to seek out, identify, and solve problems that have never been solved before. They are embarking on a journey, facing many unknowns. In contrast, at Simmons, the path forward had the comfort of a blueprint.

Building a Teaming Infrastructure

Soon after assuming her leadership role, Morath assembled a core team that she called the Patient Safety Steering Committee (PSSC). This was a select group of key influencers who would help design and launch the "Patient Safety Initiative." To identify those with interest and passion, as well as to communicate widely with as many people in the hospital as possible, she delivered a series of formal presentations about medical errors, presenting the then still unfamiliar data that as many as 98,000 people in the United States were dying annually from medical errors—higher than the number from car accidents, breast cancer, or AIDS. The PSSC was deliberately diverse—with doctors and nurses, department heads and front-line staff, union members and executives. It was a group that understood and represented the organization well.

Despite the pedigree of the PSSC and Morath's compelling delivery, many pushed back against the idea of the initiative at first, reluctant to believe that errors were a problem at Children's. They believed the national statistics, perhaps, but they did not believe that these data applied to Children's. Tempting as it must have been to Morath to simply reiterate her message more forcefully—given that she understood that *all* hospitals, because of their operational complexity, were vulnerable to error—she did not try to argue the point. Instead, she thoughtfully responded to the resistance with inquiry. "Okay, this data may not be applicable here," she concurred. Then she asked, "Tell me, what was your own experience *this* week, in the units, with your patients? Was everything as safe as you would like it to have been?"[8]

This simple inquiry seems to have transformed the dialogue. Note its features. Her question is an invitation—one that is genuine, curious, direct, and concrete. Each caregiver is invited to consider his or her own patients, his or her own experiences, in his or her own unit, in the prior few days. Moreover, the question is aspirational—not, "Did you see things that were unsafe?" but rather, "Was everything as safe as you would like it to have been?" It both respects others' experience and invites aspiration.

Too many would-be leaders forget about the power of inquiry, and instead rely on forceful advocacy to bring others along. As Morath showed, inquiry respects and invites. As people began to discuss incidents with her and with others that they had thought were unique or idiosyncratic, they realized that most of their colleagues had experienced similar events. As Morath put it, "I found that most people had been at the center of a health care situation where something did not go well. They were quick to recognize that the hospital could be doing better."[9] She led as many as eighteen focus groups throughout the organization to allow people to air their concerns and ideas.

To build the psychological safety needed for the inevitably difficult conversations about errors and failures, Morath frequently described her philosophy on patient safety—to anyone who would listen. In her words: "Health care is a very complex system, and complex systems are, by their very nature, risk-prone. The culture of health care must be one of everyone working together to understand safety, identify risks, and report them without fear of blame. We must look at ways to change the whole system when we manage to zero defects."[10] By emphasizing the systemic nature of failures, she sought to help people move away from a tendency to find and blame individual culprits.

Complex systems, as Morath recognized, also meant no easy path forward. She was passionate about her vision to direct the organization toward 100 percent patient safety but did not know how it would be accomplished. Admitting that she did not have all the answers, she enlisted everyone's help to work together to "look at ways to change the system."

Health care has had a long and painful history surrounding medical mistakes. Often called the "ABC's of Medicine"—Accuse, Blame, Criticize—the culture of medicine emphasized individual incompetence as a source of mishap, rather than careful analysis of where systems may have broken down. This mindset made blame, shame, and disciplinary action the logical approach to producing high-quality care. Unfortunately, however, this approach neither produced error-free care nor pointed the way to reducing medical errors, even during a period of heightened scrutiny. The ABC mindset is not conducive to honest, rigorous investigations into what causes the failures that occur, but rather seeks individuals to blame. Moreover, it does not take into account the belief held by an increasing number of health care professionals: that many medical errors can be traced to a fault in the system rather than to any one individual.

In fact, what the ABC mindset did best, I would argue, was to silence *reporting* of errors. Most health care workers are rightfully protective of their reputations and jobs. Especially when an error resulted in patient harm, doctors and nurses involved in the patient's care were frequently too afraid or too traumatized to discuss it. This left many dedicated and talented clinicians burdened with an internal sense of shame and nagging self-doubt about their value to the profession.

Stimulating constructive dialogue required a fundamental shift on many fronts: organizational structure, processes, norms and values, and leadership styles. Psychological safety's most important role in a health care setting is to allow increased accident reporting, a necessary first step if a hospital is to learn from its mistakes and improve over time. Health care also has a long, entrenched history of professional hierarchy. Those on lower echelons often do not feel psychologically safe enough to speak up to superiors with questions and suggestions.[11]

Morath knew firsthand about the aftershock and emotional pain of medical accidents for health care workers. She never forgot one she'd witnessed thirty years earlier, when she was a young nurse: a four-year-old patient died from an anesthesia error. What Morath remembered, even more than the devastation of the child's death, was that "the nurse who felt responsible 'went home that day and never returned,' guiltily giving up the career she loved. Doctors and other nurses 'just shut down' and never talked to one another about what happened. The hospital's attorneys swooped in to do damage control. 'It just didn't sit right and it plagued me,'" Morath said, decades later.[12]

So she introduced a new system for reporting medical incidents called "blameless reporting." The idea was to allow people to communicate confidentially or anonymously about medical accidents without being punished for doing so, so as to bring as many of these problems as possible to light, to determine their underlying causes, and to keep caring professionals in their positions. To support the new policy, members of the PSSC created a new Patient Safety Report form that asked caregivers to describe an incident in their own words rather than to simply check off appropriate boxes as they had in the past. Questions such as: "How did it happen? What was the chain of events?" and "What were the contributing factors? What could prevent future occurrences of the event?" trained the reporter to reflect deeply on the accident and to provide a full explanation.

Morath also instituted new language to discuss safety issues, encouraging people to, for example, substitute "study" or "examination" for "investigation." She thought of an examination as learning how systems work and how the pieces fit together. An investigation, on the other hand, was more like a police line-up, assigning blame to someone or something in a linear search to determine a single cause. Although Morath emphasized avoiding words that implied blame and encouraged language conducive to learning from failures, the psychological safety this promoted was rooted in her vision that "accidents" (a term preferable to "error") arose from faulty systems rather than faulty persons. "Blame" was to be replaced by the word "accountable," defined as being responsible to the duties of a particular job and whatever knowledge it required, as well as to understanding the larger system in which one was a human component.

Execution-as-Learning

In a complex operation, a leader must use widespread teaming to find and solve problems. This means making changes in the organization's operational structures to reduce barriers to teaming, as well as setting up and supporting cross-functional team activities, such as incident reviews. As we saw in the case of Eitel at Simmons, an essential leadership task is persuading those with control over resources to fund changes that look costly in the short term, but prove cost-effective in the long term.

Teaming to solve safety problems at Children's started with Morath's creation of the PSSC. This was soon followed by implementing focused event studies by cross-functional temporary teams after every significant safety incident. For example, within twenty-four hours of Matthew's near-fatal overdose, Dr. Chris Robison, associate director of medical affairs, held a closed-door meeting with all those directly involved in Matthew's care. No one would be punished unless malfeasance of some sort was discovered (an exceedingly rare outcome). This helped create the psychological safety to discuss and analyze causes of a failure, to inform preventative measures. Teaming was needed, as Robison commented, because "we could not have gotten as thorough an understanding of what happened to Matthew if I had talked with people individually. There was so much point and counterpoint during the meeting. We saw the event from the nurse's perspective and then from the respiratory therapist's and the doctor's. It is not that people only perceive things consistent with their viewpoint, but that they have actually only touched one part of the elephant."[13] The teaming culture was essential in promoting execution-as-learning.

When leaders successfully engage employees in a collaborative learning journey, activities start to happen that were not designed at the top of the organization. Ideas start to bubble up, and activities start to take hold and spread. To a manager seeking to "get the job done," this process might at first seem laborious and slow. But engaging people as active thinkers and learners is truly how a complex operation achieves its goal.

Many of the changes at Children's originated from the front lines. For instance, a clinical nurse specialist named Casey Hooke came up with the idea for a "safety action team" in the Hematology/Oncology unit. This cross-functional team of eight employees decided to meet monthly to identify medication safety hazards. At one meeting, a nurse talked about a near-miss accident using a feeding bag; she had infused a large and potentially harmful amount of fluid into a patient. The group researched the question and discovered a safer feeding bag that could prevent this kind of accident in the future. The team needled and pushed and succeeded in getting the safer equipment implemented throughout the hospital. Soon, two other units, inspired by Casey's efforts, launched Safety Action Teams. After a while, the Patient Safety Steering Committee directed the manager of each clinical unit to establish a Safety Action Team of its own.

Another bottom-up initiative was the "Good Catch Log"—an idea for a literal logbook, located in locked medication rooms on each hospital floor. If a nurse "caught" a problem that could have resulted in a medication error, he or she could record the events anonymously in the log. Safety Action Team leaders periodically gathered the Good Catch Logs and summarized the information for the rest of the team. During meetings, the team discussed the information and revised policies and procedures accordingly. As nurses realized their entries often led to concrete changes, they became even more comfortable writing in the logs.

Update

Morath remained at Children's as COO for ten years, leading the organization's slow but palpable transformation. During her tenure, the hospital earned national attention as a leader in patient safety. Over time, Morath, along with countless employees, found that blameless reporting and vigilant teaming had become integrated into the way the hospital operated. The case illustrates that leading in a complex operation often means providing more good questions than good answers.

Leading Teaming for Innovation at IDEO

In innovation operations, leadership is needed to create a fertile environment for exploration and experimentation. Teaming is essential for coming up with new ideas, winnowing them down to viable options, testing and refining them, and ultimately producing novel and useful new possibilities. Examples of innovation discussed in prior chapters include pharmaceutical research at Eli Lilly, the introduction of the first hybrid vehicle by Toyota, and the creation of the Water Cube, the iconic aquatic facility, for the Beijing Olympics. In this section, I'll show how teaming works to produce innovation by looking in depth at IDEO, the most consistently innovative company I've studied.

The Context

The idea of innovators as particularly creative individuals who march to the tune of a different drummer and shrug off others' criticism and skepticism has enduring appeal. But innovation today is almost always a team sport. Innovation occurs when new ideas and new solutions emerge at the intersections between areas of expertise, which happens through teaming. Consider what happens at IDEO, the product design consultancy whose prize-winning innovations include the first computer mouse (for Apple), interactive dressing rooms at Prada, and interiors for Amtrak's Acela trains, along with a host of far more mundane household products like Crest's "Neat Squeeze" toothpaste.

IDEO originated from a 1991 merger of three industrial design companies and an engineering firm. David Kelley, an electrical engineer and Stanford professor with an infectious laugh and boundless curiosity, was the firm's founding CEO and inspirational leader. In 2000, when Kelley became chairman of the company, designer Tim Brown took over as CEO. IDEO employees bring expertise in mechanical, electrical, and software engineering, as well as industrial and interaction design, prototype machining, human factors research, interior architecture, and more. With locations around the world (Palo Alto, San Francisco, Boulder, Chicago, Boston, London, Munich, and Tokyo), IDEO serves global clients and regional companies alike. The company's talented staff, its focus on diagnosing unmet end-user needs, and its disciplined innovation process have earned it dozens of Industrial

Design Excellence Awards in categories ranging from medical and scientific equipment, to digital media, to consumer products.

The hard part of innovation, according to Brown, is not coming up with a great new idea, but successfully steering a new idea through an old organization.[14] Of course, some of us think having a great new idea is hard, too, but Brown has a point. Innovation is part creative inspiration and part persuasion; part team problem solving and part organizational change. Taking a look at how IDEO innovates serves to illuminate important features of teaming in innovation operations.

The Goal

By the late 1990s, Kelley and other leaders at IDEO recognized a growing need to help companies figure out product *areas* to innovate, rather than merely responding to requests to design a specific new product. This could be characterized as a need for design strategy rather than for design. An experiment in new services to help clients "understand the world and innovate accordingly" as the company put it, was thereby launched, which became known as Phase Zero,[15] because it would precede the other phases of innovation.

The new innovation-strategy services would set the context for further design initiatives by identifying new product or service opportunities. If a Phase Zero project was successful, it would likely generate new work for the core innovation business.

A project for Simmons became one of the early experiments in Phase Zero as a stand-alone service.[16] Rather than being asked to design a new bed, a marketing executive at Simmons hired IDEO to help the company "understand the world in a new way and innovate accordingly." Despite what appeared to be a positive response from Simmons at the project's conclusion, Douglas Dayton, the leader of IDEO's Boston office, where the Phase Zero team had worked, reluctantly recognized that the project had failed to achieve its potential. The team's ideas seemed to him creative and feasible, but Simmons was not acting on them.

What had gone wrong?

The failure was not due to a lack of energy or imagination. Conducting interviews with mattress customers of all ages, using cameras, visiting mattress stores, and even shadowing mattress delivery people, the Phase Zero team had learned a lot.[17] Its members worked hard to explore how the bed and its associated space, furniture, and other objects acted as a system to support the sleeper at different points in his life. This exploration had identified an underserved group dubbed "the nomads," hyper-mobile single 18- to 30-year-olds. Between their parents' homes and their own first home, nomads slept on futons, air mattresses, or second- or third-hand mattresses, because available bedding products were too unwieldy or expensive for their mobile lifestyles. Nomads did not want to buy large, permanent items. They expected to move frequently. They lived in small apartments or with roommates, and often used bedrooms for entertaining and studying, not just sleeping.

This idea gave rise to some product opportunities for nomadic singles. One was a self-contained integrated mattress and frame. Another was a mattress built of visually distinct, easily folded, lightweight modular layers, which could be customized and easily moved from place to place.[18] Armed with beautiful sketches and compelling text, the team went back to see its client, from whom it received genuine, but unmotivated, enthusiasm. When it came time to see ideas converted into action at Simmons, however, IDEO would be disappointed.

Let's step back. How does IDEO usually innovate so successfully?

Building a Teaming Infrastructure

At IDEO, cross-functional teams that combine engineers, designers, architects, human factor specialists, and many others are assembled and reassembled for particular projects and parts of projects. They work in an energizing, chaotic, yet surprisingly disciplined teaming process. In this process, the specifics of the many tasks that need to be done cannot be prescribed in advance, but the broad outlines of the process are clear and well understood by all.

As is characteristic of most innovation operations, IDEO teams relied on cross-fertilization. Transferring knowledge across disciplines within teams, as well as from project to project, IDEO team members routinely developed novel solutions to diverse problems. Not surprisingly, they had limited collaboration or cross-fertilization with clients. The outside world of greatest interest to IDEO was the world of end users—not the world of corporations, with their bureaucracies, hierarchies, politics, and constraints. In fact, it's fair to say that IDEO once held disdain for corporate environments.

The core innovation process at IDEO had four distinct phases, all of which relied on teaming. In Phase One, Concept Generation, a team, inspired by the study of potential end users in the field, develops numerous abstract design solutions before selecting a single one for development. Phase One thus addresses the most basic questions about the product, the problem it solves, and the cost. Phase Two, Concept Development, considers questions such as, "How will this product work? How will we make it? How will we test it?"[19] In Phase Three, Detailed Engineering, team members define product details and build and test prototypes. The output is detailed—a working design, reports and evaluations, a costed bill of materials, technical documentation, potential manufacturing vendors, and a work plan. In Phase Four, Manufacturing Liaison, an IDEO team prepares a product and supporting documentation to hand off to a client's manufacturing partners, ready for high-volume production.[20] Teaming is essential in this journey, because the team composition shifts throughout the phases, with different experts being recruited to help with different tasks to accommodate the wide range of work and areas of expertise needed in each phase.

To encourage creativity and learning, the company's leaders had long cultivated a climate of psychological safety. To say that people at IDEO speak up freely would be a gross understatement. Designers act on their ideas with little concern about what others, including bosses, might say. Meanwhile, bosses also are not shy about speaking their minds. Letting colleagues know that you think a design is flawed is a sign of respect. But not during brainstorming, where criticism is explicitly forbidden. These rules are not just widely understood; they are codified. Conference room walls at IDEO are stenciled with brainstorming slogans such as: "Be visual." "Defer judgment." "Encourage wild ideas." "Build on the ideas of others." "Go for quantity." "One conversation at a time." "Stay focused on the topic." It helps that IDEO's learning environment is one of self-proclaimed "focused chaos," where taking interpersonal risks such as offering crazy ideas is part of the game.

In this early foray into Phase Zero, the teaming did not include clients. What it would take to navigate a new product line idea through the client organization was not considered. The ideas and designs had all been developed in IDEO offices or out in the field studying end users. An important part of the innovation journey had not been traveled. What would it look like to truly *team with clients* in a Phase Zero project? Let's take a look at what IDEO subsequently did.

Team members launched a revised Phase Zero effort by including clients in a new way, clarifying the project's aims and determining the possibilities, together. One or two clients would even join an IDEO Phase Zero team. To make it work, IDEO needed more employees capable of doing the business and organizational facets of Phase Zero work. They deepened the firm's "business factors" discipline, complementing the design and technical factors experts that dominated IDEO's culture and capabilities. Business factors experts at IDEO today bring skills that include the ability to penetrate clients' bureaucratic mazes and analyze client cultures. This, in turn, allows deeper collaboration with clients. Put simply,

IDEO's prior skills lay beyond the client—near the realm of "users." Effective Phase Zero work called for IDEO to add understanding of client organizational systems to its deep understanding of user needs and technological possibility.

Execution-as-Learning

The Simmons project would, at first blush, seem a perfect Phase Zero match, given the mandate to find new opportunities for a mattress company. This is just the kind of challenge that would intrigue IDEO: take a mundane category and run with it. Indeed, the team displayed creative thinking and imaginative exploration. Yet, if a client is to implement what IDEO recommends (a product line, for example) or act on the expanded innovation space IDEO maps out, then the solutions offered would have to reflect what the *client* (not just IDEO) is capable of envisioning and executing. It is not enough to have one or a few senior executives enthusiastic about new ideas. A project would only support client innovation if it included teaming with clients. It became clear, as Tim Brown put it, that the firm had to learn more about how to usher ideas through the organizational systems through which innovations ultimately touched customers' lives.

Update

A few years after the failed Simmons project, IDEO had dramatically expanded its emphasis on business factors and reconfigured and coached teams to integrate these skills. Thirty percent or more of its revenues were coming from Phase Zero work. The firm hired and promoted more people with business knowledge, expanding its business factors practice. IDEO's evolving journey into a new kind of client collaboration showed its characteristic ability as a learning organization, innovating and expanding its expertise in new realms, cycling forward through experimentation, failure, and many unique successes.

Leadership Summary

Essential learning in organizations occurs not through individuals working alone to sort through and solve important problems but rather through people working and learning collaboratively in flexible teams. At Simmons, production, sales, and line-management teams learned to carry out the core tasks of the routine operation more efficiently and effectively, with greater skill and dignity. What looked like a leap of faith to Eitel's new colleagues was actually a well-worn path for Eitel. At Children's, clinical, managerial, and operational teams participated in the creation of new learning processes, making progress on a critically important goal in a frustratingly complex setting. At IDEO, cross-functional teams skilled at innovation also learned how to diagnose and befriend corporate systems—innovating not just a product but the company's business model.

In all three cases, leadership helped make it happen. The flavor of leadership varied, however. Eitel had a blueprint for change and was a compelling salesperson, winning support day by day for the effortful team work ahead. Morath skillfully invited coinvestigators, high and low, to help her discover processes for ensuring patient safety. And Kelley, like many innovation leaders, seems to have merely gotten out of the way to let smart, motivated people sort through failures and dream up new experiments. Of course, it's not quite that simple. Innovation thrives when leaders, such as Kelley at IDEO, provide several critical ingredients: extremely stringent hiring to find and keep unusually talented people, a diversity of projects to fuel cross-pollination, strict process guidelines, resources, and, of course, enthusiasm.

The good news is that execution-as-learning is a winning formula in almost any industry. Even in routine production, today's best practices won't be tomorrow's. The bad news is that it's an unnatural state of affairs. Working in this way requires people to fight against the desire for instructions that guarantee results.

Execution-as-learning requires accepting that every process can be improved, and some must be replaced altogether. It's not that the goal of learning is placed above the goal of meeting today's performance standards. Learning from the work is part of the work. Efficiency still matters, especially in routine operations where doing things faster and more reliably than the competition is critical. But even there, people must keep learning to achieve long-term success. And fostering a culture of trust and respect where learning flourishes pays off in even the most deadline-driven contexts. It's just not the place to *start*. Why not?

As we have seen, teaming and learning thrive when they are intensely focused on the work that must be done to find, keep, and care for customers. This was the case in all three organizations presented in this chapter. A learning-oriented culture is a valuable organizational resource, but creating such a culture is not an end in itself. I argue that a learning organization is created by focusing renewed employee attention on the work, not by trying to change the culture. A learning culture emerges as a by-product of practice with a new way of working—one that is more interdependent, more aware of others' tasks and needs, and more willing to improve—not the other way around. For example, as Simmons employees experienced a new way of working, a new empowered, high-trust culture took shape around them.

Many change efforts fail because they focus on shifting the culture, and too often people at all levels—from senior management to the front lines of customer service—have a hard time making culture change a priority, compared to the piles of work they confront. Recall from Chapter Four that Arthur Ryan wanted to change Prudential's culture to one that was psychologically safe. Although many employees liked the idea of safety for speaking up, they didn't all understand how it related to business excellence in financial services. Despite leaders' best intentions, they often don't adequately convey why a new culture is needed and how it would help employees serve customers better.

Moving Forward

For over a century, we've focused too much on relentless execution and depended too much on fear to get things done. That era is over. Underlying the notion of a simple, controllable production system was the notion of the simple, controllable employee. In the factory model of management, it was easy to monitor workers and measure their output. But work today increasingly requires the applications of specialized skills and knowledge. Workers are expected to identify issues, analyze problems, and create new solutions. This shift has changed the dynamic of the workplace and the relationship between those in charge and those doing the work. The most successful leaders in the future will be those who have the ability to develop the talents of others. At its best, teaming clarifies and magnifies human capacity. But teaming is challenging and often counterintuitive. It conflicts with many of our natural and socially developed behaviors. Cultivating the conditions in which people can speak up, learn from each other, and experiment safely expands what can be created and what can be accomplished.

What did the Chilean miners, the astronauts on the *Columbia* mission, and Matthew, the ten-year-old patient at Children's Hospital, have in common? Their very survival depended on successful teaming. Execution-as-learning is more than a new way to operate and a new way to compete. It's a new way to survive in complex endeavors. You don't need more examples of organizations today that face challenges, flounder, fail, or just make people unhappy, to understand the imperative for change. Yes, some of the practices in this book are difficult or unnatural to put into practice. (So, once, was discovering fire, organizing mass production, or creating the iPhone!) We may be hard-wired for power struggles, greed, and workplace conflicts. But as social creatures, we also derive enormous pleasure from creating, sharing, and implementing new ideas with other people. Some of the amazing accomplishments described in this book (the Chilean rescue, the Beijing Water Cube, the RAZR, Intermountain's learning system) were created through teaming. Clearly, human and organizational obstacles to teaming and learning can be overcome.

Contagious Learning

Just as management in organizations of the past gave rise to an execution-as-efficiency mindset, the knowledge economy in which today's organizations compete gives rise to expertise silos that inhibit the teaming needed to solve global-scale problems. It is becoming increasingly clear that teaming in the future will require crossing boundaries that are organizational as well as disciplinary. Few of today's most pressing social problems can be solved within the four walls of any organization, no matter how enlightened or extraordinary. Climate change, education, transportation, urbanization, and energy use are just some of the areas in which innovative solutions are needed to ensure a safe, healthy, viable future for people and organizations around the world.

Old models of competition increasingly don't serve these purposes. Businesses, as my Harvard colleague Marco Iansiti understood a while ago, thrive when they are part of healthy ecosystems.[21] Dominating and weakening one's competitors or suppliers is no longer a winning strategy. Technology companies like Microsoft and Google have been thriving in this new game. Now it's time for older industries to take ecosystems, and the cross-industry teaming they involve, seriously. Organizations within, say, the automotive industry are less likely to collaborate to find solutions to global issues like fuel efficiency and carbon emissions if they carry the old execution-as-efficiency mindset into the future. When today's efficiencies matter more than tomorrow's sustainability, teaming and innovation both lose.

When organizations operate with an execution-as-learning mindset, sharing across boundaries is natural. Toyota has long sought to teach its suppliers and even its competitors how to implement its remarkable execution-as-learning mindset and production system. Intermountain Healthcare works tirelessly to teach other hospitals how to implement its unique form of "improvement science" into the fabric of their operations, too. IDEO happily assists other companies in transforming their cultures to support innovation. When execution and learning become intertwined, the focus appears to shift naturally to increasing the size (and quality) of the pie, away from fighting over pieces and scraps. Generating ideas to solve problems is the currency of the future; teaming is the way to develop, implement, and improve those ideas.

With the rise of knowledge-based organizations in the information age, unhealthy competition can make people reluctant to share ideas or best practices with colleagues in other groups and organizations. But without teaming, new ideas cannot flourish in organizations. Teaming across distance, knowledge, and status boundaries is increasingly vital, as old models (economic, political, organizational), old technologies, and old mindsets prove cumbersome in the face of new challenges.

Transcending Boundaries

Increasingly, businesses and nations confront problems that dwarf even the largest challenges in this book, such as building sustainable cities, developing new energy sources, and evolving new behaviors in everyday life to better conserve dwindling resources. Transforming health care delivery systems, creating radically new business models, designing innovative ecosystems for collaboration, and learning new ways to live together in sustainable communities in the future are just some of the collaborative challenges we face. Few of these can be addressed by single organizations or even by single sectors (business or government)—let alone by individuals—working alone. Progress will require teaming across disciplines, companies, sectors, and nations. There is no doubt that new endeavors in these arenas will produce failures along the way. Let's learn from them.

notes

Chapter One

1. For example, Professor Richard Hackman of Harvard maintains that a bounded, stable team membership is one of the hallmarks of effective teams. See J. R. Hackman, *Leading Teams* (Boston: Harvard Business School Press, 2002); J. R. Hackman, (ed.), *Groups That Work (And Those That Don't)* (San Francisco: Jossey-Bass, 1990); J. R. Hackman, "The Design of Work Teams," in *Handbook of Organizational Behavior*, ed. J. Lorsch (Englewood Cliffs, NJ: Prentice Hall, 1987). See also J. McGrath, *Groups: Interaction and Performance* (Englewood Cliffs, NJ: Prentice Hall College Division, 1984).

2. See especially D. G. Ancona and D. F. Caldwell, "Bridging the Boundary: External Activity and Performance in Organizational Teams," *Administrative Science Quarterly* 37 (1992): 634–655.

3. See, for example, A. C. Edmondson and I. Nembhard, "Product Development and Learning in Project Teams: The Challenges Are the Benefits," *Journal of Product Innovation Management* 26, no. 2 (March 2009): 123–138; and M. B. O'Leary, M. Mortensen, and A. W. Woolley, "Multiple Team Membership: A Theoretical Model of Productivity and Learning Effects for Individuals and Teams," *Academy of Management Review* 36, no. 3 (2011): 461–478.

4. A. C. Edmondson, "The Local and Variegated Nature of Learning in Organizations: A Group-Level Perspective," *Organization Science* 13, no. 2 (2002): 128–146.

5. A. C. Edmondson, *Organizing to Learn Module Note*, Harvard Business School Module Note, Instructor Only, (2003), HBS604–031.

6. F. W. Taylor, *The Principles of Scientific Management*, comprising *Shop Management*, *The Principles of Scientific Management and Testimony Before the Special House Committee* (New York and London: Harper & Brothers, 1911).

7. UAW-CIO Ford Department. *We Work at Ford's: A Picture History* (Detroit: UAW-CIO, 1955), p. 14.

8. Ibid.

9. Personal correspondence with GM archivist.

10. P. Senge, *The Fifth Discipline: The Art and Practice of the Learning Organization* (New York: Doubleday/Currency, 1990).

11. I. M. Nembhard and A. C. Edmondson, "Making It Safe: The Effects of Leader Inclusiveness and Professional Status on Psychological Safety and Improvement Efforts in Health Care Teams," *Journal of Organizational Behavior* 27, no. 7 (2006): 941–966.

12. For more on complex adaptive systems (CAS), see J. H. Holland, "Complex Adaptive Systems," *Daedalus* 121, no. 1 (1992): 14. For research in an organizational context, see R. R. McDaniel Jr. and R. Anderson, "Managing Health Care Organizations: Where Professionalism Meets Complexity Science," *Health Care Management Review* 25, no. 1 (2000).

13. G. Parker, *Cross-Functional Teams: Working with Allies, Enemies, and Other Strangers* (San Francisco: Jossey-Bass, 2002).

14. A. C. Edmondson, "The Competitive Imperative of Learning," *HBS Centennial Issue. Harvard Business Review* 86, nos. 7/8 (2008): 60–67.

15. See the classic work by Donald Schön on how the best practitioners reflect-in-action, not just after action: *The Reflective Practitioner* (New York: Basic Books, 1983).

16. T. Mojonnier, *Reducing Risk in the Automotive Supply Chain* (2011). Available from http://www.philosophyofmanagement.com/blog/2011/03/18/reducing-risk-automotive-supply-chain-2.

Chapter Two

1. D. Schön, *The Reflective Practitioner* (New York: Basic Books, 1983).

2. A. C. Edmondson, R. Bohmer, and G. P. Pisano, "Disrupted Routines: Team Learning and New Technology Adaptation," *Administrative Science Quarterly* 46 (2001): 685–716.

3. A. Lashinsky, "RAZR'S Edge," Fortune on CNNMoney.com, 1–6. http://money.cnn.com/2006/05/31/magazines/fortune/razr_greatteams_fortune/index.htm.

4. Ibid; see also http://en.wikipedia.org/wiki/Motorola_RAZR.

5. J. R. Hackman and A. C. Edmondson, "Groups as Agents of Change," in *Handbook of Organizational Development*, ed. T. Cummings (Thousand Oaks, CA: Sage, 2007), pp. 167–186.

6. Edmondson et al., "Disrupted Routines."

7. A. L. Tucker, I. M. Nembhard, and A. C. Edmondson, "Implementing New Practices: An Empirical Study of Organizational Learning in Hospital Intensive Care Units," *Management Science* 53, no. 6 (2007): 894–907.

8. A. C. Edmondson and T. Casciaro, *"Leading Change at Simmons,"* HBS Case No. 9–406–047 (Boston: Harvard Business School, 2006).

9. E. McGirt, "How I Work." Fortune on CNNMoney.com (15 March 2006). http://money.cnn.com/magazines/fortune/fortune_archive/2006/03/20/8371781/index.htm.

10. J. R. Detert and A. C. Edmondson, "Implicit Voice Theories: Taken-For-Granted Rules of Self-Censorship at Work," *Academy of Management Journal* 54, no. 3 (2011): 461–488.

11. See especially A. C. Edmondson, "Speaking Up in the Operating Room: How Team Leaders Promote Learning in Interdisciplinary Action Teams," *Journal of Management Studies* 40, no. 6 (2003): 1419–1452.

12. See, for example, R. Nisbett and L. Ross, *Human Inference: Strategies and Shortcomings of Social Judgment* (Englewood Cliffs, NJ: Prentice Hall, 1980).

13. L. Ross, "The Intuitive Psychologist and His Shortcomings," in *Advances in Experimental Psychology*, Vol. 10, ed. L. Berkowitz (New York: Academic Press, 1977), p. 405.

14. Ibid.

15. Ibid.

16. J. Metcalfe and W. Mischel, "A Hot/Cool System of Delay of Gratification: Dynamics of Willpower," *Psychological Review* 106, no. 1 (1999): 3–19.

17. The Elite case was discussed at some length in A. C. Edmondson and D. M. Smith, "Too Hot to Handle? How to Manage Relationship Conflict," *California Management Review* 49, no. 1 (2006): 6–31.

18. See A. C. Amason, "Distinguishing the Effects of Functional and Dysfunctional Conflict on Strategic Decision Making: Resolving a Paradox for Top Management Teams," *Academy of Management Journal* 39, no. 1 (1996): 123–148; and K. M. Eisenhardt, J. L. Kahwajy, and L. J. Burgeois, "How Management Teams Can Have a Good Fight," *Harvard Business Review* 75, no. 4 (1997): 77–85.

19. For more depth on this important topic, see pioneering work by Diana McLain Smith, *Elephant in the Room: How Relationships Make or Break the Success of Leaders and Organizations* (San Francisco: Jossey-Bass, 2011).

20. For a superb guide to this topic, see D. Stone, B. Patton, S. Heen, and R. Fisher, *Difficult Conversations: How to Discuss What Matters Most*, 10th Anniversary Ed. (New York: Penguin Books, 2010).

21. J. R. Detert and A. C. Edmondson, "Implicit Voice Theories: Taken-for-Granted Rules of Self-Censorship at Work," *Academy of Management Journal* 54, no. 3 (2011).

Chapter Three

1. This chapter draws extensively on A. C. Edmondson, "Framing for Learning: Lessons in Successful Technology Implementation," *California Management Review* 45, no. 2 (2003): 34–54.

2. See Dan Goleman's *Vital Lies, Simple Truths* for an elegant discussion of self-deception and adherence to interpretations of reality that are not only erroneous but sometimes even psychologically harmful. Argyris has shown that people tacitly assume that they know others' motives and (erroneously) act accordingly. And, Orlikowski's research on new technology implementation suggests that technological frames, or how people interpret a new technology, remain stable over time. D. Goleman, *Vital Lies, Simple Truths: The Psychology of Self-Deception* (New York: Simon and Schuster, 1985); C. Argyris, *Knowledge for Action: A Guide to Overcoming Barriers to Organizational Change* (San Francisco: Jossey-Bass, 1993); W. Orlikowski, J. Wanda, and J. Deborah Hofman, "An Improvisational Model for Change Management: The Case of Groupware Technologies," *Sloan Management Review*, Winter (1997): 11–21.

3. P. L. Berger and T. Luckman, *The Social Construction of Reality* (New York: Doubleday, 1966); K. Weick, "The Collapse of Sensemaking in Organizations: The Mann Gulch Disaster," *Administrative Science Quarterly* 38, no. 4 (1993): 628–652.

4. J. R. Detert and A. C. Edmondson, "Implicit Voice Theories: Taken-for-Granted Rules of Self-Censorship at Work," *Academy of Management Journal* 54, no. 3 (2011). Also see C. Argyris, *On Organizational Learning* (Cambridge, MA: Blackwell, 1992).

5. Mental models are implicit beliefs that shape inferences, predictions, and decisions about what actions to take; shared mental models help people understand and react to the system in which they work in similar ways. See J. A. Cannon-Bowers, E. Salas, and S. Converse, "Shared Mental Models in Expert Team Decision Making," in *Individual and Group Decision Making*, ed. N. J. Castellan (Hillsdale, NJ: LEA, 1993), pp. 241–246; R. Klimoski and S. Mohammed, "Team Mental Model: Construct or Metaphor?" *Journal of Management* 20, no. 2 (1994): 403–437; P. Senge, *The Fifth Discipline: The Art and Practice of the Learning Organization* (New York: Doubleday/Currency, 1990); M. Cannon and A. C. Edmondson, "Confronting Failure: Antecedents and Consequences of Shared Beliefs About Failure in Organizational Work Groups," *Journal of Organizational Behavior* 22 (2001): 161–177.

6. Schein's work on culture describes organizational culture as a set of taken-for-granted assumptions shared by members of an organization about the nature of reality and authority. E. H. Schein, *Organizational Culture and Leadership* (San Francisco: Jossey-Bass, 1985).

7. D. L. Coutu, "How Resilience Works," *Harvard Business Review* 80, no. 5 (2002): 46–55; V. E. Frankl, *Man's Search for Meaning* (New York: Simon and Schuster, 1963).

8. C. S. Dweck and E. L. Leggett, "A Social-Cognitive Approach to Motivation and Personality," *Psychological Review* 95, no. 2 (1988): 256–273.

9. Regulatory focus theory identifies certain means accompanying promotion and prevention orientations. E. T. Higgins, "Making a Good Decision: Value From Fit," *American Psychologist* 55 (2000): 1217–1230.

10. M. Maultsby Jr., *Rational Behavior Therapy* (Appleton, WI: Seaton Foundation, 1990).

11. C. Argyris, R. Putnam, and D. M. Smith, *Action Science: Concepts, Methods, and Skills for Research and Intervention* (San Francisco: Jossey-Bass, 1985).

12. Ibid., 229; D. Schön, *The Reflective Practitioner* (New York: Basic Books, 1983).

13. Team members are likely to attend to each other's actions and responses but are particularly aware of the behavior of the leader. Research on distributive justice demonstrates that how a leader directs social processes is equally important to team members as their content; this strongly influences team members' compliance with the leader's decision. T. R. Tyler and E. A. Lind, "A Relational Model of Authority in Groups," *Advances in Experimental Psychology* 25, ed. M. Zanna (New York: Academy Press, 1992): 115–191. Beyond the team context, leaders have been distinguished from managers (who deal with complexity and pragmatic details) because of their role as meaning-makers. In particular, leaders are critical for establishing a compelling reason to change or to learn something new and challenging. J. P. Kotter, "What Leaders Really Do," *Harvard Business Review* 68, no. 3 (1990): 103–111; Maultsby, *Rational Behavior*

Therapy; A. Zaleznik, "Managers and Leaders: Are They Different?" *Harvard Business Review* 70, no. 2 (1992): 126–135.

14. Colleagues of Chris Argyris and Don Schön, Diana Smith, Bob Putnam, and Phil McArthur have identified three distinct dimensions of interpersonal frames: how one views oneself, how one perceives others, and how one understands the implicit goal in an interaction. See P. McArthur, *Learning in Action: Tools for Collaborative Decision Making* (Newton, MA: Action Design, 2002), CD-ROM.

15. A. Tucker and A. C. Edmondson, "Why Hospitals Don't Learn from Failures: Organizational and Psychological Dynamics That Inhibit System Change," *California Management Review* 45, no. 2 (2003): 55–72.

16. In particular see C. Argyris, *Reasoning, Learning and Action: Individual and Organizational* (San Francisco: Jossey-Bass, 1982), for research on frame changing in the organizational context, and Maultsby, *Rational Behavior Therapy,* for thoughtful research and frame change in the clinical realm.

Chapter Four

1. National Aeronautics and Space Administration, *Columbia Accident Investigation Board: Report Volume 1* (Washington, DC: U.S. Government Printing Office, 2003), p. 157.

2. J. Glanz and J. Schwartz, "Dogged Engineer's Effort to Assess Shuttle Damage," *New York Times,* September 26, 2003, A1.

3. T. Whitcraft, D. Katz, and T. Day (Producers), "Columbia: Final Mission," *ABC Primetime* (New York: ABC News, 2003).

4. I. L. Janis, *Groupthink: Psychological Studies of Policy Decisions and Fiascos* (Boston: Houghton Mifflin, 1982).

5. K. E. Weick and K. H. Roberts, "Collective Mind in Organizations: Heedful Interrelating on Flight Decks," *Administrative Science Quarterly* 38 (1993): 357–381. Also see J. S. Carroll, "Organizational Learning Activities in High-Hazard Industries: The Logics Underlying Self-Analysis," *Management Studies* 35, no. 6 (1998): 669–717.

6. R. Brown, "Politeness Theory: Exemplar and Exemplary," in *The Legacy of Solomon Asch: Essays in Cognition and Social Psychology*, ed. I. Rock (Hillsdale, NJ: Erlbaum, 1990), pp. 23–37.

7. M. E. Zellmer-Bruhn, "Interruptive Events and Team Knowledge Acquisition," *Management Science* 49, no. 4 (2003): 514–528.

8. F. J. Milliken, E. W. Morrison, and P. F. Hewlin, "An Exploratory Study of Employee Silence: Issues That Employees Don't Communicate Upward and Why," *Journal of Management Studies* 40, no. 6 (2003): 1453–1476.

9. E. Schein and W. Bennis, *Personal and Organizational Change Through Group Methods* (New York: Wiley, 1965).

10. E. Schein, *Organizational Culture and Leadership* (San Francisco: Jossey-Bass, 1985).

11. W. Kahn, "Psychological Conditions of Personal Engagement and Disengagement at Work," *Academy of Management Journal* 33, no. 4 (1990): 692–724.

12. Ibid., 694.

13. T. R. Tyler and E. A. Lind, "A Relational Model of Authority in Groups," *Advances in Experimental Psychology* 25 (1992): 115–191. Also see A. C. Edmondson, "Psychological Safety and Learning Behavior in Work Teams," *Administrative Science Quarterly* 44 (1999): 350–383; and I. M. Nembhard and A. C. Edmondson, "Psychological Safety: A Foundation for Speaking Up, Collaboration, and Experimentation," in *Organizational Scholarship*, ed. K. Cameron and G. Spreitzer (New York: Oxford University Press, 2011, pp. 490–503).

14. See B. Wojciszke, H. Brycz, and P. Borkenau, "Effects of Information Content and Evaluative Extremity on Positivity and Negativity Biases," *Journal of Personality and Social Psychology* 64 (1993): 327–336; T. Casciaro and M. S. Lobo, "Competent Jerks, Lovable Fools, and the Formation of Social Networks," *Harvard Business Review* 83, no. 6 (2005): 92–99.

15. G. Berns, "In Hard Times, Fear Can Impair Decision-Making," *New York Times*, December 6, 2008, BU2.

16. B. F. Chorpita and D. H. Barlow, "The Development of Anxiety: The Role of Control in the Early Environment," *Psychological Bulletin* 124 (1998): 3–21; Also see D. A. Decatanzaro, *Motivation and Emotion: Evolutionary, Physiological, Developmental, and Social Perspectives* (Englewood Cliffs, NJ: Pearson College Division, 1998).

17. D. A. Leonard, *Wellsprings of Knowledge: Building and Sustaining the Sources of Innovation* (Boston: Harvard Business School Press, 1998).

18. A. C. Edmondson, "Learning from Mistakes Is Easier Said Than Done: Group and Organizational Influences on the Detection and Correction of Human Error," *Journal of Applied Behavioral Sciences* 32, no. 1 (1996): 5–32.

19. M. A. West and N. Anderson, "The Team Climate Inventory: Development of the TCI and Its Applications in Teambuilding for Innovativeness," *European Journal of Organizational Psychology* 5, no. 1 (1996): 53–66.

20. L. M. Janes and J. M. Olson, "Jeer Pressure: The Behavioral Effects of Observing Ridicule of Others," *Personality and Social Psychology Bulletin* 26 (2000): 474–485.

21. A. C. Edmondson, R. Bohmer, and G. P. Pisano, "Disrupted Routines: Team Learning and New Technology Adaptation," *Administrative Science Quarterly* 46 (2001): 685–716.

22. I. M. Nembhard and A. C. Edmondson, "Making It Safe: The Effects of Leader Inclusiveness and Professional Status on Psychological Safety and Improvement Efforts in Health Care Teams. Special Issue on Healthcare: The Problems Are Organizational Not Clinical," *Journal of Organizational Behavior* 27, no. 7 (2006): 941–966.

23. H. Benson and M. Z. Klipper, *The Relaxation Response* (New York: HarperCollins, 2000).

24. D. A. Garvin, A. C. Edmondson, and F. Gino, "Is Yours a Learning Organization?" *Harvard Business Review* 86, no. 3 (2008).

25. J. Bagian, personal interview, 2003.

26. S. Widnall, personal interview, 2003.

27. For example, see E. Schein, *Organizational Culture and Leadership* (San Francisco: Jossey-Bass, 1985); A. C. Edmondson, "Framing for

Learning: Lessons in Successful Technology Implementation," *California Management Review* 45, no. 2 (2003), 34–54; J. P. Kotter, "Leading Change: Why Transformation Efforts Fail," *Harvard Business Review* 73, no. 2 (1995): 59–67.

28. R. P. Winter, J. C. Sarros et al., "Reframing Managers' Control Orientations and Practices: A Proposed Organizational Learning Framework," *The International Jo rnal of Organizational Analysis* 5, no. 1 (1997): 9–24.

29. A. C. Edmondson, "Learning from Mistakes Is Easier Said Than Done."

30. J. J. Gabarro, *The Dynamics of Taking Charge* (Boston: Harvard Business Press, 1987).

31. S. Macdonald, "Learning to Change: An Information Perspective on Learning in the Organization," *Organization Science* 6 (1995): 557–568.

32. P. Carroll, *Big Blues: The Unmaking of IBM* (New York: Crown, 1993).

33. R. Farson and R. Keyes, *The Innovation Paradox: The Success of Failure, the Failure of Success* (New York: Free Press, 2002).

34. M. D. Cannon and A. C. Edmondson, "Failing to Learn and Learning to Fail (Intelligently): How Great Organizations Put Failure to Work to Innovate and Improve," *Long Range Planning Journal* 38, no. 3 (2005): 299–319.

35. A. C. Edmondson, "The Local and Variegated Nature of Learning in Organizations: A Group-Level Perspective," *Organization Science* 13, no. 2 (2002): 128–146.

36. California Hospital Patient Safety Organization can be found at http://www.chpso.org/just/index.asp.

Chapter Five

1. M. D. Cannon and A. C. Edmondson, "Confronting Failure: Antecedents and Consequences of Shared Beliefs About Failure in

Organizational Work Groups," *Journal of Organizational Behavior* 22 (2001): 161–177; A. C. Edmondson and M. D. Cannon, "Failing to Learn and Learning to Fail (Intelligently): How Great Organizations Put Failure to Work to Innovate and Improve," *Long Range Planning Journal* 38, no. 3 (2005): 299–319.

2. Ibid. (Cannon and Edmondson; Edmondson and Cannon)

3. R. M. J. Bohmer and A. Winslow, *"Dana-Farber Cancer Institute,"* *HBS Case No. 669–025* (Boston: Harvard Business School Publishing, 1999).

4. A. C. Edmondson, E. Ferlins, F. Feldman, and R. Bohmer, "The Recovery Window: Organizational Learning Following Ambiguous Threats," in *Organization at the Limit: Lessons from the Columbia Disaster*, ed. M. Farjoun and W. Starbuck (Malden, MA: Blackwell, 2005).

5. M. Moss, "Spotting Breast Cancer, Doctors Are Weak Link," *New York Times*, June 27, 2002, late ed., A1; M. Moss, "Mammogram Team Learns from Its Errors," *New York Times*, June 28, 2002, late ed., A1.

6. C. Argyris, *Overcoming Organizational Defenses: Facilitating Organizational Learning* (Needham Heights, MA: Allyn & Bacon, 1990).

7. E. Goleman, *Vital Lies, Simple Truths: The Psychology of Self-Deception* (New York: Simon & Schuster, 1985); S. E. Taylor, *Positive Illusions: Creative Self-Deception and the Healthy Mind* (New York: Basic Books, 1989).

8. Edmondson and Cannon, "Failing to Learn and Learning to Fail (Intelligently)."

9. Taylor, *Positive Illusions*.

10. Ibid.

11. C. Fishman, "No Satisfaction at Toyota," *Fast Company* 111 (2006): 82.

12. S. Finkelstein, *Why Smart Executives Fail and What You Can Learn from Their Mistakes* (New York: Portfolio Hardcover, 2003), pp. 179–180.

13. Ibid.

14. F. Lee, A. C. Edmondson, S. Thomke, and M. Worline, "The Mixed Effects of Inconsistency on Experimentation in Organizations," *Organization Science* 15, no. 3 (2004): 310–326.

15. A. C. Edmondson, "Strategies for Learning from Failure," *Harvard Business Review* 89, no. 4 (2011).

16. K. E. Weick and K. H. Roberts, "Collective Mind in Organizations: Heedful Interrelating on Flight Decks," *Administrative Science Quarterly* 38 (1993): 357–381.

17. K. E. Weick and K. M. Sutcliffe, *Managing the Unexpected: Resilient Performance in an Age of Uncertainty* (San Francisco: Jossey-Bass, 2007).

18. Weick and Roberts, "Collective Mind in Organizations."

19. A. C. Edmondson and L. Feldman, *"Phase Zero: Introducing New Services at IDEO (A),"* HBS Case No. 605–069 (Boston: Harvard Business School Publishing, 2005).

20. T. S. Burton, "By Learning from Failures, Lilly Keeps Drug Pipeline Full," *Wall Street Journal*, April 21, 2004, B1.

21. Edmondson et al., "The Recovery Window."

22. A. Taylor III, "Fixing up Ford," *CNNMoney*, May 12, 2009. Available from http://money.cnn.com/2009/05/11/news/companies/mulally_ford .fortune/?postversion=2009051103.

23. S. W. Brown and S. S. Tax, "Recovering and Learning from Service Failures," *Sloan Management Review* 40, no. 1 (1998): 75–89.

24. D. A. Garvin, *Learning in Action* (Boston: Harvard Business School Press, 2000).

25. F. F. Reichhel and T. Teal, *The Loyalty Effect: The Hidden Force Behind Growth, Profits, and Lasting Value* (Boston: Harvard Business School Press, 1996), pp. 194–195.

26. Burton, "By Learning from Failures."

27. S. Thomke, *Experimentation Matters: Unlocking the Potential of New Technologies for Innovation* (Boston: Harvard Business School Press, 2003).

28. A. L. Tucker, I. M. Nembhard, and A. C. Edmondson, "Implementing New Practices: An Empirical Study of Organizational Learning

in Hospital Intensive Care Units," *Management Science* 53, no. 6 (2007): 894–907.

29. Lee et al., "The Mixed Effects of Inconsistency."

Chapter Six

1. F. Rashid, D. Leonard, and A. C. Edmondson, *"The 2010 Chilean Mining Rescue (A),"* HBS Case No. 412–046 (Boston: Harvard Business School Publishing, 2010); and F. Rashid, D. Leonard, and A. C. Edmondson, *"The 2010 Chilean Mining Rescue (B),"* HBS Case No. 412–047 (Boston: Harvard Business School Publishing, 2010). See also J. Franklin, *33 Men: Inside the Miraculous Survival and Dramatic Rescue of the Chilean Miners* (New York: Penguin Group, 2011).

2. R. Robbins, "Quecreek Rescue Still Inspires Wonder." *TRIBLive News*, 2007. Available from http://www.pittsburghlive.com/x/pitts burghtrib/news/cityregion/s_519299.html.

3. N. Vanderklippe, "Chile's CEO Moment," *The Globe and Mail*, October 16, 2010.

4. Rashid et al., "The 2010 Chilean Mining Rescue (A)"; Rashid et al., "The 2010 Chilean Mining Rescue (B)."

5. Ibid.

6. Ibid.

7. Vanderklippe, "Chile's CEO Moment."

8. Ibid.

9. A. Morrow, "Fenix: Rocket Ship to Freedom," *The Globe and Mail*, October 14, 2010. http://www.theglobeandmail.com/news/technology /science/fenix-rocket-ship-to-freedom/article1756376/.

10. M. Useem, *The Leadership Moment: Nine True Stories of Triumph and Disaster and Their Lessons for Us All* (New York: Random House, 1998).

11. D. Dougherty, "Interpretive Barriers to Successful Product Innovation in Large Firms," *Organization Science* 3, no. 2 (1992): 179–202.

12. See especially G. Stasser and W. Titus, "Pooling of Unshared Information in Group Decision Making: Biased Information Sampling During Discussion," *Journal of Personality and Social Psychology* 48, no. 6 (1985): 1467–1478.

13. D. A. Harrison and K. J. Klein, "What's the Difference? Diversity Constructs as Separation, Variety, or Disparity in Organizations," *Academy of Management Review* 32, no. 4 (2007): 1200.

14. A. C. Edmondson, "*Transformation at the Internal Revenue Service,*" HBS Case No. 9–603–010 (Boston: Harvard Business School Publishing, 2002).

15. I. M. Nembhard and A. C. Edmondson "Making It Safe: The Effects of Leader Inclusiveness and Professional Status on Psychological Safety and Improvement Efforts in Health Care Teams," *Journal of Organizational Behavior* 27, no. 7 (2006): 941–966.

16. A. L. Tucker, I. M. Nembhard, and A. C. Edmondson, "Implementing New Practices: An Empirical Study of Organizational Learning in Hospital Intensive Care Units," *Management Science* 53, no. 6 (2007): 894–907.

17. See J. R. Detert and A. C. Edmondson, "Implicit Voice Theories: Taken-for-Granted Rules of Self-Censorship at Work," *Academy of Management Journal* 54, no. 3 (2011).

18. R. J. Ely and D. A. Thomas, "Cultural Diversity at Work: The Moderating Effects of Work Group Perspectives on Diversity," *Administrative Science Quarterly* 46 (2001): 229–273.

19. J. Aronson and C. M. Steele, "Stereotypes and the Fragility of Human Competence, Motivation, and Self-Concept," in *Handbook of Competence & Motivation*, ed. C. S. Dweck and E. Elliot (New York: Guilford, 2005).

20. S. L. Gaertner, J. D. Dovidio, J. A. Nier, G. Hodson, and M. Houlette, "Aversive Racism: Bias Without Intention," in *Affirmative Action: Rights and Realities*, ed. R. L. Nelson and L. B. Nielson (London: Oxford University Press, 2005).

21. A. C. Edmondson, B. Moingeon, V. Dessain, and D. Jensen, "*Global Knowledge Management at Danone (A),*" HBS Case No. 608–107 (Boston: Harvard Business School Publishing, 2007).

22. Ibid.

23. Ibid.

24. B. R. Staats, M. Valentine, and A. C. Edmondson, "Using What We Know: Turning Organizational Knowledge into Team Performance," HBS Working Paper No. 11–031, 2010.

25. Nembhard and Edmondson, "Making It Safe."

26. A. Tucker and A. C. Edmondson, "*Cincinnati Children's Hospital Medical Center,*" *HBS Case No. 609–109* (Boston: Harvard Business School Publishing, 2009), p. 10.

27. Note that this is a pseudonym; for the study, see D. Sole and A. C. Edmondson, "Situated Knowledge and Learning in Dispersed Teams," *British Journal of Management* 13 (2002): 17–34.

28. D. Ancona, H. Bresman, and K. Kaeufer, "The Comparative Advantage of X-Teams," *Sloan Management Review* 43, no. 3 (2002): 33–39.

29. Sole and Edmondson, "Situated Knowledge."

30. Tucker and Edmondson, "Cincinnati Children's Hospital Medical Center," p. 13.

31. P. Carlile, "A Pragmatic View of Knowledge and Boundaries: Boundary Objects in New Product Development," *Organization Science* 13, no. 4 (2002): 442–445.

32. B. A. Bechky, "Sharing Meaning Across Occupational Communities: The Transformation of Understanding on a Production Floor," *Organization Science* 14, no. 3 (2003): 312–330.

33. B. LePatner, *Broken Buildings, Busted Budgets: How to Fix America's Trillion-Dollar Construction Industry* (Chicago: University of Chicago Press, 2007).

34. A. C. Edmondson and F. Rashid, "*Integrated Project Delivery at Autodesk, Inc. (A),*" *HBS Case No. 610–016* (Boston: Harvard Business School Publishing, 2009). See also A. C. Edmondson and F. Rashid, "*Integrated Project Delivery at Autodesk, Inc. (B),*" *Harvard Business School Supplement No. 610–017,* 2009; A. C. Edmondson and F. Rashid, "*Integrated Project Delivery at Autodesk, Inc. (B),*" *Harvard Business School Supplement No. 610–018,* 2009; also see

F. Rashid and A. C. Edmondson, "Risky Trust: How Multi-Entity Teams Develop Trust in a High Risk Endeavor," Harvard Business School Working Paper No. 11–089, 2011.

35. E. Schein, *Organizational Culture and Leadership*, 4th ed. (San Francisco: Jossey-Bass, 2010): pp. 155–176 [chap 21].

36. R. G. Eccles, A. C. Edmondson, and D. Karadzhova, *"Arup: Building the Water Cube,"* HBS Case No. *410–054* (Boston: Harvard Business School Publishing, 2010).

37. See C. B. Gibson and S. G. Cohen, *Virtual Teams That Work: Creating Conditions for Virtual Team Effectiveness* (San Francisco: Jossey-Bass, 2003). See also Sole and Edmondson, "Situated Knowledge"; and A. C. Edmondson, "A Safe Harbor: Social Psychological Factors Affecting Boundary Spanning in Work Teams," in *Research on Groups and Teams*, eds. B. Mannix, M. Neale, and R. Wageman (Greenwich, CT: Jai Press, 1999).

Chapter Seven

1. A. C. Edmondson, "The Local and Variegated Nature of Learning in Organizations: A Group-Level Perspective," *Organization Science* 13, no. 2 (2002): 128–146; A. C. Edmondson and I. M. Nembhard, "Product Development and Learning in Project Teams: The Challenges Are the Benefits," *Journal of Product Innovation Management* 26, no. 2 (2009): 123–138.

2. J. H. Gittell, *The Southwest Airlines Way* (New York: McGraw-Hill, 2005).

3. The names of both the company and the individuals in this story are pseudonyms, and many of the details are fictional, but the management situation they depict is based on one experienced in a real organization.

4. D. Schön, *The Reflective Practitioner* (New York: Basic Books, 1984).

5. To learn more about cyclical models of individual learning, see D. Kolb, *Experiential Learning: Experience as the Source of Learning and Development* (Englewood Cliffs, NJ: Prentice Hall, 1984). For more on team learning, see A. C. Edmondson, J. R. Dillon, and K. Roloff,

"Three Perspectives on Team Learning: Outcome Improvement, Task Mastery, and Group Process," in *The Academy of Management Annals*, ed. J. P. Walsh and A. P. Brief (Linthicum, MD: Psychology Press, 2007).

6. See Edmondson et al., "Three Perspectives on Team Learning," for a review of the research.

7. F. X. Frei and A. C. Edmondson, *"Yum! Brands, Inc: A Corporate Do-Over,"* HBS Case No. 606–041 (Boston: Harvard Business School Publishing, 2005).

8. A. C. Edmondson and C. B. Hajim, *"Large Scale Change at The WSSC,"* HBS Case No. 603–056 (Boston: Harvard Business School Publishing, 2003).

9. M. K. Christianson, "Practice Makes Perfect: Using Simulation to Help Teams Learn to Coordinate." University of Toronto Working Paper, presented at the Academy of Management Conference, August 2011, San Antonio, TX.

10. R. G. Eccles, A. C. Edmondson, and D. Karadzhova, *"Arup: Building the Water Cube,"* HBS Case No. 410–054 (Boston: Harvard Business School Publishing, 2010), p. 7.

11. J. Liker, *The Toyota Way* (New York: McGraw-Hill, 2003).

12. S. J. Spear and H. K. Bowen, "Decoding the DNA of the Toyota Production System," *Harvard Business Review* (1999): 1–13.

13. E. Catmull, "How Pixar Fosters Collective Creativity," *Harvard Business Review* (2008): 1–12.

14. N. Bunkley, "Recall Study Finds Flaws at Toyota," *New York Times*, May 23, 2011.

15. P. M. Senge, *The Fifth Discipline: The Art and Practice of the Learning Organization* (New York: Doubleday/Currency, 1990).

Chapter Eight

1. T. Casciaro and A. C. Edmondson, *"Leading Change at Simmons (C),"* HBS Case No. 406–046 (Boston: Harvard Business School Publishing, 2005), p. 5.

2. L. Wilson and H. Wilson, *Play to Win! Choosing Growth Over Fear in Work and Life* (Austin, TX: Bard Press, 2004).

3. H. Ford and S. Crowther, *My Life and Work* (Garden City, NY: Garden City Publishing, 1922).

4. Casciaro and Edmondson, "Leading Change at Simmons (B)," 2.

5. All of the names of individuals in this story, which is told in A. C. Edmondson, M. Roberto, and A. L. Tucker, *"Children's Hospital and Clinics (A),"* HBS Case No. 302–050 (Boston: Harvard Business School Publishing, 2001) and is based on a real incident, are pseudonyms.

6. Ibid.

7. Ibid.

8. Ibid.

9. Ibid.

10. Ibid., 5.

11. I. M. Nembhard and A. C. Edmondson, "Making It Safe: The Effects of Leader Inclusiveness and Professional Status on Psychological Safety and Improvement Efforts in Health Care Teams," *Journal of Organizational Behavior* 27, no. 7 (2006): 941–966.

12. Edmondson et al., "Children's Hospital and Clinics (A)."

13. Ibid., 10.

14. A. C. Edmondson and K. Roloff, *"Phase Zero: Introducing New Services at IDEO (B),"* HBS Case No. 606–123 (Boston: Harvard Business School Publishing, 2006), p. 3.

15. A. C. Edmondson and L. Feldman, *"Phase Zero: Introducing New Services at IDEO (A),"* HBS Case No. 605–069 (Boston: Harvard Business School Publishing, 2005), p. 1.

16. The timing of this project occurred very near the beginning of Charlie Eitel's tenure as CEO at Simmons. Eitel, perhaps unfortunately, was not involved with the project, which was authorized by a marketing executive.

17. Edmondson and Feldman, "Phase Zero: Introducing New Services at IDEO (A)."

18. Ibid.

19. Ibid., 4–5.

20. Ibid.

21. M. Iansiti, *The Keystone Advantage: What the New Dynamics of Business Ecosystems Mean for Strategy, Innovation, and Sustainability* (Boston: Harvard Business Press, 2004).

acknowledgments

This book is about teaming, and teaming made it possible. I am grateful to everyone behind the scenes who played a role in helping me, and hope I can do justice to your diverse and complementary contributions.

This book pulls together findings, insights, and frameworks from twenty years of field research. I want to express my appreciation for the hundreds of people in the many organizations—managers, nurses, physicians, CEOs, and front-line associates alike—who generously gave up some of their time to be interviewed and studied. I hope that one or two of them will find their way to this book and recognize that they taught me something important. I also wish to thank the Division of Research at Harvard Business School for generous financial support that funded the many studies that underlie this book.

But, long before I was a business school professor, I was an engineer working for Buckminster Fuller, helping him with some of his final design projects. When I wasn't calculating strut lengths for a new geodesic dome, I spent my time listening to Bucky (everyone called him that) talk and teach. This is where I first learned to see large social problems (famine, pollution, housing, energy) as collective-learning challenges. Bucky thought about collaborative learning at a planetary level. All of us were crew-members aboard Spaceship Earth, he said, and we had to learn to work together to make this world work.

Planets being somewhat ambitious targets for large-scale change, it was a relief when I met entrepreneur and author Larry Wilson a few years later. Larry introduced me to the idea that organizations can learn. Moreover, organizations played a crucial role in "making this world work," as Bucky had put it. Now I had something I could sink my teeth into. As a researcher/consultant at Pecos River Learning Centers working closely with Larry, I started to observe much of what my later research confirmed. Larry's ideas are everywhere in mine. I dedicate this book to him because his passion for making a difference in organizations ignited mine.

I have been fortunate in mentors. Richard Hackman's extraordinary research and teaching led me to consider teams the right unit of analysis for my studies. Years ago, Richard chaired my dissertation committee, introduced me to the hospital as a worthy site for research, and influenced my ideas in more ways than I can recount. Chris Argyris and Peter Senge also guided my work and my aspirations in important ways. They both encouraged me to tackle questions that mattered, and I hope that parts of this book will indicate to them I have done so.

Ed Schein has become an increasingly important mentor and friend over the years, and he was the first person from whom I recall hearing the word "teaming." In a seminar at MIT, I heard Ed say that we ought to focus on teaming rather than on teams. He certainly caught my attention! I am deeply grateful to Ed for writing the thoughtful and generous foreword to this book, and to giving me incredibly helpful feedback on the manuscript, which improved it greatly.

Kathe Sweeney at Jossey-Bass played a vital role in getting this project launched and just as vital a role in getting it finished. Kathe believed in the book far more than its progress warranted. I am grateful for her enthusiasm and for her coherent thinking about teams and organizations.

Of the many people who contributed to getting this book into shape, Jeff Leeson was by far the most important. I learned a lot from Jeff's systematic approach to shaping, organizing, clarifying and structuring ideas to produce an integrated whole. Jeff bravely entered the landscape of my research papers and cases and helped me build something meaningful. I am indebted to him for his editing expertise, for his patience with my schedule, and for his high standards. Karen Propp played an essential role in the early stages of writing and shaping the book. Her thoughtful voice, perceptive insights, and creative suggestions of examples are sprinkled throughout these pages.

Susan Salter Reynolds was my most diligent, thoughtful, and creative reader, editor, colleague, and friend. She's always been there for me, and I've always appreciated her gifts as a writer and critic. Now I appreciate them even more. When she started to work on this project in its final weeks, she brought certain sections to life, and made work fun again.

Sheba Raza shouldered some of the toughest work of all, handling references, permissions, and the endless details that go into a project like this with skill, precision, and remarkable good cheer. Several research assistants provided invaluable help in the field research, case writing, and paper development that inform this book, including Laura Feldman, Corey Hajim, Dilyana Karadzhova, Stacy McManus, and Kate Roloff. Much of the research reported in this book was collaborative, and my colleagues and coauthors on several projects must be acknowledged for their vital roles, especially Richard Bohmer, Tiziana Casciaro, Jim Detert, Frances Frei, Bertrand Moingeon, Ingrid Nembhard, Gary Pisano, Faaiza Rashid, Deborah Sole, Anita Tucker, and Melissa Valentine. Diana Smith is a colleague who deserves special mention as a mentor, friend, coauthor, and cheerleader. She is one of the people who made sure I wrote this book.

Finally, my husband, George, put up with and took care of me as I put more and more time into writing. He was unfailingly supportive and caring. His love and confidence sustained me and made writing this book possible. Further, he was there every step of the way for the past eighteen years, hearing about the research projects that were going well, and not so well, and never seeming to lose faith in me or in my work. Our young sons, Jack and Nick, growing up in the Internet age, were extremely patient, often curling up with a book nearby while I typed away. Their love of books gave me hope that it was still worth writing one.

about the author

Amy C. Edmondson is the Novartis Professor of Leadership and Management at the Harvard Business School, a chair established to support the study of human interactions that lead to the creation of successful enterprises that contribute to the betterment of society. Edmondson joined the Business School faculty in 1996 and has taught courses in leadership, organizational learning, and operations management in the MBA and Executive Education programs. Her writings on organizational learning and leadership have been published in more than sixty articles in academic and management journals, and she has consulted widely on these topics for organizations around the world. In 2003, the Academy of Management's Organizational Behavior division selected Edmondson for the Cummings Award for outstanding achievement, and in 2000, it selected her article "Psychological Safety and Learning Behavior in Work Teams" for its annual award for the best published paper in the field. Her article with Anita Tucker, "Why Hospitals Don't Learn from Failures: Organizational and Psychological Dynamics That Inhibit System Change," received the 2004 Accenture Award for significant contribution to management practice.

Before her academic career, she was director of research at Pecos River Learning Centers, where she worked with founder and CEO Larry Wilson to design and implement change programs in large companies. In the early 1980s, she worked as chief engineer for architect/inventor Buckminster Fuller, and her book *A Fuller*

Explanation: The Synergetic Geometry of R. Buckminster Fuller (Boston: Birkhauser, 1987) clarifies Fuller's mathematical contributions for a nontechnical audience. Edmondson received her PhD in organizational behavior, AM in psychology, and AB in engineering and design, all from Harvard University. She lives outside Boston, Massachusetts, with her husband, George Daley, and their two sons.

index

in today's business environment,
19–24, 285–287; organizing for,
26–30; across the Process
Knowledge Spectrum, 32–38, 231;
study of, 3–4; teaming as engine of,
14–15, 24–26; tools of, 231.
See also Execution-as-learning;
Learning
Organizational performance, teaming
and, 58–59
Organizations: factors in, that inhibit
learning from failure, 157–158;
psychological safety and
accountability in, 129–131, 139,
144–145, 146; tacit knowledge in,
206–208, 217
Organizing to execute: background
on, 15–19; characteristics of, 28;
management approaches of, 28;
organizing to learn *versus*, 27–30,
234–240; across the Process
Knowledge Spectrum, 32–38;
shifting from, to organizing to learn
approach, 236–240; in "Telco" case
study, 235–236, 254–255
Organizing to learn: boundary
spanning and, 185–217;
characteristics of, 28; failure and,
149–184; framing and, 76–77,
83–113; leadership actions for,
75–78, 80; management approaches
of, 28; mindset of, 26–30;
organizing to execute *versus*,
27–30, 237–239; across the Process
Knowledge Spectrum, 32–38;
psychological safety and, 115–148;
in "Telco" case study, 237–240
Orlikowski, W., 293n.2
Ownership: framing of team members'
roles for, 96–98; participation and,
247–248

P

Parker, G., 22
Participation, inviting, 139, 140–141,
205–206

Past experience, cognitive frames
based on, 84–85
Patient safety improvement, 254,
266–276. *See also* Children's
Hospital and Clinics, Minneapolis
Perceptual biases, 64–66, 155,
158–160, 175, 293n.2
Performance, psychological safety
and, 129–131
Performance frame, 86
Performance improvement, teaming
for, 58–59
Performance measurement: in
complex operations, 244–245; in
routine operations, 28, 243–244
Performance teams, 12–13
Perfusionists, 98
Personal computer company,
operational diversity in, 39
Perturbations, 23
Pfizer, 164
Pharmaceutical companies, 163, 164,
177–178, 242–243, 277
Physical distance, teaming across,
197, 198–199, 201–205
Pilot experiments, 179, 181–182, 261
Piñera, S., 190, 192
Pixar, 251
Pizza Hut, 244
Planning: in execution-as-learning,
241, 242, 243, 245–247;
operational context differences
and, 231
Polaroid, 21
Positive illusions, 154–155
Post-it notes, development of, 142
Post-mortems, 149
Power differences, 198–199. *See also*
Hierarchy; Status
Practice sessions, 105
Prada, 277
Preparation, for change
implementation, 105, 106, 107
Preventable failures, 165, 166–167,
180; strategies for learning from,
172, 173, 176

framing of change projects and,
89–104; framing of roles in, 96–99;
for medical event studies, 275;
trend toward, 13–14
Terrorist attacks, 152, 259
Tertiary care hospital, 34. *See also*
Hospitals
Thin Book of Appreciative Inquiry, The
(Hammond), 88
"Three Perspectives on Team
Learning" (Edmondson et al.),
304–305n.5
3M, 142
Time and motion studies, 263
Time pressures, 196–197, 252
Time zone differences, 204
"Too Hot to Handle?" (Edmondson
and Smith), 292n.17
Top-down leadership. *See* Command-
and-control management
Total quality management (TQM),
176, 246
Toyota Motor Company: complacency
and quality problems at, 252–253;
execution-as-learning at, 223–224,
250, 252–253, 286–287; GM
compared to, 20; lean production
in, 263; learning from failure at,
156–157, 161; operational diversity
of, 36–38, 277; relentless reflection
at, 250; supply chain management
of, 37–38, 286–287
Toyota Production System (TPS),
161, 263, 287
Traffic control facilities, 162
Training: for change project, 105; in
hospital error reporting, 270–271;
organizing-to-execute *versus*
organizing-to-learn approaches to,
28, 29; professional, 208; team, 60
Trials: for change implementation,
106, 107; reflection and, 251;
unsuccessful, 180, 231. *See also*
Experimentation
Trust: building, for teaming, 262–263;
building, in relationship conflict,

73–74; for psychological safety,
118–120, 129; in virtual teams,
204–205
Tucker, A., 35, 109
Tversky, A., 88
20 Percent Time, at Google, 178–179

U

Uncertainty: acknowledging, 139,
140; complex adaptive systems and,
22–24; conflict and, 68, 69;
corporate giants and, 20–21;
diagnosing, 230–233; failure and,
159, 163, 167; in hospitals, 266;
learning frame for, 103–104;
organizing to learn and, 26; across
the Process Knowledge Spectrum,
33, 34–36, 230–233; thriving in
the face of, 21–22
Union Carbide, 21
Unique information, 195–196
Unique trials, 251
Uniroyal, 21
United Auto Workers, 17
U.S. Army, 55, 175
U.S. Department of Defense, 115–116
U.S. Internal Revenue Service (IRS)
call centers, 198–199, 206, 259
U.S. National Aeronautics and Space
Administration. *See* NASA
U.S. Security and Exchange
Commission, 152
U.S. Steel, 21
Universities, operational diversity of,
39
Urzúa, L., 186–187

V

Values, conflict of, 68, 69, 71–72, 73
Variety diversity, 197, 200, 217
Vertical silo organization, in hospitals,
46–47
Viagra, 164
Virtual teams, 52, 198–199, 201–205;
face-to-face meetings of, 204–205;
tacit knowledge and, 207–208